Lecture Notes in Computer Science   11116

Commenced Publication in 1973
Founding and Former Series Editors:
Gerhard Goos, Juris Hartmanis, and Jan van Leeuwen

More information about this series at http://www.springer.com/series/7408

Kyriakos Kritikos · Pierluigi Plebani
Flavio de Paoli (Eds.)

Service-Oriented and Cloud Computing

7th IFIP WG 2.14 European Conference, ESOCC 2018
Como, Italy, September 12–14, 2018
Proceedings

 Springer

Editors
Kyriakos Kritikos ⓘ
ICS_FORTH
Heraklion
Greece

Flavio de Paoli
Università di Milano-Bicocca
Milan
Italy

Pierluigi Plebani ⓘ
Dipartimento di Electronica
Fondazione Politecnico di Milano
Milan
Italy

ISSN 0302-9743   ISSN 1611-3349 (electronic)
Lecture Notes in Computer Science
ISBN 978-3-319-99818-3   ISBN 978-3-319-99819-0 (eBook)
https://doi.org/10.1007/978-3-319-99819-0

Library of Congress Control Number: 2018952649

LNCS Sublibrary: SL2 – Programming and Software Engineering

This Springer imprint is published by the registered company Springer Nature Switzerland AG
The registered company address is: Gewerbestrasse 11, 6330 Cham, Switzerland

Preface

Service-oriented and cloud computing have made a huge impact both on the software industry and on the research community. Today, service and cloud technologies are applied to build large-scale software landscapes as well as to provide single software services to end users. Services today are independently developed and deployed as well as freely composed while they can be implemented in a variety of technologies, a quite important fact from a business perspective. Similarly, cloud computing aims at enabling flexibility by offering a centralized sharing of resources. The industry's need for agile and flexible software and IT systems has made cloud computing the dominating paradigm for provisioning computational resources in a scalable, on-demand fashion. Nevertheless, service developers, providers, and integrators still need to create methods, tools, and techniques to support cost-effective and secure development as well as the use of dependable devices, platforms, services, and service-oriented applications in the cloud.

The European Conference on Service-Oriented and Cloud Computing (ESOCC) is the premier conference on advances in the state of the art and practice of service-oriented computing and cloud computing in Europe. The main objectives of this conference are to facilitate the exchange between researchers and practitioners in the areas of service-oriented computing and cloud computing, as well as to explore the new trends in those areas and foster future collaborations in Europe and beyond. The seventh edition of ESOCC, ESOCC 2018, was held at the city of Como in Italy during September 12–14, 2018, under the auspices of University of Milano-Bicocca. ESOCC 2018 was a multi-event conference aimed at both an academic and industrial audience. The main research track represented the core event in the conference that focused on the presentation of cutting-edge research in both the service-oriented and cloud computing areas. In conjunction, an industrial track was also held attempting to bring together academia and industry through showcasing the application of service-oriented and cloud computing research, especially in the form of case studies, in industry. Overall, 33 submissions were received out of which ten outstanding full and five short papers were accepted.

Each submission was peer-reviewed by three main reviewers, either directly from the Program Committee (PC) members or their colleagues. Owing to the high quality of the manuscripts received, additional discussions were conducted, both between the PC members as well as between the two PC chairs before the final selection was performed. The PC chairs would like to thank all the reviewers who participated in the reviewing process not only for helping to increase the quality of the received manuscripts but also for sharing particular ideas on how the respective work, even if rejected in its current form for the ESOCC conference, could be substantially improved. ESOCC 2018 included two special tracks devoted to "Business Process Management in the Cloud" as well as "Service and Cloud Computing in the Era of Virtualisation." The former had the goal to bring forward the notion of business process as a service

(BPaaS), i.e., of a business process that is offered in the form of a service in the cloud, as well as to explicate the various research directions that need to be followed in order to not only realise but also properly support and improve this new cloud offering. The second track aimed at examining how the design, development, and execution of service-based applications is influenced by the different virtualisation levels that exist today, which might also exhibit different levels of latency, scalability, manageability, and customizability.

The attendees of ESOCC had the opportunity to follow two outstanding keynotes that were part of the conference program. The first keynote was given by Omer Rana, Full Professor and Head of Complex Systems Research Group in the School of Computer Science and Informatics at Cardiff University. This keynote concerned the presentation of a novel data-processing architecture across different infrastructure layers that enables the migration of core functionality at the edges of the network to support the more efficient use of datacentre and intra-network resources. The second keynote was given by Valerie Issarny, Senior Research Scientist at Inria, who is also a co-founder of the Ambientic start-up as well as a scientific manager of the Inria@Sillicon Valley program. Dr. Issarny discussed in her keynote the new possibilities of mobile distributed computing systems and explained the main breakthroughs that her MIMOVE team has achieved at Inria with respect to urban participatory mobile systems concerning the leverage of mobile collaborative sensing and computing to enhance the effectiveness of these systems with respect to the delivery of quality of service.

The additional events held at ESOCC 2018 included the PhD symposium, enabling PhD students to present their work in front of real experts, as well as the EU projects track, supplying the opportunity to researchers to present the main research results that they have achieved in the context of currently operating EU projects. Further, ESOCC 2018 included the organization of three workshops, namely, the First International Workshop on Optimization in Modern Operating Systems (OptiMoCS 2018), the 4th International Workshop on Cloud Migration and Architecture (CloudWays 2018), and the 14th International Workshop on Engineering Service-Oriented Applications and Cloud Services (WESOACS 2018), for which the respective proceedings will be published separately.

The PC chairs and the general chair would like to gratefully thank all the persons involved in making ESOCC 2018 a success. This includes both the PC members and their colleagues that assisted in the reviews as well as the organizers of the industry track, the PhD symposium, the EU projects track, and the three workshops. A special applause should also go to the members of the local Organizing Committee for their devotion, willingness, and hospitality. Finally, we would cordially like to thank all the authors of all the manuscripts submitted to ESOCC 2018, the presenters of the accepted papers who made interesting and fascinating presentations of their work, as well as the active attendees of the conference who initiated interesting discussions and gave fruitful feedback to the presenters. All these persons not only enabled a very successful organization and execution of ESOCC 2018 but also formulate an active and vibrant community that continuously contributes to the research in service-oriented and cloud computing. This also encourages ESOCC to continue contributing with new research outcomes to further facilitate and enlarge its community as well as have a greater impact and share in both service-oriented and cloud computing research.

September 2018   Kyriakos Kritikos
Pierluigi Plebani
Flavio de Paoli

Organization

ESOCC 2018 was organized by the University of Milano-Bicocca, Italy

Organizing Committee

General Chair

Flavio De Paoli   University of Milano-Bicocca, Italy

Program Chairs

Kyriakos Kritikos   ICS-FORTH, Greece
Pierluigi Plebani   Politecnico di Milano, Italy

Industry Track Chairs

Marco Brambilla   Politecnico di Milano, Italy
Erik Wilde   CA Technologies API Academy, Switzerland

Workshop Chairs

Wolf Zimmermann   Martin Luther University Halle-Wittenberg, Germany
Maria Fazio   University of Messina, Italy

EU Project Space Chairs

Federico Facca   Martel Innovate, Switzerland
Dumitru Roman   SINTEF/University of Oslo, Norway

PhD Symposium Chairs

Vasilios Andrikopoulos   University of Groningen, The Netherlands
Massimo Villari   University of Messina, Italy

Website Chair

Marco Cremaschi   University of Milano-Bicocca, Italy

Steering Committee

Antonio Brogi   University of Pisa, Italy
Schahram Dustdar   TU Wien, Austria
Paul Grefen   Eindhoven University of Technology, The Netherlands
Kung Kiu Lau   University of Manchester, UK
Winfried Lamersdorf   University of Hamburg, Germany
Frank Leymann   University of Stuttgart, Germany

Flavio de Paoli   University of Milano-Bicocca, Italy
Cesare Pautasso   University of Lugano, Switzerland
Ernesto Pimentel   University of Malaga, Spain
Ulf Schreier   Hochschule Furtwangen University, Germany
Stefan Schulte   TU Wien, Austria
Massimo Villari   University of Messina, Italy
John Erik Wittern   IBM T.J. Watson Research Center, USA
Olaf Zimmermann   HSR FHO Rapperswil, Switzerland
Wolf Zimmermann   Martin Luther University Halle-Wittenberg, Germany

Program Committee

Marco Aiello   University of Groningen, The Netherlands
Vasilios Andrikopoulos   University of Groningen, The Netherlands
Farhad Arbab   CWI, The Netherlands
Luciano Baresi   Politecnico di Milano, Italy
Boualem Benatallah   The University of New South Wales, Australia
Antonio Brogi   University of Pisa, Italy
Giacomo Cabri   University of Modena and Reggio Emilia, Italy
Marco Comuzzi   Ulsan National Institute of Science and Technology,
                             South Korea
Frank de Boer   CWI, The Netherlands
Schahram Dustdar   TU Wien, Austria
Robert Engel   IBM Almaden, USA
Rik Eshuis   Eindhoven University of Technology, The Netherlands
George Feuerlicht   Prague University of Economics, Czech Republic
Marisol Garca-Valls   Universidad Carlos III de Madrid, Spain
Ilche Georgievski   University of Groningen, The Netherlands
Claude Godart   University of Lorraine, France
Paul Grefen   Eindhoven University of Technology, The Netherlands
Heerko Groefsema   University of Groningen, The Netherlands
Thomas Gschwind   IBM Zurich Research Lab, Switzerland
Martin Henkel   Stockholm University, Sweden
Knut Hinkelmann   FHNW University of Applied Sciences and Arts,
                             Northwestern, Switzerland
Einar Broch Johnsen   University of Oslo, Norway
Oliver Kopp   University of Stuttgart, Germany
Ernoe Kovacs   NEC Europe Network Labs, Germany
Patricia Lago   VU University Amsterdam, The Netherlands
Winfried Lamersdorf   University of Hamburg, Germany
Kung-Kiu Lau   University of Manchester, UK
Frank Leymann   University of Stuttgart, Germany
Zoltan Adam Mann   University of Duisburg-Essen, Germany
Roy Oberhauser   Aalen University, Germany
Guadalupe Ortiz   University of Cadiz, Spain
Claus Pahl   Free University of Bozen-Bolzano, Italy

Contents

When Service-Oriented Computing Meets the IoT: A Use Case in the Context of Urban Mobile Crowdsensing
Invited Paper

Valérie Issarny[1](✉), Georgios Bouloukakis[1], Nikolaos Georgantas[1],
Françoise Sailhan[2], and Géraldine Texier[3]

[1] Inria, Paris, France
{valerie.issarny,georgios.bouloukakis,nikolaos.georgantas}@inria.fr
[2] CNAM, Paris, France
francoise.sailhan@cnam.fr
[3] IMT Atlantique/IRISA/UBL, Rennes, France
geraldine.texier@imt-atlantique.fr

Abstract. The possibilities of new mobile distributed systems have reached unprecedented levels. Such systems are dynamically composed of networked resources in the environment, which may span from the immediate neighborhood of the users - as advocated by pervasive computing - up to the entire globe - as envisioned by the Future Internet and one of its major constituents, the Internet of Things. This paper more specifically concentrates on urban participatory mobile distributed systems where people get involved in producing new knowledge about the urban environment. Service-oriented and cloud computing are evident baseline technologies for the target mobile distributed systems. Service orientation provides the abstraction to deal with the assembly of the relevant heterogeneous component systems. The cloud provides the infrastructure to deal with the gathering and analyses of the observations coming from the sensing infrastructure, including from people. However, cloud-based centralized solutions come at a price, regarding both resource consumption and privacy risk. Further, the high heterogeneity of the participating nodes results in diverse levels of sensing accuracy. This paper provides an overview of our past and ongoing research to overcome the challenges facing urban participatory mobile distributed systems, which leverages mobile collaborative sensing, networking and computing. The experience with the Ambiciti platform and associated mobile app for monitoring the individual and collective exposure to environmental pollution serves as an illustrative use case.

Keywords: IoT · Interoperability · Middleware
Mobile crowdsensing · Urban sensing systems · Multiparty calibration

© IFIP International Federation for Information Processing 2018
Published by Springer Nature Switzerland AG 2018. All Rights Reserved
K. Kritikos et al. (Eds.): ESOCC 2018, LNCS 11116, pp. 1–16, 2018.
https://doi.org/10.1007/978-3-319-99819-0_1

1 Introduction

The Service Oriented Computing –SOC– (or Service Oriented Architecture – SOA) paradigm has proved particularly appropriate for ubiquitous and mobile computing systems [14]. Through the abstraction of networked devices and their hosted applications as services delivered and consumed on demand, the SOA approach enables the assembly of systems whose component systems can be retrieved and composed statically as much as dynamically, thanks to service discovery and service interaction protocols. While mobile services incorporate and apply the fundamental principles of SOA, they present a number of specifics that push certain challenges related to service oriented systems to their extreme and additionally introduce new unique research challenges. Such specifics relate to: (i) dynamism – open mobile environments are much more volatile than typical service environments, with services emerging and disappearing in arbitrary ways without prior notification; (ii) heterogeneity – a direct consequence of ad hoc mobile environments is that no safe assumption can be made about the technological and business features of the services encountered; and (iii) the equation among QoS expectations on services, scalability, and required resources is hard to solve, due to the resource constraints of mobile environments. Dealing with the identified specifics gets even more complex if we consider both traditional computing services and services attached to the physical world by means of sensors and actuators, i.e., Things [9].

This paper specifically focuses on the design of service-oriented systems supporting the analysis of urban-scale phenomena through the composition of the diverse relevant sensing services, from services supported by urban infrastructure networks to services gathering observations from end-users (Fig. 1). The related research challenges are numerous, including the ones due to the aforementioned specifics of mobile services. Here, we concentrate on the challenges that we have been investigating in relation with the development and deployment of an urban service monitoring the individual and collective exposure of the population to environmental pollution (Sect. 2). Thanks to the sensors that people may increasingly "hold" and/or "wear" while moving, we are potentially

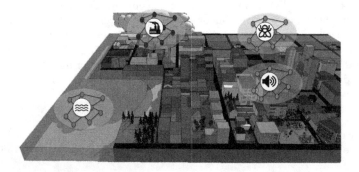

Fig. 1. Monitoring the urban environment using the fixed and mobile IoT.

able to monitor urban phenomena at a very fine grain across time and space. However, while the potential is high and examples in the area of traffic monitoring evidences it, the ability to monitor diverse urban phenomena at scale is far from being straightforward. There are indeed many hurdles arising, among which the following ones that we have been and are currently investigating:

- The monitoring of urban phenomena involves analyzing observations across time and space, but also across application domains (e.g., BMS, traffic, health). As a result, the thorough analysis of urban phenomena involves the ability to compose services across horizontal (location dependent) and vertical (application dependent) boundaries. In addition, the urban system architecture must ease such a composition of services at scale. Toward that goal, we investigate system architectures that build upon the pub/sub communication paradigm, which has proven well suited for open, large-scale dynamic systems. Further, we adopt the edge computing paradigm, which includes leveraging the processing power of the mobile nodes. Moreover, the system architecture must ease the integration of highly heterogeneous Things, which goes along with supporting interaction across diverse protocols (Sect. 3).
- While the SOC paradigm together with semantic technologies allow exposing the capabilities of the connected Things despite their high heterogeneity, the large diversity of Things also manifests itself from the standpoint of the accuracy of the delivered observations. It is then essential to assess the quality of the provided observations, which may result in either filtering out or correcting part of the observations. Obviously, the ability to correct observations leads to gathering more knowledge, for which we study automated, collaborative multi-party calibration (Sect. 4).
- The scale of the urban systems significantly challenges the networking and computing infrastructures, especially when the system keeps monitoring phenomena over time. The adoption of the pub-sub communication paradigm together with edge computing in our architecture contributes to overcoming the challenge by fostering communication and computing within the relevant geographical area(s). In addition, the mobility of nodes is worth exploiting to cross geographical regions and/or application domain boundaries. In that direction, we explore the offloading of the urban WSN-based IoT infrastructure networks to "peer" mobile nodes that act as crowdsensors in the same application domain. This allows saving the energy due to communication in the WSN and thereby increasing the WSN lifetime (Sect. 5).

The above list is only a subset of the challenges that IoT-based systems need to face to enable a thorough analysis of urban phenomena. This paper then concludes with an overview of other challenges that we and/or others are investigating and for which service-oriented and cloud computing are essential baseline technologies but that need to be revisited to handle the specifics of IoT-based systems.

2   Monitoring the Exposure to the Urban Environmental Pollution: A Use Case

According to the EU 1996 Pollution Directive (www.eea.europa.eu/policy-documents/council-directive-96-61-ec-ippc), *"'Pollution' shall mean the direct or indirect introduction as a result of human activity, of substances, vibrations, heat or noise into the air, water or land which may be harmful to human health or the quality of the environment, result in damage to materiel property, or impair or interfere with amenities and other legitimate uses of the environment."* With the majority of the population now living in cities, it is increasingly critical to be able to monitor the exposure to environmental pollution in urban centers. In particular, the research community suggests that the social cost of noise and air pollution in EU -including death and disease- could be nearly EUR 1 trillion, while the social cost of smoking in the EU has been estimated to be EUR 544 billion [17].

The development of the IoT, including the one of the sensing technologies that smartphones now embed, together with advancements in machine learning, allow for the deployment of cloud-based platforms that collect and aggregate the many relevant urban data sources to produce street-level hourly maps about the environmental pollution (e.g., [21]). Also, mobile apps that serve collecting observations about the environmental pollution enable to inform users about their individual exposure and related impact on their health [7]. As part of our research, we have developed a cloud-based platform and related mobile app for monitoring the individual and collective exposure to the environmental pollution [6]. In particular, the app implements noise sensing using the phone's microphone while accounting for the relatively low accuracy of the resulting observations [22]. In a nutshell, the mobile app implements a crowdsensing application that periodically transfers the collected observations to the cloud server, which filters out the observations that are not deemed accurate enough. The cloud server implements data assimilation techniques to integrate observations from various data sources with mathematical models to simulate the state of a system of an urban phenomenon [20].

The research resulted in the Ambiciti solution (ambiciti.io) that enables monitoring the individual exposure to noise and air pollution (Fig. 2-Left), while producing street-level maps about environmental pollution (Fig. 2-Right). In summer 2015, we deployed the first version of Ambiciti, which initially supported noise pollution monitoring only. Since autumn 2016, Ambiciti also monitors the exposure to air quality. The urban-scale deployment of Ambiciti -especially in Paris- has led us to identify a number of recommendations for the IoT-based sensing system and supporting architecture [10,12], which we have been and are still investigating. The major challenge to face is to enable and promote the gathering of observations of sufficient quality at scale so as to enable the thorough analysis of urban phenomena. The following reports on our complementary studies toward that goal. All these studies focus on developing distributed collaborative protocols that contribute to increasing the accuracy of the knowledge

Fig. 2. Monitoring the exposure to environmental pollution using Ambiciti.

produced at the edge, while reducing the overall resource consumption associated with data processing and communication.

3 System Architecture for the Urban IoT

Ubiquitous computing devices featuring sensing capabilities are deployed in a variety of *application domains*, such as smart cities, smart factories, resource management, intelligent transportation and healthcare to name a few. This enables analyzing observations of different domains across time and space in the so called *urban environment*. However, enacting IoT urban systems is still raising tremendous challenges for the supporting infrastructure from the networking up to the application layers. Key challenges [1,18] relate to *deep heterogeneity*, *high dynamicity*, *scale*, and many others.

To support the deployment of large-scale, heterogeneous and dynamic IoT urban systems we rely on the architecture depicted in Fig. 3. This comprises the following layers:

- **Device**: This layer serves applications from multiple domains. Each application involves heterogeneous devices and processing capabilities in mobile nodes.
- **Edge**: At this layer, we adopt the Edge computing paradigm to collect multi-domain data from end-users being in several regions. We define a region as a bounded geographical area with common features (e.g., a university campus). Additionally, to deal with the heterogeneity of IoT applications (exposed as services), we deploy *software interoperability artifacts* at this layer.

– **Cloud:** Several domains of IoT applications require powerful processing capabilities (e.g., for executing machine learning algorithms) and thus, at this layer we enable the use of Cloud computing resources.

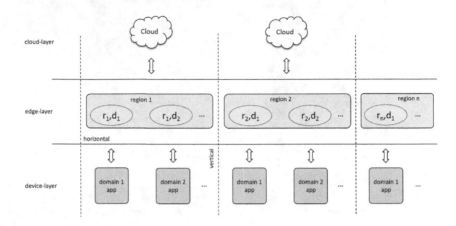

Fig. 3. System architecture for the urban IoT.

3.1   Supporting Wide-Scale IoT Apps

Mobile IoT applications are typically deployed on resource-constrained devices with intermittent network connectivity. To support the deployment of such applications, the pub/sub interaction paradigm is often employed, as it decouples mobile peers in both time and space. In a pub/sub system, multiple peers interact via an intermediate *broker* entity – publishers produce *events* characterized by a specific *filter* to the broker. Subscribers subscribe their interest for specific filters to the broker, which maintains an up-to-date list of subscriptions.

To support distributed applications spanning a wide-area, the pub/sub system has to be implemented as a set of independent, communicating brokers, forming the *broker overlay*. Let $B = \{b : i \in [1..|B|]\}$ be the set of pub/sub brokers. As depicted in Fig. 4, in such architectures [3], peers can access the system through any broker that becomes their home broker. Then, based on the peers' input, the pub/sub system ensures the delivery of the events produced towards the interested subscribers. As still shown in Fig. 4, a message broker can be assigned to support a specific region or one or more application domains inside a region. This depends on the corresponding administration of the related region's vertical markets.

Building an IoT application over a pub/sub infrastructure, requires the selection of an appropriate protocol (e.g., MQTT). Such a protocol enables IoT devices to access the broker overlay and push/receive events. Additionally, to create the pub/sub broker overlay, the corresponding *message broker* implementation (e.g., VerneMQ, HiveMQ, etc.) must be selected. Each message broker

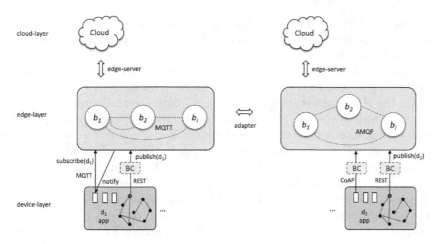

Fig. 4. Multi-domain/region pub/sub system.

technology has different capabilities, such as: compatibility with different protocols, support for clustering (i.e., forming a broker network), provision of performance features, etc. To enable the interconnection between message brokers that employ different protocols for message routing (e.g., MQTT and AMQP in Fig. 4), *adapter* software components can be utilized. Usually, such components are supported by the corresponding message broker technology (e.g., VerneMQ). An important design-time decision is the provision of resources for message broker deployment. In this work we assume the deployment of brokers at the Edge. To enable the interconnection between a message broker (Edge) and the cloud, we employ an intermediate *edge-server* which corresponds to a pub/sub subscriber that collects data and forwards them to the cloud.

3.2 Supporting Heterogeneous IoT Apps

Mobile environments can be very heterogeneous, both locally but also when reaching out to the whole IoT. Service heterogeneity concerns both business semantics and communication middleware. The former issue has led to a wide use of ontologies and related technologies in SOA. As for the latter issue, it is due to the fact that mobile IoT devices may use different communication contexts. This calls for support for heterogeneous interaction styles, namely message-driven, event-driven, and data-driven styles. Different interaction styles apply to different needs; for instance, asynchronous, event-based pub/sub is more appropriate for highly dynamic environments with frequent disconnections of involved entities. This fact makes the various service bindings supported by most service technologies too stringent, since they comply with a single (client/server) message-based interaction style. Service models should be able to abstract and comprehensively specify the various service bindings of mobile IoT devices. This further implies extending the notion of service and introducing adequate service interaction modeling. Moreover, interoperability mechanisms are required between heterogeneous interaction styles based on transformation mappings between their models.

Our work in this context has focused on the problem of interconnecting systems that employ different interaction styles or paradigms [5]. We include in particular the client/server, publish/subscribe, data streaming and tuple space paradigms, which cover the majority of communication middleware protocols enabling system interaction. Our overall approach generalizes the way to design and implement service-oriented distributed applications, where the employed interaction paradigms are explicitly represented and systematically integrated.

As a first step, we identified the semantics of the four principal interaction paradigms and elicited a connector model for each paradigm. Our models represent the essential semantics of interaction paradigms, concerning *space coupling*, *time coupling*, *concurrency* and *synchronization coupling*. These four categories of semantics are of primary importance, because these are end-to-end semantics: when interconnecting different interaction paradigms, we seek to map and preserve these semantics. Inside each interaction paradigm, we identify further one or more of four *interaction types*: one-way, two-way synchronous, two-way asynchronous and *two-way streaming* interaction. These interaction types incorporate the above semantics of end-to-end interactions.

Following the previous step, we introduced a higher-level connector model that comprehensively represents the semantics of various middleware protocols that follow the four base connector models, hence it can represent the majority of the existing and possibly of the future middleware protocols. In particular, this connector models the four interaction types supported by the base connector models in an abstract way. Furthermore, we introduced a generic interface description language for specifying interfaces in an abstract way. This language enables the definition of operations provided or required by an application component that follow the four interaction types.

By relying on the above abstractions, we have introduced a solution to seamlessly interconnect IoT devices that employ heterogeneous interaction protocols at the middleware level [2]. Interconnection is performed via one or more message brokers lying at the Edge as presented in the previous section. More specifically, a dedicated software component called a *Binding Component (BC)* performs the conversion between the middleware protocol of an IoT device and the message broker protocol as depicted in Fig. 4.

Based on our modeling abstractions, we have developed a systematic approach for the automated synthesis of BCs. The development of BCs is a tedious and error-prone process, which can highly benefit from our automated systematic support. This can help application developers integrate heterogeneous IoT devices inside complex applications. Furthermore, the automated BC synthesis is essential for applications relying on the dynamic runtime composition of heterogeneous devices, where there is no human intervention. Our solution was introduced as a core component of the H2020 CHOReVOLUTION project (chorevolution.eu) to enable heterogeneous interactions in services &

Things choreographies. Currently, it supports the following middleware protocols: REST, CoAP, MQTT, WebSockets, SemiSpace and DPWS. It is released as open source software (gitlab.inria.fr/zefxis).

4 Overcoming the Low Accuracy of Mobile Crowdsensors

Current crowdsensing approaches are primarily focused on collecting data at a large scale, as in particular supported by the pub/sub system architecture of the previous section. However, without any suitable calibration mechanism, smartphones tend to disclose inaccurate readings. To tackle this issue, we propose to collaboratively and automatically calibrate in the field, the sensors embedded in and/or connected to the smartphones. Thus, when some mobile sensors are in the same spatial vicinity, uncalibrated sensors get automatically calibrated –without involving the end users. Compared to existing solutions that iteratively calibrate one by one a unique mobile sensor at a given time, our approach supports the joint calibration of several uncalibrated sensors, thus reducing the overall calibration delay. This leads to a multi-party, multi-hop calibration for which the history of calibrated sensors is used to assess the best calibration hyperpath, which is the one that minimizes the accumulated calibration error. Our approach towards accurate urban sensing further distinguishes from the traditional WSN setting by enabling mobile, consumer-centric smartphones to interact with both stationary and mobile sensors in their proximity so as to calibrate the smartphones' sensors. In particular, our solution leverages the presence of two types of sensors:

- *Reference sensors* correspond to high fidelity sensors (e.g., a sound meter in the case of noise sensing) that are regularly calibrated by experts. Reference sensors are typically government-run (see Fig. 2 in [13] for an illustration of the few reference sensors measuring noise in the city of Paris) and their measurements are generally made publicly available. They are wirelessly networked [16] as detailed in the next section.
- *Mobile sensors* correspond to low cost and less accurate sensors that are owned by individuals (they typically include the sensors embedded in smartphones) and that need to be remotely calibrated.

Then, the reference sensors that belong to the urban infrastructure support the calibration of any mobile sensor that is within sensing range. And, in turn, the newly calibrated sensors may be used to calibrate the uncalibrated sensors they meet (as they move). The following outlines our solution whose detailed presentation may be found in [15].

Multi-party Calibration. During a rendezvous, any uncalibrated sensor i attempts to calibrate using the calibrated measurements provided by the m nearby sensors, for which we leverage multivariate linear regression.

As illustrated in Fig. 5, there is a linear dependency between the measurements produced by a non-calibrated sensor and the m surrounding calibrated sensors. Thus, any reading $y_i(t)$ of the uncalibrated sensor i at time t can be expressed as the following linear function:

$$y_i(t) = \beta_0 + \beta_1 x_1(t) + \beta_2 x_2(t) + \cdots + \beta_m x_m(t) + e_i(t) \tag{1}$$

where: $x_j(t)$ ($j \in [1, \cdots, m]$) denotes the calibrated measurements of the m sensors; $\beta_0, \cdots, \beta_m$ represent the unknown (and fixed) regression coefficients; and $e_i(t)$ is the residual noise, with $t \in [t_1, \cdots, t_p]$. The goal is to find the regression coefficients $\beta_0, \beta_1, \cdots + \beta_m$ that minimizes the residual noise. For this, we rely on the least square method, which minimizes the sum of the squared distance of the data points from the line measured perpendicular to the x axis (see Fig. 5).

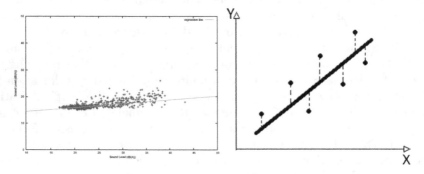

Fig. 5. An uncalibrated smartphone calibrates using the calibrated measurement of one calibrated smartphone. Regression lies in fitting a straight line to bivariate data using least square regression. The regression minimizes the vertical residual (dashed line on the right figure) by keeping to a minimum the squared vertical distance from each data point to the line.

Multi hops, multi-party calibration. Thanks to the above multivariate linear regression, the calibration coefficients of an uncalibrated smartphone sensor i may be estimated based on the readings provided by the surrounding sensors that are met during a multiparty rendezvous. However, sensor i should not systematically (re-)calibrate: it must do so only if the quality of the regression is sufficient. In particular, a high residual error (i.e., e_i in Eq. 1) reflects a poor correlation between the readings provided by the surrounding sensors, and in such a case, the conditions are not met for an effective calibration. This may occur when some smartphones are in bags/pockets and others are handheld.

Another aspect to consider for assessing the relevance of a given multiparty calibration relates to the history of past calibrations. We must compare the quality of the calibration parameters computed in the current rendezvous against the quality of the previous calibrations (if any). We thus maintain the history of multiparty calibrations using a weighted directed *hypergraph*: a multiparty rendezvous between sensor i and K sensors is represented by an *hyperedge* between sensor i and the K sensors. The quality of the regression established by i based on the readings provided by the K sensors is reflected by the weight of the directed hyperedge between i and the K sensors. Ultimately, the preferred calibration is the one that results in the lowest cumulated weight.

Summarizing the proposed multiparty calibration method, any smartphone (embedding a sensor) i participating in the collaborative calibration periodically performs the following process:

1. Smartphone i detects the presence of nearby sensing device(s), i.e., devices in the shared sensing range.
2. If any eligible rendezvous, i exchanges its sensing measurements (i.e., time series) in a synchronized manner so as to establish the linear relationship between the measurements of the nearby sensors and the raw measurements obtained locally.
3. The best calibration path is determined and the calibration function is set.

Overall, the key feature of the calibration system is to enhance the accuracy of the raw data sensing provided by a self-selected and potentially unskillfulness or distrustful crowd. As few anomalies or discordant observations may contaminate the overall knowledge, it is critical to identify, detect and treat such anomalies. To tackle this issue, we attempt to combine two complementary approaches: (i) we harness the power of the crowd to collaboratively sense and calibrate, (ii) we coordinate with city-owned sensors so as to support an initial bootstrapping calibration.

5   When Crowdsensing Meets the Infrastructured IoT Networks

The previous section shows how the participatory sensing benefits from an interaction with smart city sensing infrastructures to bootstrap the calibration of the crowdsensors and deliver more accurate measurements. This cooperation can be deepened to achieve a mutual benefit for crowdsensing and the urban IoT infrastructures. For this, we advocate the possibility of direct interactions between crowd smartphones and the infrastructured sensors that surround them. First – as illustrated in the previous section–, such interactions can benefit smartphones by allowing them to quickly and directly retrieve (higher quality) measurements taken around them. Second, smartphones can push their participatory engagement further: in addition to making their smartphone's sensors available, they can also offer to share part of their network interconnection to offload the WSN and relay part of its data (as shown in Fig. 7).

In general, urban measurement infrastructures are implemented by Wireless Sensor Networks (WSN), which are more or less extensive and distributed in the city. The sensors perform measurements and send them towards a gateway (the WSN's sink) in charge of publishing to the pub/sub system the collected data through its Binding Component (BC) as shown in Fig. 6. To do this, the WSN implements convergecast communication to allow the sink to collect data generated by each sensor in the network. With the exception of the leafs, each

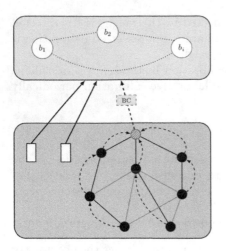
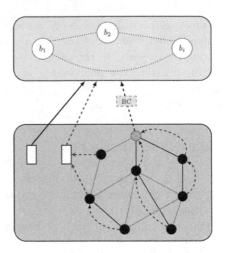

Fig. 6. Classical convergecast data collection in the WSN.

Fig. 7. Smartphone offloading data from the WSN.

sensor sends its parents both the data it generates and the data transmitted to it by its children. The worst case is that of the nodes near the sink: the emission of the measurements they generate represents only a small fraction of their communications since they spend most of their time relaying their children's data.

But, due to high deployment constraints in urban environments, sensors in the WSNs are often battery powered, which limits the lifetime of the whole urban sensing infrastructure. However, the definition of the WSN lifetime depends on the policy of the network operator. If it does not tolerate any failure, the lifetime of the network is limited by the exhaustion of the energy of at least one sensor. Another strategy is to tolerate a given number of sensors that no longer work, in which case the lifetime of the network is determined by the number of sensors that remain connected to the sink despite the death of a subset of sensors. Whatever lifetime definition is chosen, a smartphone can help the infrastructure survive longer by giving it the ability to relay some of its data. Note that this requires that smartphones can connect to infrastructured sensors, for example via protocols such as Zigbee, 802.15.4 or Bluetooth Low Energy (BLE). The fact is that sensors are increasingly able to communicate and we believe that lack of compatibility is less a technical problem than a market problem. So, although with the exception of BLE, most smartphones do not yet integrate the main interfaces supported by the sensors, we think that this will evolve within a reasonable time. Therefore, we consider that direct communication between the infrastructure and smartphones is not an obstacle for our work and will be available in the future.

Many studies have sought to optimize the lifetime of networks. They can be classified according to the techniques they propose. Some solutions seek to maximize the network lifetime by enhancing RPL energy efficiency [11]. For example with a RPL metric that integrates the available energy of the WSN nodes [8] to ensure that the nodes solicited for relaying data are the ones with the highest energy budget. However, using a routing protocol with such a very dynamic metric implies great routing instability. Other solutions are based on Delay Tolerant Networks communication techniques. In particular, the optimization of the data collection by a mobile node, usually through the optimization of the mobile node's trajectory based on variants of the traveling salesman problem [4].

In [19], we have presented how the cooperation of the crowd smartphones and the urban WSN can extend the measurement infrastructure's lifetime based on both optimization and traffic engineering techniques. We proposed a model to integrate the crowd smartphones as mobile sinks able to offload a portion of the WSN data transmissions. We optimize the routing to take advantage of the path diversity offered by the WSN topology. With a simple energy model (each sensor has an energy budget given by the capacity of its batteries), we determine the number of communications a sensor is able to perform before exhausting its energy. We can also compute the network lifetime, in our case the time before at least one sensor runs out of energy. Our linear program determines the quantity of data that a sensor should send to each of its neighbors (including mobile nodes) to maximize the network lifetime. Although the efficiency of the solution is strongly linked to the location of mobile nodes, we have shown on a realistic example that when we allow a subset of network sensors to communicate with a mobile node, we can increase the lifetime of the network in significant proportions (in our example, we multiplied the lifetime of the network by 7). Our work opens several research issues that we are exploring as part of our ongoing and future work. One of these issues relates to our load balancing strategy that requires the introduction of proportional routing into the WSN routing mechanism. This modification also makes it possible to support temporary failures of the sensors by offering next alternative jumps if a node having to relay the information is not available at the time of emission.

6   Conclusion

The IoT holds the promise of blending the physical with the virtual world, while the power of the crowd enables gathering knowledge at unprecedented scales across both time and space. However, the vision raises tremendous challenges for the supporting system architectures, among which keeping pace with the target scale and overcoming the heterogeneity of the IoT nodes. The literature has shown that service-oriented and cloud computing are evident baseline technologies: service orientation brings abstraction to overcome heterogeneity and the cloud brings the computing infrastructure to aggregate the knowledge sensed within the IoT. However, this puts high demand on the networking infrastructure, while collaborative networking and computing at the edge allow for significant resource saving. Our research focuses on such collaborative distributed

IoT-based system architectures at the edge, where we build upon our experience on developing and deploying an urban-scale system for the monitoring of the individual and collective exposure to environmental pollution.

This paper has outlined our most recent research in the area, spanning the study of: (1) a publish-subscribe system architecture enriched with software interoperability artifacts to support the interconnection of applications implementing heterogeneous communication paradigms; (2) in-network multi-party, multi-hop calibration so as to overcome the low accuracy of low cost sensors, and especially of the sensors embedded in smartphones; and (3) collaboration between the smartphones running crowdsensing apps and the urban WSN-based IoT infrastructures toward increasing the lifetime of the WSN networks.

Crowdsensing- and IoT-based system architectures, from networking up to the middleware and application layers, have been studied extensively over the last ten years, while we have focused our presentation on our specific contributions over the last couple of years. The interested reader is referred to the bibliography provided in the cited references for an overview and analysis of related work.

We have many research challenges ahead of us and some of them have been mentioned along the sections. Among our ongoing research, we would like to stress the study of privacy-aware crowdsensing systems due to the tension that the topic creates: (1) On the one hand, we know that the more accurate and precise knowledge we get about the urban environment, the more we will be able to develop effective solutions to enhance the people's well-being and reduce urban resource consumption; (2) On the other hand, gathering such a precise knowledge also goes along with the ability to infer knowledge about people and even individuals. Part of the solution lies in policy making as for instance illustrated by the recent GDPR data protection policy by the EU. Further, crowdsensing systems must be designed to enforce privacy preservation. Distributed collaborative crowdsensing systems where the individual knowledge remains at the edge and ultimately on the user's device contribute to it. Still, the systems must support the appropriate tradeoffs so that relevant urban-scale knowledge may be computed to inform the city development.

Acknowledgments. The authors would like to thank the support of: the Inria@SiliconValley International Lab, CityLab@Inria Project lab, and the EIT Digital innovation activity Env&You. They also gratefully acknowledge the major contribution of their Inria colleagues, Vivien Mallet, Pierre-Guillaume Raverdy and Kinh Nguyen, to the development of the Ambiciti system solution.

References

1. Al-Fuqaha, A., Guizani, M., Mohammadi, M., Aledhari, M., Ayyash, M.: Internet of things: a survey on enabling technologies, protocols, and applications. IEEE Commun. Surv. Tutorials 4(17), 2347–2376 (2015)
2. Bouloukakis, G.: Enabling emergent mobile systems in the IoT: from middleware-layer communication interoperability to associated QoS analysis. Ph.D. thesis (2017)

3. Bouloukakis, G., Georgantas, N., Kattepur, A., Issarny, V.: Timeliness evaluation of intermittent mobile connectivity over pub/sub systems. In: Proceedings of the 8th ACM/SPEC on International Conference on Performance Engineering (2017)
4. Garraffa, M., Bekhti, M., Létocart, L., Achir, N., Boussetta, K.: Drones path planning for WSN data gathering: a column generation heuristic approach. In: IEEE Wireless Communications and Networking Conference (WCNC) (2018)
5. Georgantas, N., Bouloukakis, G., Beauche, S., Issarny, V.: Service-oriented distributed applications in the future internet: the case for interaction paradigm interoperability. In: Lau, K.-K., Lamersdorf, W., Pimentel, E. (eds.) ESOCC 2013. LNCS, vol. 8135, pp. 134–148. Springer, Heidelberg (2013). https://doi.org/10.1007/978-3-642-40651-5_11
6. Hachem, S., Mallet, V., Raphaël, V., Raverdy, P.G., Pathak, A., Issarny, V., Bhatia, R.: Monitoring noise pollution using the urban civics middleware. In: IEEE Big Data Service (2015)
7. Hachem, S., Mathioudakis, G., Pathak, A., Issarny, V., Bhatia, R.: Sense2Health: a quantified self application for monitoring personal exposure to environmental pollution. In: SENSORNETS (2015)
8. Iova, O., Theoleyre, F., Noel, T.: Using multiparent routing in RPL to increase the stability and the lifetime of the network. Ad Hoc Netw. **29**, 45–62 (2015)
9. Issarny, V., Bouloukakis, G., Georgantas, N., Billet, B.: Revisiting service-oriented architecture for the IoT: a middleware perspective. In: 14th International Conference on Service Oriented Computing (ICSOC) (2016)
10. Issarny, V., Mallet, V., Nguyen, K., Raverdy, P.G., Rebhi, F., Ventura, R.: Dos and Don'ts in mobile phone sensing middleware: learning from a large-scale experiment. In: Proceedings of the 2016 International Middleware Conference (2016)
11. Kamgueu, P.O., Nataf, E., Ndie, T.D.: Survey on RPL enhancements: a focus on topology, security and mobility. Comput. Commun. **120**, 10–21 (2018)
12. Lefèvre, B., Issarny, V.: Matching technological & societal innovations: the social design of a mobile collaborative app for urban noise monitoring. In: 4th IEEE International Conference on Smart Computing (2018)
13. Maisonneuve, N., Stevens, M., Ochab, B.: Participatory noise pollution monitoring using mobile phones. Inf. Polity - Gov. 2.0 Making Connections Between Citizens Data Gov. **15**(1,2), 51–71 (2010)
14. Papazoglou, M.P., Traverso, P., Dustdar, S., Leymann, F.: Service-oriented computing: state of the art and research challenges. Computer **40**(11), 38–45 (2007)
15. Sailhan, F., Issarny, V., Tavares Nascimento, O.: Opportunistic multiparty calibration for robust participatory sensing. In: MASS 2017 - IEEE 14th International Conference on Mobile Ad Hoc and Sensor Systems (2017)
16. Santini, S., Ostermaier, B., Vitaletti, A.: First experiences using wireless sensor networks for noise pollution monitoring. In: Proceedings of the Workshop on Real-world Wireless Sensor Networks (REALWSN) (2008)
17. SEP: Links between noise and air pollution and socioeconomic status - in-depth report 13 produced for the European commission, DG environment by the science communication unit, UWE, Bristol. Technical report, Science for Environment Policy (2016). http://ec.europa.eu/science-environment-policy
18. Teixeira, T., Hachem, S., Issarny, V., Georgantas, N.: Service oriented middleware for the internet of things: a perspective. In: ServiceWave - European Conference on a Service-Based Internet (2011)
19. Texier, G., Issarny, V.: Leveraging the power of the crowd and offloading urban IoT networks to extend their lifetime. In: LANMAN 2018: IEEE International Symposium on Local and Metropolitan Area Networks (2018)

20. Tilloy, A., Mallet, V., Poulet, D., Pesin, C., Brocheton, F.: BLUE-based NO_2 data assimilation at urban scale. J. Geophys. Res. **118**(4), 2031–2040 (2013)
21. Ventura, R., Mallet, V., Issarny, V., Raverdy, P.G., Rebhi, F.: Estimation of urban noise with the assimilation of observations crowdsensed by the mobile application Ambiciti. In: INTER-NOISE 2017–46th International Congress and Exposition on Noise Control Engineering Taming Noise and Moving Quiet (2017)
22. Ventura, R., Mallet, V., Issarny, V., Raverdy, P.G., Rebhi, F.: Evaluation and calibration of mobile phones for noise monitoring application. J. Acoust. Soc. Am. **142**(5), 3084 (2017)

True Concurrent Management
of Multi-component Applications

Antonio Brogi, Andrea Canciani, and Jacopo Soldani[(✉)]

Department of Computer Science, University of Pisa, Pisa, Italy
soldani@di.unipi.it

Abstract. Complex applications orchestrate multiple components and services, which are independently managed by different teams (e.g., DevOps squads). As a consequence, various services may happen to be updated, reconfigured or redeployed concurrently, possibly yielding unexpected/undesired management effects. In this paper, we show how the true concurrent management of multi-component applications can be suitably modelled, analysed and automated, also in presence of faults.

1 Introduction

The efficient exploitation of cloud computing peculiarities depends on the degree of management automation of the applications shipped to cloud platforms [20]. As cloud applications typically integrate various heterogeneous components, the problem of automating the management of multi-component applications is currently one of the major concerns in enterprise IT [21].

To automate the management of a multi-component application, the concurrent deployment, configuration, enactment and termination of its components must be properly coordinated. Even if this may be done by different independent teams (e.g., DevOps squads), it must be done by considering all dependencies occurring among the components of an application. As the number of components grows, and the need to reconfigure them becomes more frequent, application management becomes more time-consuming and error-prone [5].

The components forming a multi-component application, as well as the dependencies occurring among such components, can be conveniently represented by means of topology graphs [3]. A component is represented as a node in a topology graph, while a dependency between two components can be represented by an arc interconnecting the corresponding two nodes. More precisely, each node models an application component by indicating the operations to manage it, its requirements, and the capabilities it offers to satisfy the requirements of other nodes. Each oriented arc models the dependency of a component on another, by connecting a requirement of the former to a capability of the latter.

Management protocols [6,7] enable the modelling and analysis of the management of multi-component applications, faults included. Each node is equipped with its own management protocol, i.e., a finite state machine whose transitions

© IFIP International Federation for Information Processing 2018
Published by Springer Nature Switzerland AG 2018. All Rights Reserved
K. Kritikos et al. (Eds.): ESOCC 2018, LNCS 11116, pp. 17–32, 2018.
https://doi.org/10.1007/978-3-319-99819-0_2

and states are associated with conditions on the requirements and capabilities of such node. Conditions on transitions indicate which requirements must be satisfied to perform a management operation. Conditions on states define state consistency, by indicating which requirements of a node must be satisfied in a state, as well as which capabilities the node is actually providing in such state. Management protocols also allow indicating how a node reacts to faults, which occur whenever the condition of consistency of a state is violated. The management behaviour of a multi-component application can then be derived by composing the management protocols of its nodes (according to the interconnections defined in its topology). The obtained behaviour can be exploited to automate various useful analyses, from checking whether a management plan is valid, to automatically determining management plans allowing to recover applications that are stuck because of mishandled faults or because of components behaving differently than expected.

Management protocols (as per [6, 7]) rely on an interleaving semantics. Transitions are considered as atomic, and consistency is only checked on states. This means that management protocols do not support the analysis of the true concurrent execution of management operations. Consider for instance the concurrent reconfiguration of two components, with one component requiring a capability of the other to successfully complete its reconfiguration. The latter may however stop providing the desired capability during the execution of its reconfiguration operation, even if such capability is provided right before and after executing such operation. While this may result in one of the two reconfiguration operations failing, an interleaving semantics (checking consistency only on states) would not be able to detect such failure.

In other words, faults can happen both after and *during* the concurrent execution of management operations [9]. In this paper, we extend management protocols to permit indicating how nodes react to faults happening while transiting from one state to another. We then show how to derive the management behaviour of a multi-component application by considering the true concurrent execution of the management operations of its components, and how this enables the analysis and automation of their concurrent management.

The rest of this paper is organised as follows. Section 2 illustrates an example motivating the need for extending management protocols to support true concurrency. The extension is then presented in Sect. 3, and Sect. 4 shows how to use it to analyse the true concurrent management behaviour of applications. Sections 5 and 6 discuss related work and draw some concluding remarks, respectively.

2   Motivating Example

Consider the web application in Fig. 1. The frontend of the application is implemented in JavaScript, it is hosted on a node container, and it exploits a backend component to provide its functionalities. The backend component is instead implemented in Java, it is hosted on a maven container, and it manages the application data stored by a mongo container.

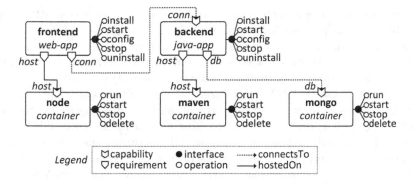

Fig. 1. Topology of the application in our motivating example. The topology is depicted according to the TOSCA graphical notation [18].

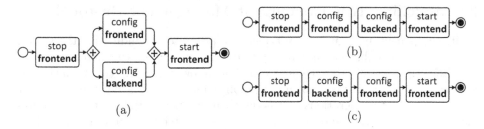

Fig. 2. Three management plans for reconfiguring backend and frontend, depicted by following the BPMN graphical notation [19].

Figure 1 explicitly represents the requirements and capabilities of the components of the considered application, the management operations they offer, as well as all inter-component dependencies. The latter are represented as relationships connecting each requirement of each node with the capability satisfying such requirement (e.g., the requirements host and conn of frontend are connected with the homonym capabilities of node and backend, respectively).

Suppose now that we wish to orchestrate the re-configuration of the frontend and backend of our application, by developing a dedicated management plan to be executed when the application is up and running. It is easy to see that one may end up in producing invalid management plans. For instance, while Fig. 2 illustrates three seemingly valid plans, only (b) and (c) are valid. Plan (a) is not valid because the concurrent execution of the operations config of frontend and backend may cause a failure in frontend. frontend indeed requires the endpoint offered by backend to successfully complete its config operation. However, backend stops providing its endpoint during the execution of its config operation. This means that the concurrent execution of both operations may result in a failure of frontend, which may not successfully complete its config operation.

The above issue is not recognised even if application components are equipped with the management protocols in [6,7] to describe their management behaviour.

Management protocols currently support an analysis of the management of applications based on an interleaving semantics, which prescribes to analyse plan (a) by considering all its sequential traces (differently interleaving concurrently performed operations). As such traces correspond to the valid management plans (b) and (c), we would end up in considering also plan (a) as valid.

We however know that (a) is not valid, because of the fault that can occur during the true concurrent execution of the operations to configure frontend and backend. Such fault is due to a node stopping to provide its capabilities, while another node is actually relying on such capabilities during the execution of one of its management operations. Management protocols must hence be extended by allowing to indicate how nodes react to the occurrence of a fault *while* executing a management operation, as this would enable the modelling and analysis of the true concurrent management of multi-component applications.

3 Modelling True Concurrent Management Protocols

Multi-component applications are typically represented by indicating the states, requirements, capabilities and management operations of the nodes composing their topology [3]. Management protocols allow specifying the management behaviour of the nodes composing an application, by indicating the behaviour of the management operations of a node, their relations with its states, requirements and capabilities, and how a node reacts to a failure in a state.

We hereby present an extension of management protocols, geared towards enabling the analysis of a true concurrent management of the components of an application. Intuitively speaking, the essence of the extension is to consider the execution of management operations as transient states, instead of as atomic transitions. The extension indeed allows to indicate which capabilities are concretely maintained during a transition, which requirements are needed to continue to perform a transition, and how a node reacts when a failure happens while executing a transition.

Management protocols allow specifying the management behaviour of a node N (modelling an application component), by indicating (i) whether/how each management operation of N depends on other management operations of N, (ii) whether/how it depends on operations of the nodes that provide capabilities satisfying the requirements of N, and (iii) how N reacts when a fault occurs.

Dependencies of type (i) are described by relating the management operations of N with its states. A transition relation τ_N indeed describes the order of execution of the operations of N, by indicating whether a given management operation can be executed in a state of N, and which state is reached if its execution is successfully completed.

Dependencies of type (ii) are instead described by associating (possibly empty) sets of requirements with both states and transitions. The requirements associated with a state/transition of N must continue to be satisfied in order for N to continue to work properly (i.e., to continue to reside in a state/to successfully complete the execution of a management transition). As a requirement is satisfied when the corresponding capability is provided, the requirements associated with states and transitions actually indicate which capabilities must continue to be provided in order for N to continue to work properly. The description of a node N is then completed by associating its states and transitions with (possibly empty) sets of capabilities that indicate the capabilities that are actually provided by N while residing in a state and while executing a transition.

Finally, faults occur when N is in a state/transition assuming some requirements to be satisfied, and one or more of the capabilities satisfying such requirement stop being provided by the corresponding nodes. To describe (iii), i.e., how N reacts to faults, a transition relation φ_N models the explicit fault handling of N, by indicating the state it reaches when a fault occurs while it is residing in a state or executing a transition.

Definition 1 (Management protocols). *Let* $N = \langle S_N, R_N, C_N, O_N, \mathcal{M}_N \rangle$ *be a node, where* S_N, R_N, C_N, *and* O_N *are the finite sets of its states, requirements, capabilities, and management operations.* $\mathcal{M}_N = \langle \overline{s}_N, \tau_N, \rho_N, \chi_N, \varphi_N \rangle$ *is a finite state machine defining the* management protocol *of* N, *where:*

- $\overline{s}_N \in S_N$ *is the initial state,*
- $\tau_N \subseteq S_N \times O_N \times S_N$ *models the transition relation,*
- $\rho_N : (S_N \cup \tau_N) \to 2^{R_N}$ *indicates which requirements must hold in each state* $s \in S_N$ *and during each transition* $\langle s, o, s' \rangle \in \tau_N$,
- $\chi_N : (S_N \cup \tau_N) \to 2^{C_N}$ *indicates which capabilities of* N *are offered in each state* $s \in S_N$ *and during each transition* $\langle s, o, s' \rangle \in \tau_N$, *and*
- $\varphi_N \subseteq (S_N \cup \tau_N) \times S_N$ *models the fault handling for a node.*

Example. The management protocols of the components of the application in our motivating example are illustrated in Fig. 3.

Consider the management protocol (b), which describes the management behaviour of backend. The states of backend are unavailable (initial), available, running and damaged. No requirements and capabilities are associated with states unavailable, available and damaged, which means that backend does not require nor provide anything in such states. The same does not hold for the running state, which is the only state where backend concretely provides its conn capability, and where backend assumes its host requirement to continue to be satisfied. If host is faulted while backend is running, backend goes back to its available state.

The transitions of the management protocol of backend indicate that all its operations need the host requirement to be satisfied during their execution, and that they do not feature any capability while being executed. If host is faulted while executing start or stop, backend enters in its state available. If host is instead faulted while executing install, uninstall or config, backend gets damaged. □

It is worth noting that (as per Definition 1) management protocols allow to introduce some inconsistencies and non-determinism while being defined. To inhibit concerns due to such a kind of inconsistencies/non-determinism,

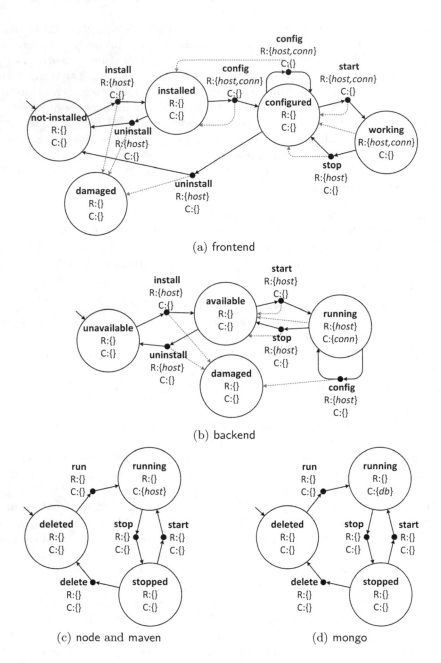

Fig. 3. Management protocols of (a) frontend, (b) backend, (c) node and maven, and (d) mongo. White circles represent states, solid arrows and black circles represent management transitions, and dashed arrows represent fault handling transitions. Labels in bold indicate names of states/operations, while R and C indicate the sets of requirements and capabilities associated with states and transitions.

we assume management protocols to enjoy some basic properties, i.e., we assume them to be well-formed, deterministic, race-free and complete[1].

4 Analysing True Concurrent Application Management

In this section, we illustrate how the true concurrent management behaviour of a multi-component application can be determined by composing the protocols of its nodes according to the application topology (Sect. 4.1). We also describe how to exploit such management to analyse and automate the concurrent management of multi-component applications, faults included (Sect. 4.2).

4.1 True Concurrent Management Behaviour of Applications

Consider a multi-component application $A = \langle T, b \rangle$, where T is the finite set of nodes in the application topology, and where the (total) binding function

$$b : \bigcup_{N \in T} R_N \to \bigcup_{N \in T} C_N$$

describes the connection among the nodes in T, by associating each requirement of each node with the capability that satisfies such requirement[2].

The true concurrent management behaviour of A is defined by a labelled transition systems over configurations that denote the states of the nodes in T. We first define the notion of *global state* for a multi-component application, which denotes the current situation of each node N forming an application, where each N is either residing in one of its states or executing a management operation.

Definition 2 (Global state). *Let $A = \langle T, b \rangle$ be a multi-component application, and let $\langle S_N, R_N, C_N, O_N, \mathcal{M}_N \rangle$ be the tuple corresponding to a node $N \in T$, with $\mathcal{M}_N = \langle \overline{s}_N, \tau_N, \rho_N, \chi_N, \varphi_N \rangle$. A global state G of A is defined as:*

$$G \subseteq \bigcup_{N \in T} (S_N \cup \tau_N) \ \textit{such that} \ \forall N \in T \,.\, |G \cap (S_N \cup \tau_N)| = 1.$$

Remark 1. The right hand condition in Definition 2 ensures that a global state G contains exactly one state/transition for each node in T. This is because a node cannot be in two different situations at the same time, i.e., it cannot be in two different states, nor it can simultaneously execute two different operations, nor it can be both residing in a state and simultaneously executing an operation. □

---

[1] The notions of well-formedness, determinism and race-freedom of management protocols, as well as the techniques for automatically completing them, can be defined as the natural extensions of those presented in [7].

[2] We assume that the names of states, requirements, capabilities, and operations of a node are all disjoint. We also assume that, given two different nodes in a topology, the names of their states, requirements, capabilities, and operations are disjoint.

We also define a function F to denote the set of *pending faults* in a global state G. The latter is the set of requirements that are assumed in G even if the corresponding capabilities are not provided.

Notation. Let G be a global state of a multi-component application $A = \langle T, b \rangle$. We denote with $\rho(G)$ the set of requirements assumed to hold by the nodes in T when A is in G, and with $\chi(G)$ the set of capabilities provided by such nodes in G. Formally:

- $\rho(G) = \bigcup_{N \in T} \{r \in \rho_N(e) \mid e \in G \cap (S_N \cup \tau_N)\}$, and
- $\chi(G) = \bigcup_{N \in T} \{c \in \chi_N(e) \mid e \in G \cap (S_N \cup \tau_N)\}$.

Definition 3 (Pending faults). *Let $A = \langle T, b \rangle$ be a multi-component application, and let G be a global state of A. The set of pending faults in G, denoted by $F(G)$, is defined as:*

$$F(G) = \{r \in \rho(G) \mid b(r) \notin \chi(G)\}.$$

The management behaviour of a multi-component application $A = \langle T, b \rangle$ can then be defined as a labelled transition system, whose configurations are the global states of A. The transition system is characterised by three inference rules, namely op_{start} and op_{end} for operation execution and *fault* for fault propagation. Rule op_{start} models the start of the execution of a management operation o on a node $N \in T$, which can happen only when there are no pending faults and all the requirements needed by N to perform o are satisfied (by the capabilities provided by other nodes in T). Rule op_{end} instead models the successful completion of the execution of a management operation, also happening when there are no pending faults. Finally, rule *fault* models the execution of fault handling transitions to handle pending faults.

Definition 4 (True concurrent management behaviour). *Let $A = \langle T, b \rangle$ be a multi-component application, and let $\langle S_N, R_N, C_N, O_N, M_N \rangle$ be the tuple corresponding to a node $N \in T$, with $M_N = \langle \overline{s}_N, \tau_N, \rho_N, \chi_N, \varphi_N \rangle$. The true concurrent management behaviour of A is modelled by a labelled transition system whose configurations are the global states of A, and whose transition relation is defined by the following inference rules:*

$$\frac{s \in G \quad \langle s, o, s' \rangle \in \tau_N \quad F(G) = \varnothing}{G \xrightarrow{o_{start}} (G - \{s\}) \cup \{\langle s, o, s' \rangle\}}(op_{start})$$

$$\frac{\langle s, o, s' \rangle \in G \quad F(G) = \varnothing}{G \xrightarrow{o_{end}} (G - \{\langle s, o, s' \rangle\}) \cup \{s'\}}(op_{end})$$

$$\frac{\begin{array}{c} e \in G \quad \langle e, s' \rangle \in \varphi_N \quad \rho_N(e) \cap F(G) \neq \varnothing \quad \rho_N(s') \subseteq (\rho_N(e) - F(G)) \\ \nexists \langle e, s'' \rangle \in \varphi_N.\ \rho_N(s') \subsetneq \rho_N(s'') \wedge \rho_N(s'') \subseteq (\rho_N(e) - F(G)) \end{array}}{G \xrightarrow{\perp_e} (G - \{s\}) \cup \{s'\}}(fault)$$

Rules op_{start} and op_{end} indicate how to update the global state of an application A when a node N starts executing a transition $\langle s, o, s' \rangle \in \tau_N$ and when such transition terminates, respectively. Both rules can be applied in a global state G only if there are no pending faults (i.e., $F(G) = \varnothing$). Rule op_{start} updates the global state by changing current state of N from s to the transient state corresponding to $\langle s, o, s' \rangle$ (i.e., $G' = (G - \{s\}) \cup \{\langle s, o, s' \rangle\}$). Rule op_{end} instead updates the global state by changing current state of N from the transient state corresponding to $\langle s, o, s' \rangle$ to s' (i.e., $G' = (G - \{\langle s, o, s' \rangle\}) \cup \{s'\}$). Both updates may also result in triggering novel faults to be handled (if $F(G') \neq \varnothing$).

The *fault* rule instead models fault propagation, by indicating how to update the global state of an application A when executing a fault handling transition $\langle e, s' \rangle$ of a node N. Such transition can be performed only if the following conditions hold:

- $\rho_N(e) \cap F(G) \neq \varnothing$, which means that some of the requirements assumed by N in e are faulted,
- $\rho_N(s') \subseteq (\rho_N(e) - F(G))$, which ensures that $\langle e, s' \rangle$ handles all faults pending in G and affecting N, and
- $\nexists \langle e, s'' \rangle \in \varphi_N . \rho(s') \subsetneq \rho(s'') \wedge \rho(s'') \subseteq \rho(e) - F(G)$, which ensures that, among all executable fault handling transitions, $\langle e, s' \rangle$ is the transition whose target state s' assumes the biggest set of requirements[3].

4.2   Analysing True Concurrent Management Plans

The modelling of the management behaviour of a multi-component application A (Sect. 4.1) sets the foundation for analysing its true concurrent management. To concretely perform such analysis, we introduce a "simple profile" of the labelled transition system modelling the management behaviour of A. The objective of the simple profile is to observe only the start and termination of management operations, by hiding all transitions corresponding to fault reaction/propagation, and by considering operations as terminated if they completed with success or if their execution has faulted.

Definition 5 (Simple profile of management behaviour). *Let $A = \langle T, b \rangle$ be a multi-component application, and let $\langle S_N, R_N, C_N, O_N, \mathcal{M}_N \rangle$ be the tuple corresponding to a node $N \in T$, with $\mathcal{M}_N = \langle \overline{s}_N, \tau_N, \rho_N, \chi_N, \varphi_N \rangle$. The simple profile of the true concurrent management behaviour of A is modelled by a*

---

[3] In this way, the fault handling transition is guaranteed to handle all the faults on the node, while at same time minimising the amount of requirements that stop being assumed (even though the corresponding capabilities continue to be provided).

labelled transition system whose configurations are global states of A, and whose transition relation is defined by the following inference rules:

$$\frac{G \xrightarrow{o_{start}} G'}{G \xmapsto{\bullet o} G'}(op_{init}) \qquad \frac{G \xrightarrow{o_{end}} G'}{G \xmapsto{o\bullet} G'}(op_{success})$$

$$\frac{G \xrightarrow{\perp_{\langle s,o,s'\rangle}} G' \quad \langle s,o,s'\rangle \in \tau_N}{G \xmapsto{o\bullet} G'}(op_{fault})$$

$$\frac{G \xmapsto{\alpha} G' \quad G' \xrightarrow{\perp_s} G'' \quad s \in S_N}{G \xmapsto{\alpha} G''}(absorption)$$

Rules op_{init} and $op_{success}$ model the start and successful completion of a management operation o, respectively. Rules op_{fault} and *absorption* differentiate the observation of faults. Rule op_{fault} allows to observe faults on management operations, to consider the execution of such operations as terminated. Rule *absorption* instead hides all fault handling transitions executed to react to the faults on states due to the execution of an action α (corresponding to the start $\bullet o$ or termination $o\bullet$ of a management operation o).

The simple profile of the management behaviour of a multi-component application A enables the analysis of plans orchestrating its management. A management plan P_A defines a partial ordering on the management operations of the nodes in A (i.e., it indicates which operations must be completed before starting the execution of another operation). The partial ordering can be visualised as a DAG, whose nodes model the start/termination of an operation, and where each arc indicates that the action corresponding to its source node must be executed before that corresponding to its target node. The DAG also models the obvious fact that $\bullet o$ always occurs before $o\bullet$, for each operation o in the plan.

Example. Consider the management plan in Fig. 2(a). Such plan indicates that stop frontend must be completed before executing config frontend and config backend, which can then be executed concurrently, and which must both be completed before starting the execution of start frontend. The corresponding partial ordering is displayed as a DAG in Fig. 4.   □

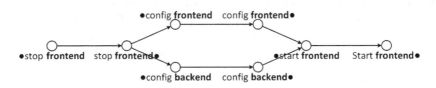

Fig. 4. DAG defined by the management plan in Fig. 2(a).

The *validity* of a management plan P_A can be defined in terms of all possible sequencing of $\bullet o$ and $o\bullet$ (for each operation o in P_A), which respects the ordering constraints defined in P_A, as well as that $\bullet o$ must obviously always occur before $o\bullet$. Such sequences correspond to the topological sorts of the DAG modelling the partial order defined by P_A.

Definition 6 (Valid plan). *Let $A = \langle T, b \rangle$ be a multi-component application. The sequence $\alpha_1 \alpha_2 ... \alpha_n$ (with $\alpha_i \in \{\bullet o, o\bullet \mid o \in O_N, N \in T\}$) is a valid management sequence in a global state G_0 of A iff*

$$\exists G_1, G_2, ... G_n : G_0 \overset{\alpha_1}{\longmapsto} G_1 \overset{\alpha_2}{\longmapsto} G_2 \overset{\alpha_3}{\longmapsto} ... \overset{\alpha_n}{\longmapsto} G_n.$$

A management plan P_A is valid in G_0 iff all its sequential traces[4] are valid management sequences in G_0.

Example. Consider again the management plans in our motivating scenario (Fig. 2). While one can readily check that the sequential plans (b) and (c) are valid, the same does not hold for plan (a).

The sequential traces of plan (a) correspond to all possible topological sorts of the DAG in Fig. 4. One of such traces is hence the following:

$\bullet$stop frontend · stop frontend$\bullet$ · $\bullet$config frontend · $\bullet$config backend ·

config frontend$\bullet$ · config backend$\bullet$ · $\bullet$start frontend · start frontend$\bullet$

If executed when all components of the application in our motivating scenario are up and running, the above trace corresponds to the evolution of global states in Fig. 5. From the figure we can observe that the execution of $\bullet$config backend causes a failure in the node frontend. The handling of such failure results in frontend getting to its installed state, where it cannot perform $\bullet$start frontend (i.e., it cannot start executing the operation start—Fig. 3(a)). This means that the considered sequential trace is not valid, hence the management plan in Fig. 2(a) is not valid either.   □

It is worth noting that the notion of validity for management plans (Definition 6) is the natural adaptation of the corresponding notion in [7] to consider the true concurrent execution of management operations. A similar approach can be used to naturally adapt all analyses presented in [7], from checking whether management plans are deterministic or fault-free, to automatically planning the management of applications (e.g., to recover applications that are stuck because a fault was not handled properly, or because misbehaving components)[5].

5   Related Work

The problem of automating the management of multi-component applications is one of the major concerns in enterprise IT [21]. This is also witnessed by the proliferation of so-called "configuration management systems", such as Chef (https://www.chef.io) or Puppet (https://puppet.com). Such systems provide

---

[4] A sequential trace of P_A is one of the sequencing of $\bullet o$ and $o \bullet$ (with o in P_A) obtained by topologically sorting the DAG modelling the partial ordering defined by P_A.

[5] Due to space limitations, we are not including the natural adaptation of all such notions and techniques in this paper.

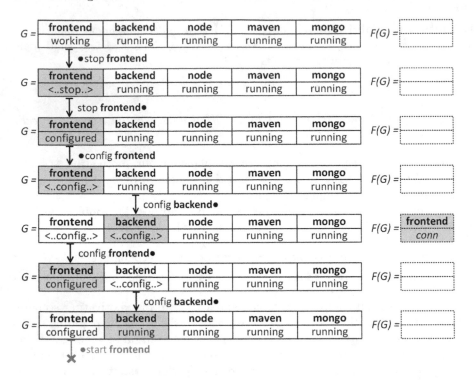

Fig. 5. Evolution of the application in our motivating example, corresponding to the execution of a sequential trace of the management plan in Fig. 2 (a) when the application is up and running. Global states and pending faults are represented as tables associating node names with their actual state, and with their faulted requirements, respectively. Transitions are displayed as labelled arrows, and each update due to the execution of a transition is highlighted in grey in the target global state.

domain-specific languages to model the desired configuration for an application, and they employ a client-server model to ensure that such configuration is met. However, the lack of a machine-readable representation of how to effectively manage cloud application components inhibits the possibility of performing automated analyses on their configurations and dependencies.

A first solution for modelling the deployment of multi-component applications was the Aeolus component model [11]. Aeolus [11] shares our idea of describing the management behaviour of the components of an application through finite-state machines, whose states are associated with conditions describing what is offered and required in a state. The management behaviour of an application can then be derived by composing those of its components. Aeolus however differs from our approach as it focuses on automating the deployment and configuration of a multi-component application. Management protocols instead focus on allowing to model and analyse the true concurrent management of a multi-component application, including how its components react to failures, as well as how to recover a multi-component application after one or more of its components were faulted.

Engage [14] takes as input a partial installation specification, and it is capable of determining a full installation plan, which coordinates the deployment and configuration of the components of an application across multiple machines. Engage however differs from our approach since it focuses on determining a fault-free deployment of applications. We instead focus on the true concurrent management of applications, by also allowing to explicitly model faults, analysing their effects, and reacting to them to restore a desired application state.

[12] proposes a fault-resilient solution for deploying and reconfiguring multi-component applications. [12] models a multi-component application as a set of interconnected VMs, each provided with a module managing its lifecycle. An orchestrator then coordinates the deployment and reconfiguration of an application, by interacting with the configurators of the virtual machines of its components. [12] is related to our approach as it focuses managing multi-component applications by taking into account failures and by specifying the management of each component separately. It however differs from our approach since it only considers environmental faults, while we also deal with application-specific faults. Similar considerations apply to the approach proposed in [13].

Other approaches worth mentioning are those related to the rigorous engineering of fault tolerant systems. [4,22] provide facilities for fault-localisation in complex applications, to support re-designing such applications by avoiding the occurrence of identified faults. [16] illustrates a solution for designing applications by first considering fault-free applications, and by then iteratively refining their design by identifying and handling the faults that may occur. [4,16,22] however differ from our approach as their aim is to obtain applications that "never fail", because potential faults have already been identified and handled. Our approach is instead more recovery-oriented [8], as we consider applications where faults can (and probably will) occur, in order to enable the design of applications that can be recovered.

Similar arguments apply to [2,15,17]. They however share with our approach the basic ideas of indicating which faults can affect components, of specifying how components react to faults, and of composing obtained models according to the dependencies occurring among the components of an application (i.e., according to the application topology).

In summary, to the best of our knowledge, ours is the first approach allowing to analyse and automate the management of multi-component applications, by considering that faults can occur during their concrete management. It does so by allowing to customise the management behaviour of each component of an application (including the specification of how it will react to the occurrence of a fault), and by considering the true concurrent management of the components forming an application.

It is finally worth noting that our work was inspired by [10], which illustrates how to provide CCS with a true concurrent semantics. The baseline idea in [10] is to define a partial ordering among the sequential parts of CCS agents, and to exploit such ordering to infer a true concurrent semantics of CCS agents (where concurrency is represented as the absence of ordering). This is closely related to what we did to provide management protocols with a true concurrent semantics, even if we consider additional constraints given by the conditions on requirements and capabilities associated with the states and transitions of management protocols.

It is also worth noting that we also investigated the possibility of employing composition-oriented automata (like *interface automata* [1]) to model the valid management of an application as the language accepted by the automaton obtained by composing the automata modelling the management protocols of its components. The main drawbacks of such an approach are the size of the obtained automaton (which in general grows exponentially with the number of application components), and the need of recomputing the automaton whenever the management protocol of a component is modified or whenever a new component is added to an application.

6   Conclusions

We presented a solution for modelling, analysing and automating the true concurrent management of multi-component applications. More precisely, we have extended management protocols [7] to permit indicating how application components react to faults occurring while they are executing management operations. We have also shown how to derive the management behaviour of a multi-component application by considering the true concurrent execution of the management operations of its components, and how this enables the analysis and automation of its concurrent management.

The presented extension is a fundamental milestone towards the exploitation of management protocols for a fully asynchronous, distributed coordination of the management of multi-component applications. As components can now evolve asynchronously (with one component executing a management operation while another component is executing another operation), the management of multi-component applications can be decentralised, e.g., by distributing its orchestration over the components forming an application. The investigation of such a kind of solutions is in the scope of our future work.

In the scope of our future work we also plan to follow two other interesting directions. On the one hand, we plan to validate our approach by implementing a prototype supporting the modelling and analysis of true concurrent management protocols, and by assessing our approach with case studies and controlled experiments, similarly to what we did in [7]. On the other hand, we plan to further extend management protocols to account for QoS attributes, including cost, so as to enable determining the best plan to achieve a management goal.

References

1. de Alfaro, L., Henzinger, T.A.: Interface automata. In: Proceedings of the 8th European Software Engineering Conference Held Jointly with 9th ACM SIGSOFT International Symposium on Foundations of Software Engineering, ESEC/FSE-9, pp. 109–120. ACM (2001)
2. Alhosban, A., Hashmi, K., Malik, Z., Medjahed, B., Benbernou, S.: Bottom-up fault management in service-based systems. ACM Trans. Internet Technol. **15**(2), 7:1–7:40 (2015)
3. Bergmayr, A., et al.: A systematic review of cloud modeling languages. ACM Comput. Surv. **51**(1), 22:1–22:38 (2018)
4. Betin Can, A., Bultan, T., Lindvall, M., Lux, B., Topp, S.: Eliminating synchronization faults in air traffic control software via design for verification with concurrency controllers. Autom. Softw. Eng. **14**(2), 129–178 (2007)
5. Binz, T., Breitenbücher, U., Kopp, O., Leymann, F.: TOSCA: portable automated deployment and management of cloud applications. In: Bouguettaya, A., Sheng, Q., Daniel, F. (eds.) Advanced Web Services, pp. 527–549. Springer, New York (2014). https://doi.org/10.1007/978-1-4614-7535-4_22
6. Brogi, A., Canciani, A., Soldani, J.: Fault-aware application management protocols. In: Aiello, M., Johnsen, E.B., Dustdar, S., Georgievski, I. (eds.) ESOCC 2016. LNCS, vol. 9846, pp. 219–234. Springer, Cham (2016). https://doi.org/10.1007/978-3-319-44482-6_14
7. Brogi, A., Canciani, A., Soldani, J.: Fault-aware management protocols for multi-component applications. J. Syst. Softw. **139**, 189–210 (2018)
8. Candea, G., Brown, A.B., Fox, A., Patterson, D.: Recovery-oriented computing: building multitier dependability. Computer **37**(11), 60–67 (2004)
9. Cook, R.I.: How complex systems fail. Cognitive Technologies Laboratory, University of Chicago. Chicago IL (1998)
10. Degano, P., Nicola, R.D., Montanari, U.: A partial ordering semantics for CCS. Theoret. Comput. Sci. **75**(3), 223–262 (1990)
11. Di Cosmo, R., Mauro, J., Zacchiroli, S., Zavattaro, G.: Aeolus. Inf. Comput. **239**(C), 100–121 (2014)
12. Durán, F., Salaün, G.: Robust and reliable reconfiguration of cloud applications. J. Syst. Softw. **122**(C), 524–537 (2016)
13. Etchevers, X., Salaün, G., Boyer, F., Coupaye, T., DePalma, N.: Reliable self-deployment of distributed cloud applications. Softw. Pract. Experience **47**(1), 3–20 (2017)
14. Fischer, J., Majumdar, R., Esmaeilsabzali, S.: Engage: a deployment management system. In: Proceedings of the 33rd ACM SIGPLAN Conference on Programming Language Design and Implementation, PLDI 2012, pp. 263–274. ACM (2012)
15. Grunske, L., Kaiser, B., Papadopoulos, Y.: Model-driven safety evaluation with state-event-based component failure annotations. In: Heineman, G.T., Crnkovic, I., Schmidt, H.W., Stafford, J.A., Szyperski, C., Wallnau, K. (eds.) CBSE 2005. LNCS, vol. 3489, pp. 33–48. Springer, Heidelberg (2005). https://doi.org/10.1007/11424529_3
16. Johnsen, E., Owe, O., Munthe-Kaas, E., Vain, J.: Incremental fault-tolerant design in an object-oriented setting. In: Proceedings of the Second Asia-Pacific Conference on Quality Software, APAQS, p. 223. IEEE Computer Society (2001)
17. Kaiser, B., Liggesmeyer, P., Mäckel, O.: A new component concept for fault trees. In: Proceedings of the 8th Australian Workshop on Safety Critical Systems and Software, SCS, vol. 33, pp. 37–46. Australian Computer Society, Inc. (2003)

18. Kopp, O., Binz, T., Breitenbücher, U., Leymann, F.: Winery – a modeling tool for TOSCA-based cloud applications. In: Basu, S., Pautasso, C., Zhang, L., Fu, X. (eds.) ICSOC 2013. LNCS, vol. 8274, pp. 700–704. Springer, Heidelberg (2013). https://doi.org/10.1007/978-3-642-45005-1_64
19. OMG: Business process model and notation (bpmn), version 2.0. https://www.omg.org/spec/BPMN/2.0/ (2011)
20. Pahl, C., Brogi, A., Soldani, J., Jamshidi, P.: Cloud container technologies: a state-of-the-art review. IEEE Trans. Cloud Comput. (2017, in press) https://doi.org/10.1109/TCC.2017.2702586
21. Pahl, C., Jamshidi, P., Zimmermann, O.: Architectural principles for cloud software. ACM Trans. Internet Technol. **18**(2), 17:1–17:23 (2018)
22. Qiang, W., Yan, L., Bliudze, S., Xiaoguang, M.: Automatic fault localization for BIP. In: Li, X., Liu, Z., Yi, W. (eds.) SETTA 2015. LNCS, vol. 9409, pp. 277–283. Springer, Cham (2015). https://doi.org/10.1007/978-3-319-25942-0_18

Runtime Evolution of Multi-tenant Service Networks

Indika Kumara[1]([✉]), Jun Han[2], Alan Colman[2],
Willem-Jan van den Heuvel[1], and Damian A. Tamburri[1]

[1] Tilburg University, Warandelaan 2, 5037 AB Tilburg, Netherlands
{I.P.K.WeerasinghaDewage,wjheuvel,d.a.tamburri}@uvt.nl
[2] Swinburne University of Technology, PO Box 218,
Hawthorn, VIC 3122, Australia
{jhun,acolman}@swin.edu.au

Abstract. In a multi-tenant service network, services relate to each other and collaborate to support the functional and performance requirements of multiple tenants. Such a service network evolves over time as its services and tenants change. Consequentially, the composite application that enacts the service network also needs to evolve at runtime, which is problematic. For example, different types of changes to the application, and their consequential impacts need to be realized and managed at runtime. In this paper, we present an approach to evolving multi-tenant service networks. We identify the types of runtime changes to a service network composite application and their impacts, and present a middleware support for realizing and managing the identified changes and impacts. A software engineer can specify the desired changes to the running application, and enact the change specification to modify it. We show the feasibility of our approach with a detailed case study.

Keywords: Service network · Multi-tenancy
Change management · Evolution

1 Introduction

A business service network is a web of business services connected according to the capabilities provided and consumed by them [1,2]. The business services support business activities of enterprises or individuals (e.g., claim handling and roadside assistance). To achieve economies of scale via runtime sharing of services among tenants, a *multi-tenant service network* simultaneously hosts a set of virtual service networks (VSNs), each for a separate tenant, on the same physical service network [3,4]. The tenants generally have common and variable functional and performance requirements, and thus their VSNs share some services in the service network while also using different services as necessary.

© IFIP International Federation for Information Processing 2018
Published by Springer Nature Switzerland AG 2018. All Rights Reserved
K. Kritikos et al. (Eds.): ESOCC 2018, LNCS 11116, pp. 33–48, 2018.
https://doi.org/10.1007/978-3-319-99819-0_3

A composite service application (hosted in a middleware runtime) can generally enact a multi-tenant business service network. It needs to connect services based on their relationships, to route and regulate the message exchanges between them, and to form VSNs over the service network. As the service network evolves, for instance, by adding a new service or tenant, or by changing the capabilities of an existing service, this composite application also needs to be evolved at runtime, which is a complex problem. Firstly, the different classes of changes that can potentially occur to the application, and the potential consequential impacts of each such change need to be identified. Secondly, a change and its impacts need to be realized and managed at runtime by the middleware without disturbing the operations of those tenants unaffected by the change.

Most existing works on service networks consider modeling and analysis of service networks from specific aspects [2] such as value flows [5], business processes [6], and service relationships [2,7]. The composite applications that enact service networks need to use service composition approaches such as BPMN (Business Process Management Notation) and BPEL (Business Process Execution Language) [1], which provide little or no direct support for the abstractions in multi-tenant service networks such as services, their relationships, message routing and regulation, and VSNs. Moreover, the existing works lack the support for two key change management activities [8] for multi-tenant service networks: identifying the impacts of a change, and realizing the change and its impacts.

In [3,4], we have proposed an approach called *Software-Defined Service Networking (SDSN)* that can deploy, enact, and manage multi-tenant service networks (composite applications). SDSN provides a programming model (a set of architectural abstractions to naturally represent a multi-tenant service network), a domain specific language (DSL), a middleware environment, and a set of tools. A software engineer can design the multi-tenant service network with the DSL, and enact and manage the designed network with the middleware at runtime.

This paper focuses on the above-mentioned two key activities of change management for a composite application that realizes a multi-tenant service network using our SDSN approach. We first identify the types of runtime changes to the application and their potential impacts. Second, we present the change management system in our SDSN middleware, including its architecture and its support for the controlled propagation of changes and impacts. The middleware also provides an ECA (event-condition-action) rules based language to specify and schedule the enactment of changes to the runtime models (*models@runtime* [9]) of the application. We present a set of guidelines that a software engineer can use to create a change specification for an evolution scenario systematically. We show the feasibility of our approach with a case study that implements common evolution scenarios for variant-rich applications (e.g., product lines and multi-tenant systems). We analyze the case study results to assess change impacts of evolution scenarios, and quantify the time taken to realize changes at runtime.

In this paper, we motivate our research and present the key requirements for a change and impact management support for multi-tenant service networks in Sect. 2. Section 3 provides an overview of our SDSN approach to realizing multi-tenant service networks. Section 4 discusses our change and impact management

support in detail. Section 5 presents the prototype and evaluation of our approach. Section 6 presents related work, and Sect. 7 concludes the paper while
providing the directions for further research.

2 Motivating Scenarios and General Requirements

Consider RoSAS (Road-Side Assistance Service) service network that offers roadside assistance to its tenants such as travel agencies and vehicle sellers by composing business services such as repairers and towing providers (see Fig. 1). Due
to the benefits of the multi-tenancy, RoSAS shares the services among its tenants. Each tenant has a virtual service network (VSN) in RoSAS service network
to coordinate roadside assistance for their users such as travelers and motorists.

The capabilities and capacities of services as well as the functional and performance requirements of tenants can exhibit commonalities and variations, which
lead to the commonalities and variations in the VSNs of the tenants. For example, HappyTours and EuroCars require rental vehicle, while AnyTrucks prefers
accommodation. Thus, the VSNs of the former tenants use the rental vehicle
provider SilverVehicles, and the VSN of the later tenant uses the accommodation provider AmayaHotel. HappyTours' VSN uses the repairer MacRepair (for
3 days repair time) and the other two tenants' VSNs use AutoRepair (for 6 days).
Compared with MacRepair, AutoRepair does not have parts internally. Thus,
the VSNs of AnyTrucks and EuroCars include the part supplier JackParts. The
towing provider TomTow has the limited capacity (the number of new tows per
day), and cannot support the capacity requirements of both tenants AnyTrucks
and EuroCars. Thus, the VSN of AnyTrucks also includes the towing provider
SwiftTow. Note that the capacities of business services (e.g., towing capacity)
cannot be changed by simply managing the computation resources used by them.

Let us consider two key requirements for the runtime management of the
roadside assistance multi-tenant service network.

1. *Supporting Runtime Changes to Multi-tenant Service Networks.* The services
   and the requirements of the tenants and the service network provider can
   change over time. For instance, after two months, EuroCars requests the taxi

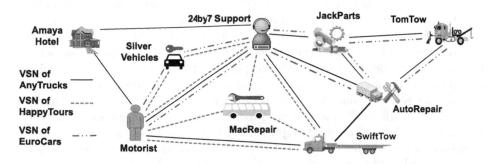

Fig. 1. Roadside assistance multi-tenant service network

hiring capability instead of the rental vehicle, and HappyTours requests 25 additional assistance cases per day. After one year, RoSAS decides to provide legal assistance for vehicle accidents. A new company starts to offer the repair assessment for vehicles, and the RoSAS provider needs to use it. To respond to or utilize these changes at the service network, a software engineer should be able to modify the RoSAS composite application at runtime. Thus, the middleware that hosts the application should support the classes of runtime changes that can occur to the application during its lifetime.

2. *Managing Consequential Change Impacts.* A change to the RoSAS composite application can further affect the application and its tenants. For example, a change to the representation of the repairer AutoRepair in the application can affect some other elements in the application and the VSNs of HappyTours and EuroCars. The middleware that hosts the composite application needs to enable a software engineer to identify such change impacts and then design and perform the controlled propagation of each change and impact.

3   Realizing Multi-tenant Service Networks: An Overview

A multi-tenant service network simultaneously hosts a set of virtual service networks on the same physical service network at runtime. In [3, 4], we have proposed a novel approach, SDSN (Software-Defined Service Networking), to realize multi-tenant service networks (or cloud applications). SDSN provides a programming model, a domain specific language, and a middleware for designing and enacting multi-tenant service networks. This section provides an overview of the runtime abstractions of multi-tenant service networks in our SDSN approach.

The service network is an overlay network over the services. A *node* in the service network is a proxy to a service, and acts as a router where the messages from the other services are routed to the corresponding service via the node, and vice versa. A *link* between two nodes models the relationship between the corresponding two services, and acts as the messaging channel between the two nodes. A node has a set of *tasks* to represent the capabilities of the service. A link has a set of *interaction terms* to capture the interactions between the services.

The service network includes a set of *regulation enforcement points (REPs)* to intercept and regulate the interaction messages between services, and to monitor and enforce the performance constraints (response time and capacity) on service capabilities. There are four types of REPs: *synchronization* (at each node), *routing* (at each node), *pass-through* (at each link), and *coordinated-pass-through* (across links). The synchronization REP of a node synchronizes a subset of incoming interactions from the adjacent nodes before executing a task (sending a request to the node's service). The routing REP of a node routes a received response or request from the node's service to a subset of the adjacent nodes. The pass-through REP in a link can process the interaction messages between two nodes, and generate *events* representing the states of the interactions. The coordinated-pass-through is to regulate the interactions across different pairs of nodes. Each REP has a *knowledgebase* and a *regulation table*. The former contains event-condition-action (ECA) rules that implement regulation decisions using a number of *regulation mechanisms* such as admission control and load balance. The latter maps a message flow to a set of rules in the knowledgebase, which decide what to do with the message flow.

Each tenant has a *virtual service network (VSN)*, which is a specific service composition in the service network that meets the functional and performance requirements of the tenant. The VSNs of tenants simultaneously coexist on the same service network. Multiple business processes can exist in a VSN. Each process is a service network path, which is a subset of the service network topology. A service network path is represented by the entries in the relevant regulation tables. A table entry at a REP maps the messages belonging to a process to a subset of the regulation rules in the knowledgebase of the REP. Each such rule applies a set of regulation functions to the messages. The isolation of VSNs/processes is achieved by keeping the messages associated with a process instance isolated. Then, the isolated messages are routed and regulated on the service network path of the process instance. As the message flow continues over the network path, the business process is enacted as an event-driven business process, where events trigger the execution of tasks.

VSNs of multiple tenants share some service network elements for their common requirements, and use some other service network elements for their distinctive requirements. The elements include nodes, links, tasks, interaction terms, regulation rules/mechanisms, and services. The interested reader is referred to [3] for more details on the design and enactment of multi-tenant service networks.

Example. Figure 2 shows a part of the RoSAS service network. It consists of a number of nodes (e.g., MO, SC, and TC1) connected by links (e.g., MO-TC1, MO-SC, and SC-TC1), and supports the coordination of the interactions between the services (e.g., motorist, 24by7Support, and SwiftTow) to meet the roadside assistance requirements of the tenants. The nodes include the relevant tasks, for example, *tPickUp* of the node TC1 (to pick up a broken down vehicle). The links include the relevant interaction terms, for example, *iPickUp* of the link MO-TC1 (to represent the motorist's request for collecting the vehicle). Each

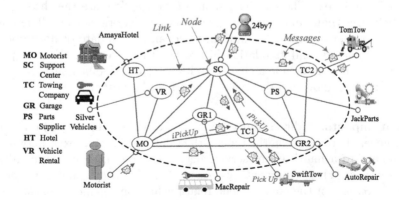

Fig. 2. Realization of the roadside assistance multi-tenant service network

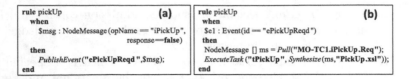

Fig. 3. (a) a pass-through rule (link MO-TC1), (b) a synchronization rule (node TC1)

node and link also include the relevant REPs. The messages are routed and regulated over the service network via these REPs. Figure 3 shows two regulation rules. The pass-through rule generates the event *ePickUpReqd*, which triggers the synchronization rule, which creates a service request from the relevant interaction messages, and sends the request to SwiftTow to ask to collect the vehicle.

4 Change and Impact Management for Multi-tenant Service Networks

This section considers two key (runtime) change management activities [8] for multi-tenant service networks realized using our SDSN approach: (1) identifying types of changes and their consequential impacts, and (2) designing and implementing the identified changes and impacts. We discuss the types of changes and their impacts, the change management middleware system, and the process of designing a change management policy for realizing change scenarios.

4.1 Types of Changes and Impacts

A change can occur at any element of the multi-tenant service network. A given change to an element can further cause changes to that element and/or other elements as *direct consequential* impacts of the change (see Fig. 4).

Types of Changes. The *addition*, *removal*, and *update* are the three general types of changes that can occur to a given service network element. The update to an element can include the addition, removal, and update of its properties, its children elements, and its relationships with other elements. For example, an update to a node can include a change to its service endpoint reference, adding a new task, and removing a reference to a link with another node.

Types of Impacts. A direct impact of a given change to an element on another element generally depends on the type of the relationships that exist between the two elements. In a multi-tenant service network, there are four common types of relationships: (1) *containment*, (2) *association*, (3) *usage*, and (4) *representation/realization*. In the containment relationship, one element contains some other elements. For example, a node has a set of tasks. In the association relationship, one element is connected to some other elements. For example, a node is

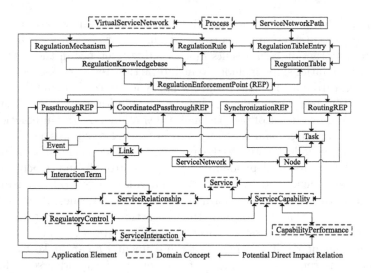

Fig. 4. Changeable elements and their potential direct impact relations

connected to another node via a link. The two nodes have references to the link. In the usage relationship, one element depends on or use some other elements for its behavior or existence. For example, an event may exist due the presence of an interaction term, and the execution of a task depends on the occurrence of some events. In the representation relationship, an element in the composite application represents a domain concept. For example, a node represents a service, and a regulation rule realizes a regulation decision.

The containment relationships include service-service capability, service relationship -service interaction/regulatory control, service capability-capability performance, service network-node/link, service network-coordinated pass-through REP, node-task, link-interaction terms, node-(routing/synchronization)REP, link-passthrough REP, REP-knowledgebase, REP-regulation table, knowledgebase-rules, regulation table-table entry, and VSN-process. The addition of a new container element generally requires new contained elements. The removal of the container element removes its contained elements. The removal of the contained elements can make the container element obsolete. For example, a new regulation knowledgebase requires new rules, the removal of a link removes its interaction terms, and the removal of the tasks of a node makes the node obsolete.

The association relationships include service-service relationship, service capability -service interaction, regulatory control-service interaction/service capability, node-link, task-interaction term, regulation rule-mechanism/event, regulation table entry-rule, and service network path-table entry. Consider the element type A and the element type B has a unidirectional association (from A to B). A new element $a1$ (type A) may require an element $b1$ (type B). The removal of $a1$ can make $b1$ obsolete if no other elements use it. The removal of *b1* makes the reference to it in *a1* dangling. For example, a new task requires the references to the interaction terms to be consumed/produced, and the removal of a referred interaction term results in a dangling reference in the task.

The usage relationships include event-interaction term, task-event, interaction term-passthrough rule, and task-routing/synchronization rule. In addition, there are mutual usage dependencies between regulation rule types. A synchronization rule requires a set of pass-through rules to analyze the interaction messages to be synchronized, and generate the events. It also requires a set of routing rules at the source nodes to initiate the interactions to be synchronized. Similarly, a routing rule has usage dependences with pass-through and synchronization rules. The events generated by a pass-through rule are generally consumed by some synchronization rules and coordinated pass-through rules. A pass-through rule also needs a routing rule to create the interaction messages that it processes.

Consider the element type *C* uses the element type *D*. A new element *c1* requires an element *d1*. The removal of the element *c1* can make the element *d1* obsolete. The removal or update of the element *d1* can adversely affect the behavior of the element *c1*. For example, the removal of a synchronization rule can make the relevant pass-through and routing rules obsolete. The removal of a pass-through rule requires the removal of or updating the conditions of the rules that use the events generated by it as those rules will not be activated.

The representation relationships include service-node, service relationship-link, service capability-task, service interaction-interaction term, regulatory control -regulation rule/mechanism, capability performance-regulation rule /mechanism (e.g., performance monitoring and admission control), and VSN/process-service network path. Consider the element type *E* realizes the domain concept *F*. The addition of the concept instance *f1* requires that of the element *e1*. The removal of *f1* makes the element *e1* invalid it represents a nonexistent concept instance. The update to *f1* may require the same to the element *e1*. For example, a new service requires a node, and the removal of an existing service makes the related node invalid as it represents a nonexistent service.

Due to the limited space, we did not provide the examples for each dependency, and each impact that the dependency creates. An interested reader may refer to an accompanying technical report [10] for more details.

4.2   Change Management System

To support the runtime changes to a multi-tenant service network in a controlled manner without compromising the consistency of the service network, we adopted the change management scheme proposed by Kramer and Magee [11]. We introduce a management state for each runtime element of a service network, which determines when an element can be removed, updated, or used. The middleware provides the capabilities to change management states, and generate the events at each state change. A software engineer can design change management policies in a way that a given change operation on an element is performed only when the element is in its appropriate management state (see Sect. 4.3).

In general, an element in a service network can be in three management states: *Active*, *Passive*, and *Quiescence*. The *Passive* state of an element enables the system to complete the existing process instances, and to move the element to its *Quiescence* state. If a runtime change to an element can adversely affect some existing process instances, then the change must be delayed until the element reaches its *Quiescence* state. A newly added element always in the *Passive* state, and must be moved to the *Active* state so that the process instances can use it. An element can be removed from the system when it is in *Quiescence* state.

VSNs, processes, and process instances can also have the above management states. A process instance for an instantiation request from a user of a tenant is created only if the VSN and its selected process is in *Active* state. Otherwise, the request message is queued, and later served when the state of the process becomes *Active*. A running instance is in the *Active* state. When it is paused, the management state becomes *Passive*, and the messages (in transit) belonging to the process instance are queued. When the management state becomes *Active*, the routing of the queued messages resumes. When the process instance is terminated, it is moved to the *Quiescence* state, and scheduled to be removed.

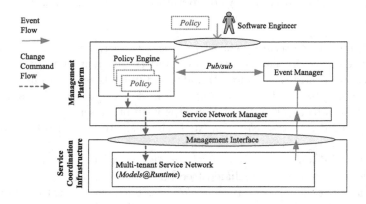

Fig. 5. Change management support in SDSN middleware

Figure 5 shows the high-level system architecture of the SDSN middleware, highlighting its change management support. It has a service coordination platform and a management platform. The former maintains multi-tenant service networks at runtime using the *models@runtime* approach, and supports the runtime changes to them (discussed in Sect. 4.1). Each change operation (e.g., *addNode* and *removeLink*) is included in the management interface, which is exposed as a Web service. The management platform includes a service network manager that uses the management Web service interface to monitor and change the running service networks, a policy engine that can maintain and enact the change management policies, and an event manager that stores the various events including management state change events. The management policies are a set of ECA rules. Generally, the conditions of a rule are events, and the actions are the change operations/commands (exposed by the management interface).

4.3 Design and Enactment of Change Management Policies

A given change can have a desired impact or an undesired impact. A direct change impact can be a consequential change or a solution (a set of intentional/designed changes) developed to utilize a desired impact, and to mitigate an undesired impact. In either case, if a change A triggers a change B as a direct impact, then to realize this impact, the change operation for propagating the change B needs to be used. A change can have a ripple effect. For example, the removal of a node may need the removal of its links with other nodes. To propagate this impact, the change operation *removeLink( )* can be used. The removal of these links can have further impacts. For example, some of the tasks may refer to the interaction terms in the removed links, and the affected tasks need to be updated using the operation *updateTask( )*.

A software engineer needs to identify each change and its impacts (see Sect. 4.1), and then specify them in a change management policy in terms of change operations/commands. We below provide some guidelines for a software engineer to develop such policies so that the desired changes are ordered and scheduled appropriately. We use the example of supporting the *taxi hire* feature in the RoSAS service network. A collaboration among a set of services realizes a feature.

1. *Identify and design service network topology changes.* The differences between the expected service network topology and the current one are designed in terms of (to be added or removed) nodes and links. Lines 12–14 in Fig. 6 show the topology changes for our example (a node to represent the taxi service, and two links to capture its relationships with other services).
2. *Identify and design task changes.* Next, the tasks to be added to or removed are designed (see Lines 15–16 in Fig. 6).
3. *Identify and design interaction term changes.* Next, the interaction terms to be added or removed are included (see Lines 18–19 in Fig. 6).
4. *Identify and design task-interaction changes.* The next step is to link or unlink tasks and interaction terms to reflect the required changes to the provided-required relationships in the service network. This is achieved by manipulating the inputs and outputs of the relevant tasks (see Line 21).
5. *Identify and design regulation rule and mechanism changes.* Once the modifications to the configuration design of the service network are designed, the changes to its regulation design can be introduced. These changes include regulation rule and mechanism changes at some REPs. The changes to the regulation mechanisms imply the changes to their implementations, which are Java modules in our prototype. The regulation rules can be defined as ECA rules (as .drl files) using Drools rule language (drools.org). Lines 29–31 show some of the relevant changes in our example, which add regulation rules at the node TX and the link SC-TX. Figure 7 shows two regulation rules that execute the task *orderTaxi*, and route the response from the service.
6. *Identify and design VSN changes.* The next step is to design the desired VSN changes, which include the regulation table entries at some REPs

(to be added, removed, and updated). Lines 45–47/33–35 show some relevant changes. As EuroCars replaces the rental vehicle with the taxi hire, the service network path of its VSN is modified by removing the path for the rental vehicle collaboration, and by adding the path for the taxi hire collaboration.

7. *Identify and design management state changes.* The changes to a multi-tenant service network can only be propagated when the relevant elements (to be affected) are in appropriate management states (see Sect. 4.2). The software engineer needs to initiate the appropriate state changes before and after making changes. In our example, the management state of the VSN/process is moved to the *Passive* state (see Line 5).

8. *Capture the dependencies between the individual policy rules.* As the changes need to be made to the system orderly, the software engineer needs to organize the enactment of the management policy into stages. Each stage can be represented as an ECA rule, whose conditions can use the enactment state of the policy (e.g., the end of a stage) and the management state change events. In general, we need to have stages for: (1) moving the elements to be changed to their desired management states, (2) propagating configuration design changes, (3) propagating regulation design changes, (4) removing the elements in their *Quiescence* state, and (5) moving the elements changed to their desired management states. The policy in Fig. 6 has these stages.

9. *Deploy designed management policies.* Finally, the software engineer can deploy the designed policy at the management platform. As the individual rules of the policy are executed (as their conditions are met), the changes described in the rules are propagated to the relevant runtime elements.

5   Prototype Implementation and Evaluation

Prototype Implementation. In [3,4], we have presented the prototype implementation of the SDSN approach. It includes a design language, tools, and middleware. The coordination engine and the management platform of the middleware are deployed on an Apache Tomcat web server as Apache Axis2 modules. The executable design language is XML-based, and the change management and regulation policy languages use Drools rule language. We use the Drools rule engine to implement the policy engines at the management platform and REPs. A software engineer can use the Drools IDE to define regulation rules and management policies. The SDSN implementation is available at https://github. com/road-framework/SDSN. The size of the project has 407356 lines of code (Github GLOC on 3/11/2018).

Evaluation. We show the feasibility of our approach with a case study that includes common change scenarios for multi-tenant service networks (adapted from the change scenarios for variant-rich applications [12,13]) (Table 1). To realize a scenario, we first identify the differences between the initial service

```
1   rule "stage1"
2     when
3       $mps : ManagementPolicyState (id =="policy1", state=="active")
4     then
5       updateProcess("EuroCars.P1","state", "passive");
6       $mps.setState("stage1_done");
7   end
8   rule "stage2"
9     when
10      $mps : ManagementPolicyState (id =="policy1", state=="stage1_done")
11    then
12      addNode("TX","http://localhost:8082/axis2/services/TaxiHireService");
13      addLink("SC-TX","SC","TX");
14      addLink("TX-MO","TX","MO");
15      addTask("TX","OrderTaxi","...");
16      addTask("SC","PayTX","...");
17      ...
18      addTerm("SC-TX","orderTaxi","AtoB");
19      addTerm("TX-MO","notifyTaxiBooking","AtoB");
20      ...
21      updateTask("SC","Analyze","outputs","add","SC-TX.orderTaxi.Req");
22      ...
23      $mps.setState("stage2_done");
24  end
25  rule "stage3"
26    when
27      $mps : ManagementPolicyState (id =="policy1", state=="stage2_done")
28    then
29      addSynchronizationRules("TX","TX_SYN.drl");
30      addRoutingRules("TX","TX_Routing.drl");
31      addPassthroughRules("SC-TX","SC-TX.drl");
32      ...
33      addSynchronizationTableEntries("EuroCars.P1","orderTaxi:TX;payTX:SC;..");
34      addRoutingTableEntries("EuroCars.P1","orderTaxiRes,sendInvoice:TX;...");
35      addPassthroughTableEntries("EuroCars.P1","orderTaxi,
36                                              orderTaxiRes:SC-TX;...");
37      $mps.setState("stage3_done");
38  end
39  rule "stage4"
40    when
41      $ms : ManagementState (id =="EuroCars.P1.VC.SYN", state=="quiescence") and
42      $ms1 : ManagementState (id =="EuroCars.P1.VC.Routing", state=="quiescence")
43      and ...
44    then
45      removeSynchronizationTableEntries("EuroCars.P1","VC, SC");
46      removeRoutingTableEntries("EuroCars.P1","VC, SC");
47      removePassthroughTableEntries("EuroCars.P1","VC-SC");
48      $mps.setState("stage4_done");
49  end
50  rule "stage5"
51    when
52      $mps : ManagementPolicyState (id =="policy1", state=="stage3_done") and
53      $mps1 : ManagementPolicyState (id =="policy1", state=="stage4_done")
54    then
55      updateNode("TX","state","active");
56      ...
57      updateProcess("EuroCars.P1","state", "active");
58      $mps.setState("quiescence");
59  end
```

Fig. 6. A fragment of the change management policy for our example

```
rule orderTaxi                                (a)   rule orderTaxiRes                              (b)
  when                                                when
    $e1 : Event(id == "eOrderTaxiReqd")                 $msg : ServiceMessage(opName== "orderTaxiRes")
  then                                                then
    NodeMessage [] msgs = Pull("SC-TX.orderTaxi.Req");    Forward("SC-TX.orderTaxi.Res",
    ServiceMessage sMsg =                                   Synthesize("OrderTaxiRes.xsl",$msg));
        Synthesize(msgs,"OrderTaxi.xsl");                Forward("TX-MO.notifyMO.Req",
    ExecuteTask("OrderTaxi", sMsg);                        Synthesize("NotifyMO.xsl",$msg));
end                                                 end
```

Fig. 7. A synchronization rule and a routing rule at the node TX

network and the target one after the realization of the scenario. Then, we design the management policy to capture the differences as change commands, and apply the created policy at the running initial service network. We compared the logs and response messages of VSN executions with those of the manually created same service network to validate the changes to the initial service network. The case study resources are at https://github.com/indikakumara/SDSN-ESOCC-2018.

We assessed the effectiveness of our support for evolution by doing a change and impact analysis. A detailed analysis of the changes and impacts for each change scenario is included in the case study resources. The scenarios together validated our support for each change type (and its impacts) to a multi-tenant service network (see Sect. 4.1). Moreover, we observed that the units of change

Table 1. Change scenarios for the roadside assistance service network

No:	Types of changes	Sub-scenarios (One functional and one performance)
1	Add/remove a mandatory feature	*Reimbursement* feature (to be used by each tenant)
		Response time <30 min and max-throughput = 150 for all assistance cases
2	Add/remove an optional feature	*Accident Tow* feature (to be used by HappyTours and the new tenant AsiaBus)
		Response time <2d and throughput = 10 for a reimbursement
3	Add/remove feature to a feature group	*TaxiHire* feature to/from the features *RentalVehicle* and *PublicTransport*
		4d repair duration in addition to the existing 2d and 3d for *Repair* feature
4	Add/remove feature dependency	The dependency *Major Repair excludes Accommodation*
		The dependency *Repair time = 3d includes Tow duration = 4* h
5	Make the optional feature	*Accident Tow* a mandatory feature
		Make *Or* repair durations 2d, 3d, and 4d *Alternative (XOR)* options
6	Modify feature implementation	Extend a *Repair* implementation to use external parts if no parts available inhouse
		Add an external assessor to a repairing implementation, increasing repair time by 6 h
7	Add/remove multiple feature implementations	One realization of *Reimbursement* to/from its other realizations
		One realization of *Accident Tow* for duration = 3 h to/from its other realizations
8	Add/Remove feature implementation dependency	*Accident Tow* with MarkTow excludes *Repair* with MacRepair
		Repair duration = 3d with AutoRepair includes *RentalVehicle* duration = 3d with SLRCars

at the domain-level are generally confined to their explicit representations in the composite application, i.e., representations of services, their collaborations, their relationships, their capabilities, the routing and regulation of interactions, and VSNs/processes. This is a key requirement to support effective evolution [14].

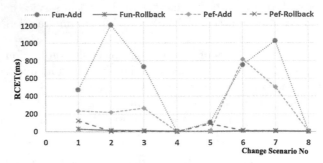

Fig. 8. Runtime change enactment time (RCET) for the change scenarios

We have also measured the run-time change enactment time (RCET) for each scenario (see Fig. 8). RCET is the time difference between the manager of the service network receiving a management policy and the service network being ready for use after applying the policy. The experiment uses a machine with an Intel i5-2400 CPU (3.10 GHz), 3.23 GB RAM, and Windows 7. The average RCET values for the functional scenarios are 537.2 ms (addition) and 12.25 ms (rollback). Those for the performance scenarios are 256.75 ms (addition) and 32.5 ms (rollback). We believe that this is reasonable.

6   Related Work

We consider the related work from variant-rich applications and service networks. We focus on the changes to the runtime artifacts of composite applications (compared with the works on design time artifacts [15] such as service specifications).

Two common types of variant rich applications are software product lines and cloud applications. Among the works from the product lines, Morin et al. [9] and Baresi et al. [12] supported modifying a business process at a set of predefined points to create variants. Bosch and Capilla [16] supported, in a smart home product line, feature-level changes by mapping a feature to a device that offers a service. The works from cloud applications considered issues such as tenant-specific variants [17,18], and tenant-specific upgrades [19]. Truyen et al. [17] used the dependency injection to bind tenant-specific variants to the variation points of a component-based cloud application. Moens et al. [18] proposed a feature-model based development of cloud applications, where a service realizes a feature. Van Landuyt et al. [19] presented a middleware support for modifying a composite cloud application by activating tenant-specific upgrades at runtime via the dynamic (re)binding of services.

In [13], we also addressed the runtime change and impact management of multi-tenant cloud applications designed as dynamic software product lines. In this paper, we considered the service network model, which is significantly different from the product-line based model in terms of runtime abstractions/elements in the composite application, and thus changes and their impacts.

Most existing works on service networks consider the modeling and analysis of service networks from specific aspects [2] such as business value flow [5], business processes [6], and service relationships [1]. Their realizations have relied on process-centric models, which fail to represent service networks naturally. That is, the domain concepts (e.g., services, service capabilities, service relationships, service interactions, interaction routing and regulation, service network paths, and virtualization) and their representations are mismatched, and the domain concepts are not directly represented or managed in the realization, limiting their utility. Regarding change and impact analysis, Kabzeva et al. [7] proposed a modeling approach to represent the entities (services, actors, and processes) in a service network, and their different relationships (e.g., consumption, competition, and ownership) at design time. They also proposed a tool to assess the impact of a change to an entity or a relationship.

Overall, there is a limited support to the runtime change and impact management for a composite service application that realizes a multi-tenant service network. The existing approaches also lack architectural abstractions to represent a multi-tenant service network naturally at runtime. They also do not provide a change and impact analysis for such runtime representations, and the middleware support for the realization and management of each change and impact. This paper addresses these limitations in the existing research.

7   Conclusions and Future Work

We have addressed the runtime evolution of a multi-tenant service network, where a single service network simultaneously hosts a set of virtual service networks for multiple tenants. We have identified different types of runtime changes to the service network and their potential impacts, and discussed our middleware support for realizing and managing those changes and impacts. A software engineer can design the controlled propagation of the desired changes. We have evaluated our approach with a case study and a performance study. The results have shown that our approach can support the runtime change and impact management of multi-tenant service networks, with little performance overhead.

In the future, we plan to develop a pattern-based formalization of the change and impact management of multi-tenant service networks, and a tool that uses the formalization to identify and assess change impacts. The generation of change management policies from high-level visual models will also be investigated.

References

1. Danylevych, O., Karastoyanova, D., Leymann, F.: Service networks modelling: an SOA & BPM standpoint. J. Univers. Comput. Sci. **16**(13), 1668–21693 (2010)
2. Razo-Zapata, P., et al.: Service network approaches. In: Handbook of Service Description: USDL and its Methods, pp. 45–274 (2012)
3. Kumara, I., et al.: Software-defined service networking: performance differentiation in shared multi-tenant cloud applications. IEEE TSC **10**(1), 9–22 (2017)
4. Kumara, I., et al.: Virtualisation and management of application service networks. In: Network as a Service for Next Generation Internet, vol. 73, pp. 357–382 (2017)
5. Allee, V.: Reconfiguring the value network. J. Bus. Strat. **21**(4), 1–6 (2000)
6. Comuzzi, M., Vonk, J., Grefen, P.: Measures and mechanisms for process monitoring in evolving business networks. Data Knowl. Eng. **71**(1), 1–28 (2012)
7. Kabzeva, A., Gtze, J., Mller, P.: Model-based relationship management for service networks. IJSSOE **5**(4), 104–132 (2015)
8. Bohner, S.A: Impact analysis in the software change process: a year 2000 perspective. In: International Conference on Software Maintenance, pp. 42–51 (1996)
9. Morin, B., et al.: Models@Runtime to support dynamic adaptation. Computer **42**(10), 44–51 (2009)
10. Kumara, I., et al.: Change and impact analysis of multi-tenant service networks. Technical report (2018). https://github.com/indikakumara/SDSN-ESOCC-2018/blob/master/TR.pdf
11. Kramer, J., Magee, J.: The evolving philosophers problem: dynamic change management. IEEE TSE **16**(11), 1293–1306 (1990)
12. Baresi, L., Guinea, S., Pasquale, L.: Service-oriented dynamic software product lines. Computer **45**(10), 42–48 (2012)
13. Kumara, I., Han, J., Colman, A., Kapuruge, M.: Runtime evolution of service-based multi-tenant SaaS applications. In: Basu, S., Pautasso, C., Zhang, L., Fu, X. (eds.) ICSOC 2013. LNCS, vol. 8274, pp. 192–206. Springer, Heidelberg (2013). https://doi.org/10.1007/978-3-642-45005-1_14
14. Tarr, P., et al.: N degrees of separation: multi-dimensional separation of concerns. In: International Conference on Software Engineering, pp. 107–119 (1999)
15. Andrikopoulos, V., Benbernou, S., Papazoglou, M.: On the evolution of services. IEEE TSE **38**(3), 609–628 (2012)
16. Bosch, J., Capilla, R.: Dynamic variability in software-intensive embedded system families. Computer **45**(10), 28–35 (2012)
17. Truyen, E., et al.: Context-oriented programming for customizable SaaS applications. In: ACM Symposium on Applied Computing, pp. 418–425 (2012)
18. Moens, H., Filip, T.: Feature-based application development and management of multi-tenant applications in clouds. In: SPLC, pp. 72–81 (2014)
19. Van Landuyt, D., Gey, F., Truyen, E., Joosen, W.: Middleware for dynamic upgrade activation and compensations in multi-tenant SaaS. In: Maximilien, M., Vallecillo, A., Wang, J., Oriol, M. (eds.) ICSOC 2017. LNCS, vol. 10601, pp. 340–348. Springer, Cham (2017). https://doi.org/10.1007/978-3-319-69035-3_24

DevOps Service Observability *By-Design*: Experimenting with Model-View-Controller

Damian A. Tamburri[1], Marcello M. Bersani[2], Raffaela Mirandola[2], and Giorgio Pea[2,3(✉)]

[1] TU/e JADS, s'Hertogenbosch, Netherlands
d.a.tamburri@tue.nl
[2] DEIB, Politecnico di Milano, Milan, Italy
{marcellomaria.bersani,raffaela.mirandola}@polimi.it
[3] Moviri S.p.A, Milan, Italy
giorgio.pea@polimi.it

Abstract. The speeding growth of the IT market and its disruptive technologies, think of DevOps or Microservices, are leading towards using typical design patterns in a completely novel fashion. We consider the Model-View-Controller (MVC) as a target for a controlled refactoring experiment aimed at making it more *observable*, that is, mutated to be more easily monitorable in line with DevOps expectations. The article illustrates and implements our proposed mutation of MVC with *observability*. Using a proof-of-concept application prototype, the article illustrates how the improved observability can impact on general application maintainability — we use common software metrics from the state of the art. We conclude that there are indeed forms for common design patterns (e.g., MVC) which are more monitorable but they are more expensive in terms of maintenance and hence require attention by the research community at large and further experimentation.

1 Introduction

The birth and the evolution of the Internet, from 2 million users and 1 Terabyte/month of traffic in 1990 to over 2 billion users and 10 Terabyte/second of traffic in 2011 [21] has sparked the development of more and more complex, large-scale, data-intensive software architectures that provide services to millions, even billions of people. At these magnitudes, monitoring quality of service [1,10,19] become even more critical. For this reason, a renewed attention recently emerged on how services should be designed to increase a property we call *observability*, that is, the ability to constantly and incrementally *observe* individual components, their granular interactions, the atomic computations and their intermediate and final results at runtime. Catering for observability allows more specific and granular refactoring, thus enabling the continuous, incremental, and iterative improvement of their functionality in a DevOps fashion [3].

© IFIP International Federation for Information Processing 2018
Published by Springer Nature Switzerland AG 2018. All Rights Reserved
K. Kritikos et al. (Eds.): ESOCC 2018, LNCS 11116, pp. 49–64, 2018.
https://doi.org/10.1007/978-3-319-99819-0_4

Starting by discussing the suitability of a classical architectural patterns like Model-View-Controller (MVC) [4] for observability, this article contributes an attempt at offering a more *observable* version of the MVC software architectural pattern that is more consistent with observability requirements for architectures in our modern DevOps contexts. We named our research solution as *oMVC*, which stands for "observable Model-View-Controller". To evaluate our research solution, we operate a proof-of-concept experiment for *oMVC* implementing the architectural pattern within a medium online multiplayer game of our own design. Concerning this proof-of-concept, we discuss how the *oMVC* abstractions and data-flow improve observability. Subsequently, we evaluate the additional *maintenance costs* of adding-in observability. More specifically, we use metrics from the state of the art in software maintenance [6] to measure the maintainability of our proof-of-concept with and without *oMVC* — this evaluation shows rather conflicting results.

On one hand, results indicate that the adoption of an improved architectural pattern, such as *oMVC*, is a trade-off between the complexity of the pattern. On the other hand, results imply that the effort required in the post-design phase of the software development, operations, maintenance and refactoring, testing, and long-term maintenance are also higher.

We conclude that observability can bring about many benefits but, like any other architecture property, it needs careful trade-off analysis [12, 22], e.g., especially in (micro)services design contexts where multiple instances of more observable architectural patterns are used[1].

Structure of the Paper. Section 2 describes the state of the art. Section 3 defines *Service Observability* and outlines the proposed solution: *oMVC*. Section 4 evaluates our research solution in terms of software metrics. Section 6 concludes our paper.

2   State of the Art: MVC and Its Variants

MVC - Classic Approach. MVC is a software architectural pattern originally introduced in the SmallTalk-80 programming language for the design and implementation of user interfaces [13]. Since its introduction in 1988 as a paradigm for building user interfaces, MVC has progressively shifted towards being a general architectural pattern for complex software architectures, especially used in web-services, and service applications designs [16–18]. The pattern defines the following three fundamental abstractions:

– *Model* groups together the "architecture's domain state and behaviour" [13] and "manages the behaviour and data of the architecture domain, respond to requests for information about its state (usually from the view), and responds to instructions to change state (usually from the controller)" [4]. In other terms, Model provides an abstraction that puts together the state of an architecture and the procedures manipulating the architecture state, everything in the context of each architecture's domain.

---

[1] https://tinyurl.com/yck9emou.

- *View* "deals with everything graphical; it requests data from their model, and displays the data." [4]. In other terms, View provides an abstraction to represent to the external world the state of an architecture.
- *Controller* "takes over the user interaction with the model and the view" and "contains the interface between their associated models and views and the input devices (keyboard, pointing device, time)" [4]. In other terms, Controllers coordinate Views and Models with the interactions produced by the user with the architecture.

Figure 1 illustrates the relationships between the different abstractions of MVC: the user interaction is managed by a Controller, which reacts to it by commanding the right Model to change the part of the state of the architecture it is responsible for; the Model notifies the Controller and the View that "depends" on it, so that they can either adapt their functionalities to the change occurred in the Model (this happens in the case of the Controller), or they render a new representation of the Model data to the external world (this happens in the case of the View). To render such data, a View requires to query their Models.

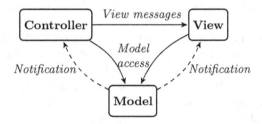

Fig. 1. Data-flow in MVC.

MVC Variants. The first variant we report for MVC is known as Model-View-ViewModel (MVVM) and is a software architectural pattern developed at Microsoft Inc. by Ken Cooper and Ted Peters for building event-driven user interfaces [7]. MVVM defines one additional abstraction in addition to the classical Model and View abstractions from classical MVC.

ViewModel. A ViewModel represents an intermediary between the View and the Model. It decouples Views from the Model by means of a local state, used by the Views to render a proper UI, and by means of a set of commands used by the Views to signal the occurrence of a user interaction. The execution of these commands causes the ViewModel to coordinate the realisation of different parts of the business logic of the architecture so that a new state for the architecture is generated. Whenever the internal data of the Model change, the ViewModel is notified and its local state is updated; in addition the Views associated to the ViewModel are notified and re-render pieces of UI to be displayed to the user (note that Views can be notified by the ViewModel not necessarily whenever the ViewModel's local state changes). The View interacts with the ViewModel by means of data-binding and commands to render a proper UI and to signal user interactions. The ViewModel reacts to commands by coordinating pieces of business logic executed by the Model. The ViewModel reacts to newly available Model data by updating its local state and by notifying associated Views about the change. The notified Views automatically query the local state of the ViewModel to display an updated UI.

Model-View-Presenter (MVP). MVP is a software architectural pattern developed by Taligent Inc. in 1996 that defines the following abstractions: *Model, Command, Selection, View, Interactor* and *Presenter.* Model is defined as the same abstraction offered by MVC but it is only focused the architecture domain data or, equivalently, the state of the architecture; the architecture behaviour is outsourced to the Command abstraction, which offers an interface for updating slices of the Model. Selection represents elements of the architecture state, or of the Model, that Commands are willing to change. View is defined as the same abstraction offered by MVC but, in this case, it is also capable to capture user interactions, by means of Interactors (in MVC user interaction is captured by the Controller). Presenter is the coordinator of all the previous abstractions.

Summary. Observability of software artifacts seems considerable. More specifically, designing applications that are inherently observable has tangible benefits in terms of product maintainability, both in the implementation phase and later in the post-release phase. Indeed, a more observable application allows for a more accurate code analizability throughout all the life-cycle of the application and, hence, a reduction of the costs. Therefore, we aim at defining a precise set of features that applications have to fulfill, in order to be observable. In addition, we design an new architecture pattern that enforces these features by construction. The baseline stems from the following principle: observability is a precursor for the possibility of: (i) reading all the relevant information defining the application state and (ii) keeping track of the changes applied to the application state and of the order among the changes throughout the execution. In our analysis, we focus on the so-called stateful applications, that are such that the application functionality can only be obtained with the maintenance and manipulation overtime of different pieces of internal information – i.e., the application state.

3   Redesigning MVC for Observability

The analysis of the architectural patterns and frameworks in the previous section allowed us to elicit 5 common properties, three of them characterizing the new architectural solutions emerging to make an architecture observable.

For design patterns to aid service observability, they should offer suitable abstractions for:

P1: the representation (i.e., logging and reporting) of the architecture or service state, intended as a human- and machine-readable representation of the set of variable values (or simply, the *observable* variables) in which the system is observed to be in any given instant during operation [2,14]. Note that, with the concept of variable, we identify any entity that can change value in the scope of the service' own computation (e.g., an integer variable or even a more complex object);

P2: the representation of the events that reflect data inputs from outside of the service and the internal events representing the effects over that data, including any of its computations – observability reflects an ordered set of data transformations [8] affecting the application state;

P3: the manipulation of the architecture state in response to the events – observability reflects the value of architecture self-organization or other self-* properties [15] enacted in response to the context variations (e.g., inputs, specific processing results, etc.);

P4: the provisioning of the architecture state to the outside environment in machine-readable format - in this case, observability reflects the ordered set of outputs that the system has produced against the inputs corresponding to those outputs;

P5: the coordination of all the previous features - in this case, observability is realized by appropriate business logic inside the architecture;

Stemming from the above, we offer the definition below:

> **Observability.** An implementation of an architectural pattern becomes observable when *its behavior can be precisely monitored, logged, and rendered for analysis* through suitable components that are instrumented by its design patterns and decisions. Hence, a software application offers *observability* (or simply, it is *observable*) when it defines explicit abstractions implementing P1, P2, and P4.

3.1   Observability Limitations for MVC and Its Variants

Based on the previous terms and definitions, we classify the architectural patterns discussed in Sect. 2 in terms of the properties P1–P5. MVC partially supports P1 and P3 as it does not define two distinct abstractions for the architecture state and for the procedures manipulating the state: Model actually groups both together. Moreover, in MVC there is no abstraction to represent external events as the state transition is enabled by generic messages, exchanged by Controller and Model. Hence, P2 is not fulfilled. Other variants of MVC, e.g., Model-View-View-Model[2] (MVVM), offer the same features as MVC with respect to the properties P1 and P3. In addition, however, MVVM defines the abstraction Command for the event exchanges between ViewModel and View but without a specific notion of event. Finally, the Model-View-Presenter (MVP) variant partially supports P2 as the pattern does not provide an abstraction representing input data availability but rather it provides an abstraction –Interactor– to signal them to the Presenter abstraction.

---

[2] The definition of MVVM can be found at https://tinyurl.com/y7qwtqkr.

3.2   Improving MVC for Observability: *o*MVC

We refactor MVC to provide for the following observability-improving behaviors according to the definition of Observability of Sect. 3.

1. Store captures the application state [P1];
2. Action represents a generic application event [P2];
3. View/Normal components intercept an architecture-relevant event and construct a proper Action [P2]; they also render the application state to the environment [P4];
4. Store propagate the Actions into the architecture [P3, P5]; it retrieves the correct Resolver and use it to obtain the Policies to be executed in response to the event described by the Action; Store executes such Policies and updates State. Store also notifies interested View/Normal components about changes in the State; all the notified View/Normal components compute a new state representation to be outputted to the rest of the application or to the external environment.

Figure 2 shows the *o*MVC pattern with its main abstractions and Fig. 3 shows the class diagram of the overall *o*MVC architecture.

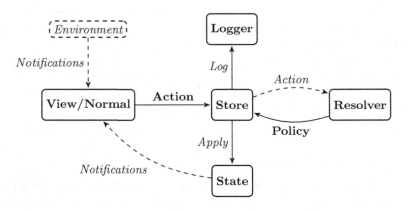

Fig. 2. Event and data-flow in *o*MVC.

The baseline component in *o*MVC pattern is implemented through the State abstraction whereby the isolation of the application state is realized. All the components that foster the improved application observability depend on it.

State Abstraction. *oMVC State*, or simply *State*, represents the state of an architecture, hence *the set of pieces of information whose maintenance over time defines completely the characteristics and the behavior of the software architecture itself, given the problem at hand.*

An atomic information is a pair datum/meaning with an associated understanding or semantic interpretation [9]. A meaning of a datum can be expressed by "appending" to it a label. For instance, (*registeredUsers, 10*).

A piece of information can be decomposed in other pieces of information, thus forming a complex information hierarchy. As State groups pieces of information we propose to structure State as a set of key-value pairs in which keys represent labels and values represent either a datum or another set of key-value pairs. Such structural model grasps the complexity of a piece of information and can be easily mapped to many efficient data structures and constructs in the world of computer science and engineering (C structures, Object oriented classes, Relational tables, Dictionaries, Hash tables, etc..).

Action Abstraction. *oMVC Action is a complete description of an internal or external event that is of interest for a software architecture.* In other terms, an Action groups all the necessary pieces of information capable of describing completely an architecture-relevant event, so that the architecture can put in motion proper processing procedures.

It is possible to characterise an architecture-relevant event by means of three distinct objects: the identifier and the category of the event in addition to some data that convey the content of the event itself. This characterisation has been proposed because of a simple reasoning concerning how human beings manage events: whenever an event occurs, we want to know what is the category of the event (e.g., good event, bad event, an event that concerns the family, etc.), what is the event (e.g., the door broke), and we want to know the details of the event (e.g., what part of the door is broken, in which way, etc.). This definition fosters an effective characterization of actions: for instance, an event "MouseClickLeft", that might belongs to category "ItemClick", can be referred to the a specific item, say "registeredUserField", that is described by the third field of the Action. Such a general description of the events allow us to propose a structural model for Actions: similarly to State, as they both group pieces of information, Actions can be shaped as a set of key-value pairs in which two pairs are fixed: the pair that expresses an event identifier, and the pair that expresses an event group identifier. The specification we provide for a *o*MVC Action underlines the fact that two different events generate two different Actions, and that two Actions are different if they refer to two different events. Therefore, a one-to-one relationship exists between Actions and architecture-relevant events: an identifier for an event is also an identifier for an Action and an identifier for the group of an event is also an identifier for the group of an Action.

View/Normal Components Abstraction. *oMVC View/Normal component is responsible for intercepting relevant internal or external events, making them available to the rest of the architecture as Actions, and producing a representation of the State of the architecture to be exposed to other components or to the external world, whenever the State changes.* More precisely, a *View component* intercepts events coming only from the external world and produces a representation of the State of the architecture to be communicated only to the external world, while a *Normal component* intercepts only events internal to the architecture and produces a representation of the State of the architecture to be communicated only to other architecture's components. This specification does not suggest a particular structural model for View/Normal components.

Nonetheless, it constraints View/Normal components to construct Actions for describing events and to observe the State of the architecture for changes through a suitable subscription mechanism.

Policy Abstraction. *oMVC Policy is a rule or a behavior that defines part of the business logic of a software architecture and that is put in motion after some event makes available some data of interest to the architecture.* Policies can be distinguished into *state Policies* and *side Policies*. The formers implements the business logic manipulating the architecture state whereas the latter consist of a non State related data manipulation. Policies are implemented through procedures, that are triggered by the occurrence of some event. State Policies accept two arguments: the current State of the architecture, as a state Policy is asked to manipulate it, and an Action. Every state Policy returns the new State.

Resolver Abstraction. *oMVC Resolver maps a given Action to the correct (state and side) Policies that should be executed upon it.* The specification of Resolver does not impose any specific implementation yet it only requires that, for every Action, at most one State Policy and at most one Side Policy are returned by means of a proper Resolver. Many Resolvers can be defined, each one mapping the Actions belonging to a given group to their proper Policies.

Store Abstraction. *oMVC Store coordinates the interaction between State, Actions, Resolvers, Policies and View/Normal components to make a software architecture work correctly.* The coordination process can be split into three functionalities: (i) a look-up mechanism allowing components to access State for the architecture state retrieval. (ii) The *Action propagation* mechanism allowing the architecture state evolve upon the occurrence of an event. (iii) A subscription mechanism allowing View/Normal components to subscribe to changes in State, and so be notified whenever they happen.

The Action propagation mechanism is *the* mechanism that View/Normal components are forced to use to make available constructed Actions to the rest of the architecture so that proper Policies can be executed to handle the event encapsulated within the Action: whenever a View/Normal component *propagates* an Action using Store, the latter performs the following actions: (i) maps the Action to a proper Resolver and use the retrieved Resolver to obtain the (state and side) Policies associated with the Action; (ii) executes the Policies and changes the application state with the one produced by running the state Policy; (iii) notifies all the (subscribed) View/Normal components that have subscribed to State changes; Akin to View/Normal components, the Store abstraction specification does not suggest a particular structural model, but the chosen one should offer the above functionalities.

Logger Abstraction. *oMVC Logger maintains the application log that stores the application behavior through a sequence of tuples (Action, State before manipulation, State after manipulation).* The Logger is activated whenever a View/Normal component propagates an Action, as the Action propagation mechanism allows for the manipulation of the State.

3.3   Relationship with MVC

State, Policies and Model. The MVC Model groups the state of an application and the procedures to manipulate it, while in *o*MVC there is a clear separation between State and Policies. The MVC pattern does not impose any restriction on the application's state implementation, and, in general, a MVC application may have more than one Model; conversely, State is a unique and centralized shared container of key-value pairs. Moreover, while MVC prescribes that Model knows the Views that depend on it, State is not aware of other abstractions nor implements a notification mechanism (a task outsourced to Store).

Resolvers, View Components, Store and Controller. The functionalities of the MVC Controller (that intercepts and interprets application-relevant events and causes the Model to change) are expressed through various *o*MVC abstractions. The Action propagation mechanism, implemented by Store, has the role of enforcing the modification of the application state, similarly to the MVC Controller. Differently from MVC, Store notifies the View components about the state change and Store commands the State to change by executing Policies, that are provided by the Resolvers. Moreover, *o*MVC assigns to View components both the functionalities of providing a representation of the application to the external world and of intercepting events, which is not the case for MVC that assigns the former to the View and the latter to the Controller.

Logger, Actions, and Side Policies, are not mapped to any MVC abstraction.

4   Evaluating Software Quality Metrics for *o*MVC

To evaluate the modifications illustrated in the previous section, we conduct an empirical evaluation of the effects of the *o*MVC pattern with software metrics that are specifically related to the source code of the architecture and that can be automatically evaluated through static analysis.

We designed a medium-sized online game. The player is assigned the mission to make users play an online software version, with some modifications, of the board game *Escape From Aliens in Outer Space* [20]. In this game, players assume either the role of humans or aliens, and, in any case, find themselves on a spaceship. The humans have the mission of escaping from the spaceship by reaching certain escape or rescuing points; the aliens have the mission of devouring as many humans as possible, possibly denying them to leave the spaceship.

The architecture is based on three patterns typically used for web-services [16], namely: (1) *client-server*, (2) *publisher-subscriber*, and, subsequently, (3) *o*MVC. The client-server pattern is used to implement the most of the online multiplayer functionality of the game. All the requests and responses involved in the synchronous communication strategy adopted by architecture can be modeled as messages that carry an identifier of the action to be performed on the server, and that carry additional data relevant for the execution of the action.

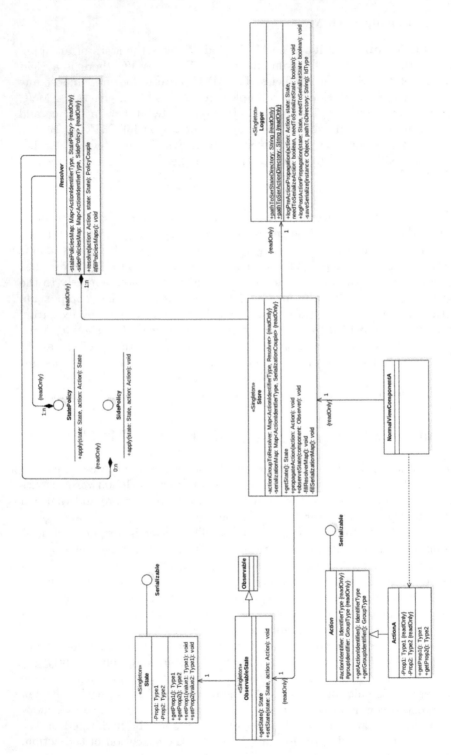

Fig. 3. Class diagram of *o*MVC architecture.

The publisher-subscriber pattern is used to implement those functionalities of the software system that require asynchronous communication between the client and the server such as, for instance, the start of a game or the display of chat messages. The *o*MVC pattern is used to implement the business logic of the entire architecture, both in the client and in the server.

Evaluation Objective. We compare key software metrics computed for the *o*MVC proof-of-concept and for an equivalent MVC architecture — metrics results are outlined in the remainder of this section.[3]

Chidamber and Kemerer (CK) metrics [6].

- LCOM (Lack of cohesion in methods) measures how tightly bound or related the internal elements of a software module are with each other.
- NOR (Number of root classes) measures how many class hierarchies are in the program.
- DIT (Depth of the inheritance tree) measures the length of a class hierarchy.
- RFC (Response for a Class) measures the number of methods and constructors invoked by objects of a class.
- CBO (Coupling between Objects) measures how many methods and instance variables of a class B the methods of a class A uses (bidirectional uses are considered only once, inheritance related connections are not considered).
- WMC (Weighted Methods per class) measures the sum of the cyclomatic complexity of the methods in a class. More complex methods usually require more tests for reasons of decision coverage.

Class dependency (CD) metrics.

- *Cyclic* (Number of cyclic class dependencies) measures, for each class c, the number of classes c directly depends on, and that in turn depend on c.
- *Dcy* (Number of dependencies) measures, for each class c, the number of classes c directly depends on.
- *Dcy** (Number of transitive dependencies) measures, for each class c, the number of classes c directly or indirectly depends on.
- *Dpt* (Number of dependants) measures, for each class c, the number of classes that directly depend on c.
- *Dpt** (Number of transitive dependants) measures, for each class c, the number of classes that directly or indirectly depend on c.

The software metrics described above have been computed using the IntelliJ MetricsReloaded plugin[4], and the complete metrics results are available in the context of the same Github organisation used for the *o*MVC proof-of-concept.

The figures in Table 1 show the values of the Chidamber and Kemerer metrics, and of the Class dependency metrics, for the server component whereas those in Table 2 show the same metrics for the client component, comparing the *o*MVC proof-of-concept (red bars) with its equivalent MVC architecture (blue bars).

---

[3] See https://github.com/StateStrategyproof-of-concept/Server and https://github.com/StateStrategyproof-of-concept/Client.

[4] https://plugins.jetbrains.com/plugin/93-metricsreloaded.

Table 1. CK metric (left) and CD metrics (right) for the server: *o*MVC-based in red and MVC-based in blue (lower metric values are better).

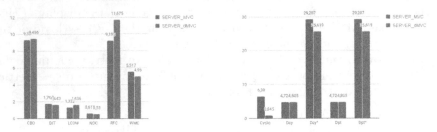

Table 2. CK metric (left) and CD metrics (right) for the client: *o*MVC-based in red and MVC-based in blue (lower metric values are better).

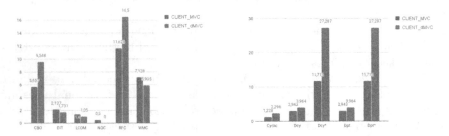

Server Side. CK metrics have similar values for both the architectures, with a slight advantage for the MVC architecture, and with the only exception of the RFC metric, which considerably favors the MVC architecture. RFC metric, unlike the others, does directly depend on the number of classes and methods defined in an architecture, hence, since *o*MVC introduces many classes for implementing its abstractions, the value of the metric is reasonably expected to be higher. The Class dependency metrics assume similar values, with a slight advantage for *o*MVC when Dcy and Dpt are considered, that becomes relevant for Cyclic metric. This trend ensues from the isolation and the reduced inter-components dependency that *o*MVC promotes.

Client Side. CK metrics show varied trends: the RFC metric is higher for the *o*MVC-based architecture. The CBO metric favors the MVC architecture — this circumstance is explained by two reasons: (a) the propagation of different Actions by the GUI components increases the CBO value of the Action class and, (b) the client of the *o*MVC-based architecture introduces more Actions than the server. Conversely, the remaining metrics favor *o*MVC since (a) the data-flow and the introduced abstractions reduce the complexity of classes by offloading the architectural business logic to the Action propagation mechanism, and (b) the LCOM, DIT, NOC, and WMC metrics are measures of class complexity and methods relatedness. Class dependency metrics always favors the MVC-based architecture. The Side Policies and the classes used for the View component introduce many transitive dependencies that considerably influence the values of *Dcy* and *Dpt**. The *o*MVC-based architecture exploits a unique

View component (i.e., GUIManager), rather than different small ones, that observes the *o*MVC State and orchestrates many different other components. Furthermore, the *o*MVC client propagates Actions inside Side Policies - that is rare in the context of the server architecture. Hence, the additional degree of recursion for the Action propagation mechanism produces more transitive and cyclic dependencies, with the consequent and perceivable metric variations.

The effect of the *o*MVC pattern on the implementation mainly affects CBO and RFC, whose values are degrading by 40% and 29%, respectively. These values indicates, in general, that the unit-testing on the classes can be at most 40% more demanding than the same testing on the MVC implementation. Conversely, the cyclomatic complexity of the server is lessened by 17%, hence yielding to smaller test cases for the coverage analysis.

---

5 Threats to Validity

Lack of Quantitative Metrics. The definition of Architecture Observability in Sect. 3 is declarative. It only outlines how an architectural pattern should be designed so that the implementing applications are observable. Observability is actually obtained because certain structural criteria (enforced through the properties P1-P5) are met. However, the observability delineated in Sect. 3 cannot be evaluated numerically as there is no a quantitative metrics that allows designers to estimate the observability of an implementation and, hence, to compare different implementations with each other. Its effect can only be measured indirectly (for instance, one can refer to the standard ISO 9126 [11] for the evaluation of some software qualities that are affected by the implementation of a specific architecture).

Implementation Complexity. The conclusions and the graphs provided in the previous section point out a generalized negative impact of *o*MVC for the majority of the Chidamber and Kemerer metrics in contrast to only few that are improved. This is not surprising, as the use of a structured pattern, which is implemented by means of various distinct entities, commonly introduces more "structural complexity" – i.e., more classes, methods and dependencies – than an unstructured design, realizing the same functionalities. On the one hand, a software entity implementing complex functionalities can benefit from a more structured implementation (consider the cyclomatic complexity of the server). The overhead introduced by the pattern can be less than, or at least comparable with, the complexity entailed by its functionality; and the greater maintainability of the final product compensates the use of the pattern. However, on the other hand, simple software implementations (e.g., the client side in our proof-of-concept) might suffer from the use of a pattern as it might introduce more "structural complexity" than the one actually needed, hence yielding a less concise software whose modification complexity can degrade.

Proof-of-Concept Evaluation. The evaluation of the observability of *o*MVC has been carried out through a proof-of-concept application of limited size. A deeper analysis is needed with the aim of comparing different implementations of *o*MVC when it is applied to small, medium and large applications. Indeed, the evaluation of the impact of a pattern in small applications can be strongly affected by the overhead that the pattern itself introduces.

***o*MVC in the Zoo of Patterns.** As outlined in Sect. 2, MVC has already been elaborated and extended various times and many versions of MVC were tailored to specific contexts. The use of the specific classes such as Policy and Resolver might actually resemble as an application of the State Machine pattern. However, the purpose of *o*MVC is different from the one of State pattern. The State pattern promotes decoupling of state-dependent functionalities from the state object itself. A state class delegates state-specific behavior to its current state object and does not care of implementing state-specific functionalities directly. *o*MVC exploits a State-like mechanism to manage the state of an application but it implements policies, actions and resolvers to enrich the State pattern with event-based features that can be used in many contexts for defining the transformation of the application state upon the occurrence of events.

Discovering Patterns vs. Creating New Ones. One of the core principle of designing patterns claims that patterns are discovered but not invented [5]. *o*MVC is designed and its structure is not elicited from the analysis of implemented solutions. However, *o*MVC ensues by construction from the MVC variants in the state-of-the-art. The five properties P1-P5, enlisted in Sect. 3 to define observability, are obtained by the analysis of the known patterns and their baseline tenets. *o*MVC, which explicitly provides abstractions that allow designers to satisfy the requirements captured by the properties, is therefore a by-construction consequence of the known solutions that improves observability.

6   Conclusions

We have re-designed the MVC software architecture pattern to be more *observable*, i.e., to be able to solve the problem of state management by providing abstractions that separate how the application state is structured, how it is manipulated, how it is represented to the external world, and how the previous activities are put together and made available *constantly* in an analysable log.

A valuable research path reflects further re-designs of patterns for a systematic comparison against *o*MVC over a more significant collection of diverse software architectures, and using more extensive quality assessment. Finally, some effort should be spent in defining a quantitative metrics for observability to be measured on actual implementation of *o*MVC and that can be automatically evaluated through static code analysis[5].

---

[5] The authors' work is partially supported by EU H2020-TWINN-2015 "DOSSIER-Cloud" no. 692251.

References

1. Aagedal, J.Ø.: Quality of service support in development of distributed systems. Ph.D. thesis, University of Oslo (2001)
2. Atlee, J.M., Gannon, J.D.: State-based model checking of event-driven system requirements. IEEE Trans. Softw. Eng. **19**(1), 24–40 (1993). http://dblp.uni-trier. de/db/journals/tse/tse19.html#AtleeG93
3. Bass, L., Weber, I., Zhu, L.: DevOps: A Software Architect's Perspective. SEI Series in Software Engineering. Addison-Wesley, New York (2015). http://my. safaribooksonline.com/9780134049847
4. Burbeck, S.: Applications programming in smalltalk-80(tm): How to use Model-View-Controller (MVC) (1987). http://st-www.cs.uiuc.edu/users/smarch/ st-docs/mvc.html
5. Buschmann, F., Henney, K., Schmidt, D.C.: Pattern-Oriented Software Architecture: On Patterns and Pattern Languages, vol. 5. Wiley, Chichester (2007)
6. Chidamber, S.R., Kemerer, C.F.: A metrics suite for object oriented design. IEEE Trans. Softw. Eng. **20**(6), 476–493 (1994)
7. Cooper, K., Peters, T.: The MVVM pattern. https://msdn.microsoft.com/en-us/ library/hh848246.aspx
8. Doerr, M.: Data transformations (2001). http://cidoc.ics.forth.gr/data_ transformations.html
9. Floridi, L.: Information: A Very Short Introduction. Very Short Introductions. OUP, Oxford (2010)
10. Horvat, G., Zagar, D., Vlaovic, J.: Evaluation of quality of service provisioning in large-scale pervasive and smart collaborative wireless sensor and actor networks. Adv. Eng. Inf. **33**, 258–273 (2017). http://dblp.uni-trier.de/db/journals/aei/aei33. html#HorvatZV17
11. Software engineering - product quality - part 1: Quality model. Standard, International Organization for Standardization, Geneva (2001)
12. Kazman, R., Klein, M., Clements, P.: ATAM: method for architecture evaluation. Technical report CMU/SEI-2000-TR-004, Carnegie Mellon Uiversity, Software Engineering Institute (2000)
13. Krasner, G.E., Pope, S.T.: A cookbook for using the model-view controller user interface paradigm in smalltalk-80. J. Object Oriented Program **1**(3), 26–49 (1988)
14. Mateescu, R.: Model checking for software architectures. In: Oquendo, F., Warboys, B.C., Morrison, R. (eds.) EWSA 2004. LNCS, vol. 3047, pp. 219–224. Springer, Heidelberg (2004). https://doi.org/10.1007/978-3-540-24769-2_18
15. Pilpre, A.: Self-* properties of multi sensing entities in smart environments. Master's thesis, MIT (2005)
16. Prazeres, C.V.S., da Graça Campos Pimentel, M., Munson, E.V., Teixeira, C.A.C.: Toward semantic web services as mvc applications: from owl-s via uml. J. Web Eng. **9**(3), 243–265 (2010). http://dblp.uni-trier.de/db/journals/jwe/jwe9.html# PrazeresPMT10
17. Prazeres, C.V.S., Teixeira, C.A.C., Munson, E.V., da Graça Campos Pimentel, M.: Semantic web services: from owl-s via uml to mvc applications. In: Shin, S.Y., Ossowski, S. (eds.) SAC, pp. 675–680. ACM (2009). http://dblp.uni-trier.de/db/ conf/sac/sac2009.html#PrazeresTMP09
18. Qiu, X.: Building desktop applications with web services in a message-based MVC paradigm. In: ICWS, p. 765. IEEE Computer Society (2004). http://dblp.uni-trier. de/db/conf/icws/icws2004.html#Qiu04

19. Reale, A.: Quality of service in distributed stream processing for large scale smart pervasive environments. Ph.D. thesis, University of Bologna, Italy (2014). Basesearch.net (ftunivbologntesi:oai:amsdottorato.cib.unibo.it:6390)
20. Santa Ragione S.r.l.: Escape from the aliens in outer space. http://www.eftaios.com/
21. Google Chrome Team: The evolution of the web. http://www.evolutionoftheweb.com/
22. Zalewski, A.: Beyond ATAM: architecture analysis in the development of large scale software systems. In: Oquendo, F. (ed.) ECSA 2007. LNCS, vol. 4758, pp. 92–105. Springer, Heidelberg (2007). https://doi.org/10.1007/978-3-540-75132-8_8. http://dblp.uni-trier.de/db/conf/ecsa/ecsa2007.html#Zalewski07

Re-architecting OO Software into Microservices
A Quality-Centred Approach

Anfel Selmadji[(✉)], Abdelhak-Djamel Seriai, Hinde Lilia Bouziane,
Christophe Dony, and Rahina Oumarou Mahamane

LIRMM, CNRS and University of Montpellier, Montpellier, France
{selmadji,seriai,bouziane,dony}@lirmm.fr,
rahina.oumarou-mahamane@etu.umontpellier.fr

Abstract. Due to its tremendous advantages, microservice architectural style has become an essential element for the development of applications deployed on the cloud and for those adopting the DevOps practices. Migrating existing applications to microservices allow them to benefit from these advantages. Thus, in this paper, we propose an approach to automatically identify microservices from OO source code. The approach is based on a quality function that measures both the structural and behavioral validity of microservices and their data autonomy. Unlike existing works, ours is based on a well-defined function measuring the quality of microservices and use the source code as the main source of information.

Keywords: Object-Oriented · Microservices
Migration · Identification

1 Introduction

Recently, microservice architectural style has become an essential element for the development of applications deployed on the cloud or for those adopting the DevOps practices [5,10]. In this style, an application consists of a set of small services which are independently deployable. Usually, each microservice can only manage its own data [10,12]. These services communicate through lightweight mechanisms and they are deployed using containers such as Docker [12–14].

For the cloud, microservices facilitate the reconfiguration of an application according to the changes that may occur at runtime [3]. These changes can be related to cloud resources (e.g. resource allocation, etc.), quality of service (e.g. scalability guarantees, etc.) or any other event (e.g. failure, etc.). For DevOps, microservices facilitate a continuous integration, delivery and deployment tasks [5].

Besides the adoption of microservice architectural style for the development of new applications, the migration of existing monolithic ones to this style allows

© IFIP International Federation for Information Processing 2018
Published by Springer Nature Switzerland AG 2018. All Rights Reserved
K. Kritikos et al. (Eds.): ESOCC 2018, LNCS 11116, pp. 65–73, 2018.
https://doi.org/10.1007/978-3-319-99819-0_5

them to benefit from all the above-mentioned advantages. The migration process consists of three steps: (1) comprehension of the existing system (i.e. reverse engineering), (2) identification of microservices and (3) packaging them.

Different works have proposed strategies to achieve this migration [4,8,9,11]. Some of these approaches propose limited and ad-hoc heuristics for identifying microservices. Indeed, they do not consider the data autonomy of microservices [4,8] or they focus on measuring internal coupling and cohesion of microservices and not their external coupling [4,11]. Finally, some others require, in addition to the source code, the use of other artifacts [8,11] that can be unavailable.

In this paper, we tackle these limitations by proposing an automatic approach to identify microservices from OO source code. Unlike existing approaches, ours considers the specificity of microservices. It is based on a quality function that measures the functional validity of a microservice and its data autonomy.

The remainder of this paper is organized as follows. Section 2 outlines related works. Section 3 presents the proposed approach for identifying microservices. Section 4 evaluates our proposal. Finally, Sect. 5 concludes the paper.

2   Related Works

An attempt at providing a structured approach to identify microservices from monolith is Service Cutter [8]. Service Cutter uses artifacts and documents related to the software engineering process to build a graph representation which is decomposed through graph cutting. The limitation of Service Cutter is that the used artifacts and documents can be unavailable or not up to date.

Levcovitz et al. [9] proposed an approach to identify microservices from monolithic enterprise applications. The approach consists of grouping each user interface with the business functionality it calls and the database tables used by this functionality in a microservice. Therefore, the main limitation of this approach is that it is based on a restrictive hypothesis about the architecture of the monolith to be decomposed (i.e. MVC architecture).

Mazlami et al. [11] proposed a formal model to extract microservices from monoliths. More precisely, the authors used three formal coupling strategies and embed those in a graph-based clustering algorithm. In this approach, some coupling strategies depend on the change history of the code. Thus, if it is unavailable or consists of a limited number of commits, the approach is unusable.

Baresi et al. [4] proposed an approach to identify microservices from an OpenAPI specification. The identification process consists of matching the terms in the specifications against a reference vocabulary to suggest possible decompositions. The limitation of this approach is relying on well-defined interfaces that provide meaningful names. Moreover, database partitioning was not handled.

In conclusion, the existing works suffer from considerable limitations in terms of the restrictions associated with the used artifacts, the exploited information, and the partitioning measures on which they are based.

3   Microservices Identification from OO Source Code

Our microservices identification approach is based on four principles: (1) It considers OO software, (2) It exploits, mainly, the source code to identify microservices, (3) It defines a function that measures the quality of a microservice. (4) It exploits the information concerning the relations between the entities of the code and the information related to the persistent data manipulated in this code.

3.1   From Microservices Characteristics Description to Characteristics Evaluation

Characteristics of Microservices: Lewis and Fowler [10] define microservices as *small* services, communicating with lightweight mechanisms. These services are *independently deployable* by *fully automated deployment* machinery. They may be written in *different programming languages* and use *different data storage technologies*. Newman [12] considers microservices as *small, autonomous* services that work together. Pujals [13] defines microservices as autonomous lightweight processes, created and deployed with relatively small effort and ceremony.

Based on these definitions and others [14], we identified microservice's main characteristics: *(1) Small and focused on one function:* a microservice is typically responsible for a simple business functionality. *(2) Autonomous:* microservices are separate entities. They communicate via network calls and each one manages its own database. *(3) Technology neutral:* with a system composed of a set of microservices, each one can use different technologies. *(4) Automatically deployed:* if the number of microservices increases, automatic deployment is required.

The above characteristics can be classified into two categories: (1) those related to the structure and behavior of microservices and (2) others related to the microservice development platform. Therefore, to measure the quality of candidate microservices, only the characteristics that define microservice structure and behavior are selected: *small and focused on one function* and *autonomous*.

Evaluation of the "Focused on One Function" Characteristic: In our approach, a microservice M is viewed as a set of classes collaborating to provide one function. This collaboration can be determined from source code through the internal coupling, that represents the degree of direct and indirect dependencies between classes. Moreover, it can be determined by the number of volatile data[1] whose use is shared by these classes. It reflects the internal cohesion. Thus, *FOne* (*Eq.* 1) evaluates the characteristic *Focused on One Function*.

$$FOne(M) = \frac{1}{2} \ \ (InternalCoupling(M) + InternalCohesion(M)) \quad (1)$$

---

[1] Attributes are an example of volatile data.

Evaluation of the Structural and Behavioral Autonomy of a Microservice: Microservices are separate entities. Thus, in order that a set of classes represents a microservices their dependencies on external classes should be minimal. This can be measured using external coupling (see *Eq. 2*).

$$FAutonomy(M) = ExternalCoupling(M) \tag{2}$$

Evaluation of the Data Autonomy of a Microservice: A microservice can be completely data autonomous if it does not require any data from other microservices. In order that a microservice require less external data, its classes need to manipulate the same data. Thus, FData (*Eq. 3*) is based on measuring data dependencies between the classes of the microservice ($FIntra$), and their data dependencies with classes not belonging to the microservice ($FInter$).

$$FData(M) = \frac{1}{2} \ (FIntra(M) - FInter(M)) \tag{3}$$

The $FIntra$ (resp. $FInter$) function applied on a microservice M represents the ratio between the number of data shared between its classes (resp. with other classes) and the total number of data manipulated in the microservice.

Global Evaluation of a Microservice: The global evaluation (*Eq. 4*) of a microservices depends on the evaluation of its characteristics.

$$FMicro(M) = \frac{1}{n} \ (\alpha FOne(M) - \beta FAutonomy(M) + \gamma FData(M)) \tag{4}$$

Where M is a microservice, α, β and γ are coefficient weights determined by software architect and $n = \alpha + \beta + \gamma$. By default, the value of each term is 1.

3.2   Evaluation of Microservice Characteristics Based on Metrics

Internal Coupling: Internal coupling evaluates the degree of direct and indirect dependencies between classes. The more two classes use each other's methods the more they are coupled. Hence, the internal coupling is measured as follows:

$$InternalCoupling(M) = \frac{\sum CouplingPair(P)}{NbPossiblePairs} \tag{5}$$

Where $P = (Cl1, Cl2)$ is a pair of classes of the microservice M, *NbPossiblePairs* is the number of possible pairs of classes in M, whereas *CouplingPair* is:

$$CouplingPair(Cl1, Cl2) = \frac{NbCalls(Cl1, Cl2) + NbCalls(Cl2, Cl1)}{TotalNbCalls} \tag{6}$$

Where *NbCalls(Cl1, Cl2)* is the number of calls of the methods of *Cl1* by those of *Cl2* and *TotalNbCalls* is the number of method calls in the application.

Indeed, measuring internal coupling using $Eq. 5$ takes into account the frequency of calls. However, it does not promote clusters in which all the classes are coupled. For this reason, we introduced the sum of the standard deviations between the coupling values in the evaluation of the internal coupling ($Eq. 7$).

$$InternalCoupling(M) = \frac{\sum CouplingPair(P) - SumStandardDev}{NbPossiblePairs} \quad (7)$$

External Coupling: External coupling evaluates the degree of direct and indirect dependencies of the classes belonging to a candidate microservices on external classes. It is measured similarly to internal coupling, with only one difference which is the set of used pairs. To measure external coupling, each pair consists of two classes such that exactly one of them belong to the microservice.

Internal Cohesion: Internal cohesion evaluates the strength of interactions between classes. Usually, two classes are more interactive if their methods work on the same attributes. Thus, internal cohesion is measured as follows:

$$InternalCohesion(M) = \frac{NbDirectConnect}{NbPossibleConnect} \quad (8)$$

Where $NbPossibleConnect$ is the possible number of connections between the methods of the classes belonging to the microservice M, whereas $NbDirectConnect$ is the number of connections between these methods. Two methods $m1$ and $m2$ are directly connected if they both access the same attribute or the call trees starting at $m1$ and $m2$ access the same attributes. Because our aim is to measure the cohesion between the classes of the microservices, the connections between the methods of the same class are not considered. Note that, this internal cohesion measurement metric is a variation of the metric TCC (Tight Class Cohesion) proposed by Bieman and Kang [7].

3.3 Clustering Process

To identify microservices from OO code, classes are grouped based on their dependencies. Hence, a hierarchical agglomerative clustering algorithm [1] is used. We consider our function to measure the quality of a microservice as the similarity function used in the algorithm. Thus, the classes that maximize the value of the quality function are grouped together. More details can be found in [1].

4 Experimentation and Validation

4.1 Research Questions and Data Collection

To validate our approach we conducted an experiment to answer the following research questions: **RQ1:** does the proposed approach produce an adequate decomposition of an OO application into microservices? **RQ2:** is the definition of the quality function, without considering data autonomy, adequate? **RQ3:** does the evaluation of data autonomy enhance the quality of microservices?

To answer these questions, we have experimented on three OO applications of different sizes: small (*FindSportMates*[2]), average (*SpringBlog*[3]) and relatively large (*InventoryManagementSystem*[4]). Table 1 provides some metrics on them.

Table 1. Applications metrics

Application	No of classes	No of classes representing database tables	Code size (LOC)
InventoryManagementSystem	104	19	13447
FindSportMates	17	5	785
SpringBlog	42	5	1615

4.2 Experimental Protocol

The answers to the research questions are based on a tool developed in Java. To answer **RQ1**, we used our tool to identify microservices. Then, we compared them to those identified manually. The protocol for answering **RQ2** is similar to the one used for **RQ1** with one difference: we set our tool to identify microservices based on a function related to the characteristics *"focused on one function"* and *"structural and behavioral autonomy"*. To answer **RQ3**, we compare the precision and recall values related to the answers of **RQ1** and **RQ2**.

4.3 Direct Results

The source code of each of the previous applications was partitioned into a set of clusters. Table 2 shows the results obtained based on the entire quality function (*FMicro*) and on a quality function without the data autonomy part (*FSem*).

Table 2. Microservice extraction results

Application	No of microservices		Average no of classes per microservice	
	FMicro	*FSem*	*FMicro*	*FSem*
InventoryManagementSystem	10	9	8.5	9.44
FindSportMates	2	2	6	6
SpringBlog	4	4	9.25	9.25

[2] github.com/chihweil5/FindSportMates.
[3] github.com/Raysmond/SpringBlog.
[4] github.com/gtiwari333/java-inventory-management-system-swing-hibernate-nepal.

To evaluate the microservices obtained by our approach, we compare them with those identified manually. Thus, we classify the microservices obtained manually in three categories: (1) Those that exactly match the ones identified by our approach. The microservices identified by our approach and are classified in this category are considered excellent. (2) Those that can be obtained by a simple composition/decomposition of the microservices identified by our approach. The microservices identified by our approach of this category are considered good. (3) Those that are neither in the first nor in the second categories. The microservices identified by our approach that are classified in this category are considered bad.

The classification results are described in Table 3 and expressed in term of precision and recall in Table 4. Precision (resp. recall) assesses the ratio between the number of good and excellent microservices to the total number of the classified ones (resp. the number of the manually identified ones).

4.4   Answers to Research Questions

The precision values obtained based on *FMicro* are greater than 83%. This shows that a large part of the manually identified microservices are identified by our approach. The recall values obtained based on *FMicro* are also greater than 75%. This means that a large part of the microservices identified by our approach are those identified manually. Thus, we answer **RQ1** as follows: our approach allows obtaining an adequate decomposition of an OO application into microservices.

In addition, similarly to *FMicro*, the precision values obtained based on the partial quality function *FSem*, are between 80% and 100%.

The interpretation of the recall values for *FSem* is the same as *FMicro* while considering that the recall values are either equal to or lower than those obtained

Table 3. Microservice classification results

Application	No of excellent microservices		No of good microservices		No of bad microservices	
	FMicro	*FSem*	*FMicro*	*FSem*	*FMicro*	*FSem*
InventoryManagementSystem	1	1	17	15	3	5
FindSportMates	0	0	3	3	1	1
SpringBlog	3	2	7	8	3	3

Table 4. Precision and recall measurement

Application	Precision		Recall	
	FMicro	*FSem*	*FMicro*	*FSem*
InventoryManagementSystem	90%	80%	85,71%	76,19%
FindSportMates	100%	100%	75%	75%
SpringBlog	83,33%	83,33%	76,92%	76,92%

by relying on *FMicro*. Based on these values, the answer to **RQ2** is the definition of the quality function, without considering data autonomy, is adequate.

The precision and recall values obtained based on *FSem* are equal to or less than those obtained based on *FMicro*. The values that are equal are related to applications that do not manipulate many persistent data. Thus, the answer to **RQ3** is the evaluation of data autonomy enhance the quality of microservices.

4.5   Threats to Validity

Threats to Internal Validity: Our approach may be affected by two internal threats. Firstly, each class belongs to only one microservice. However, in some applications, some classes may participate in several functionalities. Nevertheless, this generally concerns only certain classes that the architect can duplicate. Secondly, we rely on a hierarchical clustering algorithm. This algorithm allows obtaining values of the quality function close to optimal ones.

Threats to External Validity: There are two external threats. Firstly, the quality of the OO source code can impact the identification. Secondly, the matching between the microservices obtained by our approach and those obtained manually can vary according to the granularity of the manually identified ones.

5   Conclusion

We presented, in this paper, an approach for the identification of microservices by an analysis of OO source code. This approach is based on both the evaluation of microservice quality, using a quality function, and an algorithm for grouping classes according to the value of this quality. The conducted experimentation shows the relevance of the obtained microservices using our approach compared to those identified manually. However, the results need to be consolidated by experimentations on very large applications. Moreover, inspired by existing works [2,6], we will propose an approach to package the identified microservices and deploy them on the cloud while taking into account the dynamic reconfiguration.

References

1. Adjoyan, S., Seriai, A.D., Shatnawi, A.: Service identification based on quality metrics object-oriented legacy system migration towards SOA. In: SEKE (2014)
2. Alshara, Z., Seriai, A.D., Tibermacine, C., Bouziane, H.L., Dony, C., Shatnawi, A.: Migrating large object-oriented applications into component-based ones: instantiation and inheritance transformation. ACM SIGPLAN Not. **51**, 55–64. ACM (2015)
3. Balalaie, A., Heydarnoori, A., Jamshidi, P.: Migrating to cloud-native architectures using microservices: an experience report. In: Celesti, A., Leitner, P. (eds.) ESOCC Workshops 2015. CCIS, vol. 567, pp. 201–215. Springer, Cham (2016). https://doi.org/10.1007/978-3-319-33313-7_15

4. Baresi, L., Garriga, M., De Renzis, A.: Microservices identification through interface analysis. In: De Paoli, F., Schulte, S., Broch Johnsen, E. (eds.) ESOCC 2017. LNCS, vol. 10465, pp. 19–33. Springer, Cham (2017). https://doi.org/10.1007/978-3-319-67262-5_2
5. Bass, L., Weber, I., Zhu, L.: DevOps: A Software Architect's Perspective. Addison-Wesley Professional, Reading (2015)
6. Bastide, G., Seriai, A., Oussalah, M.: Adapting software components by structure fragmentation. In: Proceedings of the 2006 ACM Symposium on Applied Computing, pp. 1751–1758. ACM (2006)
7. Bieman, J.M., Kang, B.K.: Cohesion and reuse in an object-oriented system. ACM SIGSOFT Softw. Eng. Notes **20**, 259–262 (1995)
8. Gysel, M., Kölbener, L., Giersche, W., Zimmermann, O.: Service cutter: a systematic approach to service decomposition. In: Aiello, M., Johnsen, E.B., Dustdar, S., Georgievski, I. (eds.) ESOCC 2016. LNCS, vol. 9846, pp. 185–200. Springer, Cham (2016). https://doi.org/10.1007/978-3-319-44482-6_12
9. Levcovitz, A., Terra, R., Valente, M.T.: Towards a technique for extracting microservices from monolithic enterprise systems. arXiv preprint (2016)
10. Lewis, J., Fowler, M.: Microservices: a definition of this new architectural term. MartinFowler.com **25** (2014)
11. Mazlami, G., Cito, J., Leitner, P.: Extraction of microservices from monolithic software architectures. In: 2017 IEEE International Conference on Web Services (ICWS), pp. 524–531. IEEE (2017)
12. Newman, S.: Building Microservices: Designing Fine-grained Systems. O'Reilly Media, Inc., Sebastopol (2015)
13. Sharma, S.: Mastering Microservices with Java. Migrating to Cloud-Native Architectures Using Microservices: An Experience ReportPackt Publishing Ltd. (2016)
14. Sharma, S., Gonzalez, D.: Microservices: Building scalable software (2017)

An Encoder-Decoder Architecture for the Prediction of Web Service QoS

Mohammed Ismail Smahi[1(✉)], Fethellah Hadjila[1(✉)], Chouki Tibermacine[2(✉)], Mohammed Merzoug[1(✉)], and Abdelkrim Benamar[1(✉)]

[1] LRIT, University of Tlemcen, Tlemcen, Algeria
{i_smahi,f_hadjila,mohamed.merzoug,a_benamar}@mail.univ-tlemcen.dz
[2] LIRMM, CNRS and University of Montpellier, Montpellier, France
Chouki.Tibermacine@lirmm.fr

Abstract. Quality of Service (QoS) prediction is an important task in Web service selection and recommendation. Existing approaches to QoS prediction are based on either Content Filtering or Collaborative Filtering. In the two cases, these approaches use external data or past interactions between users and services to predict missing or future QoS scores. One of the most effective techniques for QoS prediction is Matrix Factorization (MF), with Latent Factor Models. The key idea of MF consists in learning a compact model for both users and services. Thereafter QoS prediction is simply computed as a dot product between the user's latent model and the service's latent model. Despite the successful results of MF in the recommendation area, there are still a set of problems that should be handled, like: (i) the sparsity of the input models, and (ii) the learning of the latent factors which is prone to over-fitting. In this paper, we propose an approach to solve these two problems by using a simple neural network, an auto-encoder, and by exploiting cross-validation on a well-known dataset, in order to select the ideal number of latent factors, and thereby reduce the over-fitting phenomenon.

1 Introduction

Web service recommendation and selection have attracted much attention in the service computing community these last years [1–5]. With the rapid increase of the number of services over the Internet and Cloud computing platforms, the task of recommendation became more important. One of the most important criteria taken into consideration in recommending services is their Quality of Service. Recommendation systems are based, among other artifacts, on large collections of QoS scores related to different service users and invocations over different time periods. However, these collections contain sometimes missing QoS scores. In addition, QoS scores vary substantially in time. These two facts induce an additional complexity in building recommendation systems [6,7].

To deal with the aforementioned complexity, recommendation systems leverage either Content Filtering or Collaborative Filtering (denoted CF) techniques

© IFIP International Federation for Information Processing 2018
Published by Springer Nature Switzerland AG 2018. All Rights Reserved
K. Kritikos et al. (Eds.): ESOCC 2018, LNCS 11116, pp. 74–89, 2018.
https://doi.org/10.1007/978-3-319-99819-0_6

to predict the QoS score of a given service [8]. The first technique (*i.e.* content filtering) requires external data to build the profile of users or items (the services), which is not always available. However the second one is mainly based on the past interactions between the users and the items. Through these interactions and transactions, recommendation systems can infer the missing values. Roughly speaking, there are two types of CF techniques: Nearest Neighbors approaches and Matrix Factorization approaches (also known as Latent Factor Models). The key idea of matrix factorization consists in learning a compact model for both users and services, thereafter the QoS prediction is simply computed as a dot product between the user's latent model and the service's latent model. According to [7,8] Matrix Factorization techniques are more effective (in terms of accuracy) than the Nearest Neighbors schemes. Despite the successful results of MF in the recommendation area, there are still a set of problems that should be handled, as mentioned in [7,9]; there are two major issues: (i) the sparsity of the service invocation matrix, which is the input of the recommendation system, can largely affect the predicted QoS; (ii) the learning of the latent factors is prone to over-fitting; as a result the consistency of the latent factors can be compromised. To deal with this situation, MF techniques should adopt additional mechanisms to reduce this side effect.

In this paper, we enhance MF techniques to alleviate the aforementioned issues. The main contributions of our paper are summarized as follows:

- We leveraged auto-encoders [10,11] to build the latent models of both users and services. This choice is mainly motivated by the consistent mathematical foundation of this neural network (in fact, the auto-encoder can learn the optimal decomposition of any real service invocation matrix). In addition, we divide the input data set into a set of clusters in order to reduce the data sparsity.
- To reduce the over-fitting phenomenon, we selected the ideal number of latent factors (the size of the hidden layer) according to the cross-validation principle;
- To evaluate the proposed approach, we conducted a set of experiments on a real-world Web service QoS performance (WS-DREAM) [12]. These experiments are related to different sizes of the dataset and different levels of sparsity.

The remaining of the paper is organized as follows. Section 2 introduces some background material on autoencoders. Section 3 details the proposed approach for Web service QoS prediction. Section 4 exposes the conducted experiments and discusses the obtained results. Before concluding and presenting some perspectives at the end of the paper, we present in Sect. 5 the related works.

2   Background on Autoencoders

Auto-encoder [10,11] is an unsupervised neural network that aims to learn a representation of the inputs that produces the least deformation. In general, this representation (or code) must be compact and meaningful. In terms of architecture, the auto-encoder is designed as a feed-forward non recurrent neural network (see Fig. 1), where the size of the input layer is equal to the size of the output layer (which is denoted as n). Additionally, the auto-encoder can have one or more hidden layers, among which the central hidden layer, representing the code of the inputs (its size is denoted as $code\_size$).

In terms of dynamics, the auto-encoder can be viewed as a composition of two functions: the encoding function F_1 (which produces the code) and the decoding function F_2 (which produces the reconstruction), where $F_1 : D_1^n \rightarrow D_2^{code\_size}$ and $F2 : D_2^{code\_size} \rightarrow D_1^n$.

The class of functions having D_1^n as domain and $D_2^{code\_size}$ as range is termed A. The class of functions having $D_2^{code\_size}$ as domain and D_1^n as range is termed B. Thus, the output will be : $x' = F_2(F_1(x))$, and the code is $z = F_1(x)$.

If the auto-encoder contains only one hidden layer, then the encoding/decoding functions will be defined as: $z = f(Wx + b)$ and $x' = f'(W'z + b')$, such that: f and f' are transfer functions which can be linear or non-linear (sigmoid, for instance). W and W' are two matrices having the dimensions $(code\_size, n)$ and $(n, code\_size)$ respectively. b and b' represent the bias vectors of dimension $code\_size$ and n respectively.

The auto-encoder is called linear if the transfer functions are linear, otherwise it is non-linear.

In terms of learning, the auto-encoder has to produce the closest reconstructions with respect to the inputs. To do so, it minimizes a dissimilarity function (referred to as $error$). The latter dissimilarity may leverage either the L_p norm, the *Hamming* distance, or another elementary function. Formally, the aim is to find $F_1 \in A$, $F_2 \in B$ such that:

$$error(F_1, F_2) = \sum_{t=1}^{m} \Delta(F_2(F_1(x_t)), x_t) \tag{1}$$

where: Δ : is the L_p norm, the Hamming distance or another dissimilarity function. X_t: is an example that belongs to the learning data set. m: is the size of the data set.

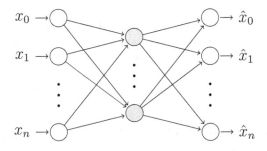

Fig. 1. Auto-encoder architecture (with one hidden layer)

It can be proven that, in case where the decoder is linear and the loss function uses the sum of the squared Euclidean distances, then the linear auto-encoder has the same performance as the non-linear auto-encoder [13] (which means that they reach the same optimum).

If we assume that the auto-encoder is linear and contains a unique hidden layer, and the delta function is the squared Euclidean distance, then the optimal encoding matrix W and the optimal decoding matrix W' will be given as follows:

$$W = \Sigma_{\leq p, \leq p}^{-1}.(U_{.,\leq p})^t \ and \ W' = (U_{.,\leq p}).\Sigma \leq p, \leq p \qquad (2)$$

where U and Σ are derived from the singular value decomposition [14] of the input matrix X (*i.e.* $X = U\Sigma V^t$). Equation 2 means that we keep the p largest singular values, where X is a real matrix of size (m, n), U is an orthonormal matrix of size (m, m), V is an orthonormal matrix of size (n, n).

3   Proposed Approach

Figure 2 depicts the global architecture of the proposed approach. First, we assume that the QoS data is collected from various sources such as social networks, third party monitoring systems, or direct feed-backs. The collected QoS data set is viewed as a matrix that contains n services on columns and m users on lines, each cell is modeled as a vector of r realizations of the corresponding QoS criterion with respect to a given user and service. We assume that these QoS realizations contain missing values which need to be predicted. To do so, the QoS data set will undergo a set of steps which are described as follows:

– Firstly (Step 1) we cluster the lines of the initial matrix according to the service location, more specifically we will perform a clustering based on the service country property and another clustering based on the service provider property. According to the works in [7,15] the services on the same country are likely to have the same infrastructure and thus similar QoS. Each cluster contains a set of lines that have the same service provider or the same country.

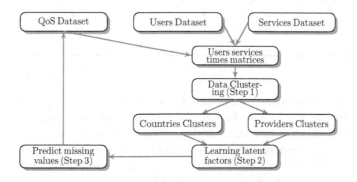

Fig. 2. Overview of the prediction system architecture

We noticed that the sparsity of the entire WS-DREAM data set [12] is 26%. However the sparsity of USA's cluster is 24%. In addition the sparsity of other clusters is less than 20% (like Australia, Argentina and others). The aim of this step is to reduce the sparsity of the input matrix. The more the matrix is dense the better the results are. In summary this step will produce a set of clusters that have the same property (either the provider ID or the country ID). Each cluster is represented with a reduced matrix that has less columns and lines with respect to the initial dataset.

- Secondly (Step 2) we perform the learning of latent factors of each reduced matrix (or cluster) by leveraging an auto-encoder. During the auto-encoder training, we also perform a cross validation in order to infer the best size of the hidden layer (the number of latent factors), we assume that all the clusters are trained with the same number of latent factors. This step will provide the hidden layer size that ensures the best validation error (the lowest error).
- At last (Step 3), the learned auto-encoder produces the missing QoS values and stores them in the initial data set.

Algorithm 1. Data clustering according to countries and providers

---

Input   : $\mathcal{P}, \mathcal{C}$ (Providers and Countries from dataset)
Output: $Cluster\_Set\_P$,▷ Countries clusters $Cluster\_Set\_C$ ▷ Providers clusters

1 **foreach** $id \in Providers(\mathcal{P})$ **do**
2 $\quad|\quad Cluster\_P_{id} = \emptyset$
3 **end**
4 **foreach** $id \in Countries(\mathcal{C})$ **do**
5 $\quad|\quad Cluster\_C_{id} = \emptyset$
6 **end**
7 $Cluster\_Set\_P =< Cluster\_P_1, Cluster\_P_2, \dots, Cluster\_P_{|P|} >$
8 $Cluster\_Set\_C =< Cluster\_C_1, Cluster\_C_2, \dots, Cluster\_C_{|C|} >$
9 **foreach** $service_i \in \mathcal{D}ataset$ **do**
10 $\quad provider\_id = get\_provider(service_i)$
11 $\quad country\_id = get\_country(service_i)$
12 $\quad Cluster\_P_{p\_id} = Cluster\_P_{p\_id} \cup \{service_i\}$
13 $\quad Cluster\_C_{c\_id} = Cluster\_C_{c\_id} \cup \{service_i\}$
14 $\quad update(Cluster\_Set\_P, Cluster\_P_{p\_id})$
15 $\quad update(Cluster\_Set\_C, Cluster\_C_{c\_id})$
16 **end**

Algorithm 1 allows the clustering of the services according to the country ID or the provider ID. In line 7 we initialize the set of clusters according to the provider criterion, the same thing is done for the country criterion in line 8. In line 9 up to 16, we update each cluster with its corresponding service.

Algorithm 2 learns the latent variables as well as their optimal size (denoted $code\_size^\star$). In line 4, we explore six possibilities for the code size (20, 40, 60, 80, 100 and 120), the first possibility is initialized in line 1. Thereafter, we extract the current cluster $Cluster_i$ (line 7) and we learn the optimal encoding/decoding matrices (in the next line). This learning function is explained later (Algorithm 3). Afterward, we average the previous validation error over the $clusters\_number$ available clusters (line 11). In line 12 up to 16, we update the minimal validation error as well as the optimal encoding/decoding matrices (W_{11}^* up to W_{p2}^*), additionally the optimal code size is also updated. In line 17, we increment the code size and we repeat the same process for the other values.

Algorithm 2. Learning latent factors

    Input : $Cluster\_Set\_j$ $\triangleright j \in \{P, C\}$
    Output: $Best\ Configuration$: $error_{min}$, $code\_size^*$, $best\_weights$

1   $code\_size = 20$
2   $cs\_max = 6$
3   $error_{min} = \infty$
4   **for** $code\_size\_value : 1 \rightarrow cs\_max$ **do**
5       $error = 0$
6   **for** $i : 1 \rightarrow |Cluster\_Set\_j|$ **do**
7           $Cluster_i = getCluster(i, Cluster\_Set\_j)$
8           $<< W_{i1}^*, W_{i2}^* >, er_i >= AeCV(Cluster_i, code\_size)$
9           $error = error + er_i$
10   **end**
11      $error = error / |Cluster\_Set\_j|$
12   **if** $error < error_{min}$ **then**
13          $error_{min} = error$
14          $best\_weights = << W_{11}^*, W_{12}^* >, < W_{21}^*, W_{22}^* >, \ldots < W_{p1}^*, W_{p2}^* >>$
15          $code\_size^* = code\_size$
16   **end**
17      $code\_size = code\_size + 20$
18 **end**

Algorithm 3, Autoencoder Cross Validation (AeCV), infers the best encoding/decoding matrices $W_{i\,1}^*/W_{i\,2}^*$ for a given $Cluster_i$ and predefined $code\_size$.

The learned auto-encoder (AE) leverages a linear transfer function in the output layer and a sigmoid transfer function in the hidden layer. In line 7, we divide the current $Cluster_i$ into eight parts. After that we perform eight learnings by training each part as a validation set (line 10) and the remaining parts as a training set (line 9). In line 10, we learn the optimal encoding/decoding matrices $W_{k\,i\,1}^*$ and $W_{k\,i\,2}^*$ (they represent the best encoding/decoding matrices related to $cluster_i$ and $folder_k$), which are related to the kth part of the $Cluster_i$. The cost function represents the squared error between the auto-encoder output and the desired value. In line 12, we compute the auto-encoder error performed on the validation set. In line 13 and 19 we sum the validation errors related to all folders and we take the mean. The statements 14 up to 17 retain the minimal validation error (*i.e.* v_error_{min}) and its corresponding encoding/decoding matrices (*i.e.*

Algorithm 3. Autoencoder cross validation (AeCV)

    Inputs : $Cluster_i, code\_size$
    Outputs: $< W^\star_{i\,1}, W^\star_{i\,2} >, mve$

1 $v\_error_{min} = \infty$ ▷ the best validation error

2 $err_k = \infty$

3 $k\_fold = 8$

4 $mve = 0$

5 $T = Cluster_i$ ▷ training set

6 $V = \emptyset$ ▷ validation set

7 $< folder_1, ..., folder_{k\_fold} >= division(Cluster_i)$

8 **for** $k : 1 \rightarrow k\_fold$ **do**

9      $T = T - folder_k$

10     $V = folder_k$

11     $< W^\star_{k\,i\,1}, W^\star_{k\,i\,2} >= \underset{\substack{\text{all possible matrices} \\ W_{k\,i\,1}, W_{k\,i\,2}}}{\operatorname{argmin}} \sqrt{\frac{1}{|T|} \sum_{m=1}^{|T|} (AE_{W_{k\,i\,1}, W_{k\,i\,1}}(S_m) - S_m)^2}$

      ▷ $S_m \in T$

12     $err_k = \frac{1}{|V|} \sum_{m=1}^{|V|} (AE_{W^\star_{k\,i\,1}, W^\star_{k\,i\,1}}(S_m) - S_m)^2$

13     $mve = mve + err_k$

14   **if** $(err_k < v\_error_{min})$ **then**

15        $v\_error_{min} = err_k$

16        $best\_weight = < W^\star_{k\,i\,1}, W^\star_{k\,i\,2} >$

17   **end**

18 **end**

19 $mve = mve/k\_fold$

$W^\star_{k\,i\,1}, W^\star_{k\,i\,2}$) also termed *best_weights*. Finally, we return the best weight as well as the mean validation error (mve).

4   Experimental Evaluation

We conducted an experimental evaluation of the performance of the proposed approach. In this section, we will show both the prediction accuracy and the impact of the technical parameters on the prediction quality.

4.1   Experimental Setup

To evaluate the proposed approach, we conducted experiments on a real-world Web service QoS performance repository[1] [12]. This data set contains series of QoS data (for both response time and throughput) which are collected from 142 users (distributed over 57 countries). These users invoke 4500 web services that are located all over the world. Each sequence of QoS data contains at most

---

[1] WS-DREAM: http://www.wsdream.net.

64 values which are measured once after a time interval in a time slot. The time slot takes 15 minutes and the duration of the time interval between two consecutive time slots is 15 min. In summary we have $142 \times 4500 \times 64$ QoS records for each criterion (response time or throughput). These QoS records contain missing or invalid information that are about 26%. Table 1 summarizes the properties of our dataset. All the learning algorithms are implemented in Tensorflow Python[2]. The experiments run on 3 different machines: i3-380M 3 GHz with 4 GB RAM, i5-4200U 1.6 GHz with 4 GB RAM and i7-3840QM 2.8 GHz with 16 GB RAM. In what follows, we present some important elements that are primordial to understand the rest of the section:

Table 1. Information of web service QoS values

Statistics	Response time	Throughput time
Scale	0–20 s	0–20 kbps
Mean all values	3.165 s	9.608 kbps
Num. of users	142	142
Num. of web services	4500	4500
Num. all values	30 287 611	30 287 611
Num. missing values	10 609 313	10 609 313

- To evaluate the approach performance, we employ two metrics: Mean Absolute Error (MAE) (formula 3) and Root Mean Square Error (RMSE) (formula 4). Since we used the cross-validation, we focus on the average of MAE (formula 5) and the average of RMSE (formula 6). The score of the last formula (6) is used as the output of Algorithm 3.

The standard MAE is specified as follows:

$$MAE_V = \frac{1}{|V|} \sum_{(u,s) \in V} \left| X_{u,s} - \hat{X}_{u,s} \right| \qquad (3)$$

where V represents the validation set. $X_{u,s}$ represents the real QoS score for service s given by user u, and $\hat{X}_{u,s}$ the predicted one.

The standard RMSE is specified as follows:

$$RMSE_V = \sqrt{\frac{1}{|V|} \sum_{(u,s) \in V} \left(X_{u,s} - \hat{X}_{u,s} \right)^2} \qquad (4)$$

The average MAE is specified as follows:

$$AverageMAE = \frac{1}{\left| \bigcup_{allV_h} V_h \right|} \sum_{allV_h} (MAE_{V_h} \cdot |V_h|) \qquad (5)$$

---

[2] Source code: https://github.com/imsld/Auto-encoder-QoS-Prediction.

Where V_h represents a validation set. The average RMSE (which is also denoted as mve in line 19 of Algorithm 3) is specified as follows:

$$AverageRMSE = \frac{1}{\left| \bigcup_{allV_h} \right|} \sum_{allV_h} (RMSE_{V_h} \cdot |V_h|) \tag{6}$$

- Before launching the clustering and the learning steps of the framework, we prepare our data set in order to improve its density. Initially the data set contains around 26% of invalid values. After the execution of the two following rules, the percentage of invalid values becomes 23%.
  - R1: For each $Qos_{i,u,s,t}$ of the data set, such as $i \in \{response\_time, throughput\}$, u is the *user ID*, s is the *service ID*, and t is the *time slot* of the QoS realization ($t \in \{1, \ldots, 64\}$). If $Qos_{i,u,s,t}$ is invalid (missing or zero) then we replace it by the average of the valid QoS values of the previous time slots: $Qos_{i,u,s,t} = \frac{1}{\left(\sum_{t \in T} valid(i,u,s,t)\right)} \left(\sum_{t \in T} Qos_{i,u,s,t} \cdot valid(i,u,s,t)\right)$
    where
    $$valid(i,u,s,t) = \begin{cases} 1 \ if \ Qos_{i,u,s,t} \ is \ available \\ 0 \ if \ Qos_{i,u,s,t} \ is \ missing \end{cases}$$
  - R2: For each $Qos_{i,u,s,t}$ of the data set, if $Qos_{i,u,s,t}$ is invalid and all its previous values (regarding time slots) are invalid, then $Qos_{i,u,s,t} = 0$.

  In what follows, we assume that this prepared data set is the official input of the proposed approach.
- We assume that the learning phase of each cluster lasts for 5000 iterations (at most). Additionally the learning will be stopped if the auto-encoder error is less than 0.01.
- We perform the clustering step by grouping the services having the same country ID (the clustering based on provider ID will be handled in future works), we obtain 70 clusters which can involved up to 1404 services per group. By doing so, we divide the initial matrix into several sub-matrices that have the same number of lines (142) and different columns. The number of columns corresponds to the size of the cluster. This step aims to reduce the number of invalid entries, and thus it improves the prediction accuracy.
- Concerning the cross validation, we divide each cluster of the data set into eight parts ($k\_fold = 8$). Each part consists of eight consecutive QoS data (*i.e.* Part $= \{Qos_{iust}, Qos_{ius(t+1)}, \ldots, Qos_{ius(t+7)}\}$. In addition, we examine 6 code size values: $code\_size \in \{20, 40, 60, 80, 100, 120\}$. This means that we perform eight trainings for each code size. Thereafter we retain the code size that provides the best validation error. We also notice that the density factor (Ds) of this scheme is $Ds = 80\%$ (density of 80% means that 80% of the entries data set are retained as training set, while the other 20% are used to test the performance of our model for each code size).

4.2   Research Questions

Our experiments aim to answer the following questions:

- Q1: Does the proposed approach provide a prediction accuracy better than well-known state of the art methods? The compared methods are the following:
  - User-based CF using PCC (UPCC) [16]: this model is a user-based prediction model.
  - Item-based CF using PCC (IPCC) [17]: this model uses similar services for the QoS prediction.
  - WSRec [18,19]: an approach which combines both UPCC and IPCC
  - AVG: this approach takes the mean of the three valid QoS data at the most recent time slots.
  - IPCC* [18]: a linear aggregation of IPCC and AVG (we take equitable weights for both sub models).
  - UPCC* [18]: a linear aggregation of UPCC and AVG (we take equitable weights for both sub models).
  - WSRec* [18]: a linear aggregation of WSRec and AVG (we take equitable weights for both sub models).
  - ARIMA [20]: this is a well-known statistical method adapted to QoS web service prediction.
  - Lasso-K20 [9]: this approach optimizes the recommendation problem by adapting the lasso penalty function.
- Q2: What is the impact of the code size on the prediction accuracy?
- Q3: What is the impact of the code size on the sensitivity to over-fitting?

4.3   Results and Discussion

Table 2 presents the MAE and the RMSE of different prediction algorithms for the response time. We assume that the density of the state of the art methods is $Ds = 80\%$.

From these results, we derive the following findings:

- According to the MAE metric, UPCC, IPCC, WSRec are less effective than the remaining approaches since they do not use the past QoS data.
- The Lasso-K20 out-performs ARIMA, AVG, UPCC*, IPCC*, and WSRec* in terms of MAE and RMSE. In addition it presents less variation of RMSE when we change the data set [9]. However ARIMA and AVG approaches show larger RMSE variations when we change the data set. We notice that, the more the variation of the model error is low the better the generalization.
- The models auto-encoder-100 and auto-encoder-120 present the highest scores for both MAE and RMSE. For instance, the auto-encoder-100 achieves about 57% improvements in MAE accuracy compared to ARIMA. Likewise it achieves about 51% improvements in MAE accuracy compared to the Lasso-K20 method.

Table 2. Accuracy comparison of prediction methods on Response Time

Approaches	MAE	RMSE
AVG	1.159	3.206
IPCC	1.467	3.032
IPCC*	1.242	2.753
UPCC	1.372	2.925
UPCC*	1.200	2.714
WSRec	1.372	2.925
WSRec*	1.200	2.716
ARIMA	1.028	2.986
Lasso-K20	0.893	2.572
Autoencoder-100	0.704	1.422
Autoencoder-120	0.681	1.369

To explain the impact of the code size (denoted as code_size in Algorithm 2) we show in Fig. 3 the variation of RMSE (the output of Algorithm 3) according to the code size and the cluster size. It can be clearly seen that the code sizes 100 and 120 out-perform the remaining values for all clusters. Furthermore, we observe that the performance of code size 100 is greater or equal than the performance of code size 120 for almost all clusters with less than 100 services. (These clusters represent the majority of services). Therefore, according to the Occam's razor principle [21], we should use a code size equal to 100 for test sets with less than 100 services. In addition, when the test set size is larger than 100 we should use 120 as code size. Broadly speaking, we can say that a model is prone to over-fitting if the prediction error highly changes when we change the data set (this model is qualified as a high variance model). Consequently, if we aim to confirm that our approach (*i.e.* the auto-encoder with 100 hidden neurons) is less sensitive to over-fitting, we should compute the prediction error (RMSE) on a new test set and derive the deviation between the validation error and the new test set error. The larger the deviation is, the higher the over-fitting

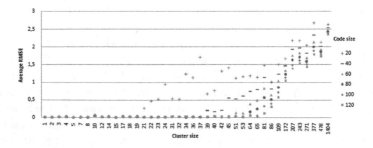

Fig. 3. The RMSE variation for response time metric

sensitivity we obtain. In Table 3 we show the mean validation error (also termed the average RMSE) as well as the RMSE related to the entire data set (*i.e.* 142 × 4500 × 64 entries) for some code sizes. It is clearly shown in this table that the code sizes 100 and 120 are the least sensitive to over-fitting, compared to the other possibilities. We also notice that the code sizes 20, 40 are less sensitive to over-fitting but they also suffer from under-fitting, since their corresponding auto-encoders have a large average RMSE.

Table 3. Over-fitting sensitivity

Code size	20	40	60	80	100	120
Average RMSE	1.939	1.684	1.564	1,487	1.422	1.369
RMSE Dataset	2.818	2.521	2.337	2.211	2.116	2.040
Deviation (absolute difference)	0.879	0.837	0.773	0.724	0.694	0.671

4.4   Threats to Validity

The way we measured RMSE may be a threat to *construct validity*. To some extent, the measurement is biased by the fact that the data set that we considered is the one that we have slightly modified (by changing some of the invalid values), instead of the original one from WS-DREAM. But since there is only 3% of values which have been changed, we are quite confident that the impact of this threat on the validity of the results is really marginal. We have started another measurement of this metric, but this takes several weeks of training and prediction. The preliminary results (on all clusters by using the auto-encoder with a code size of 20) showed that RMSE is higher, but with only 0.01 (1.79 instead of 1.78).

A potential threat to *internal validity* concerns the extent to which we may be confident with the conclusions, on sensitivity to over-fitting, which have been made from variance in prediction error when data sets are changed. We could have taken one code size and then measure the deviation on several test data sets. The comparison we have made is between the average RMSE and the RMSE of the whole data set. The evaluation on this *single* test data set may influence the results. But the fact that this was made on several code sizes (20, 40, 60, 80, 100 and 120) mitigates this risk.

A threat to the *external validity* may be the generalization of the presented results to other contexts, and more precisely to other data sets. The presence of such a large data set (WS-DREAM) enabled us to train correctly our predictor. The use of another data set may give lower accuracy. However, the use in our prediction of an auto-encoder together with a cross-validation to identify the best code size, helps in reducing the impact of using another data set on prediction error.

5   Related Works

In this section, we present some related works based on Collaborative Filtering algorithms that were proposed recently.

Many existing CF works are based on neighborhood methods. This kind of methods leverages the most similar neighbors of a service/a user to predict the missed QoS. However, this category mainly suffers from the data sparsity, small coverage and cold start problems [19,22].

The work presented in [9] assumes that QoS values depend on service invocation time. In order to make an accurate service recommendation, a time-aware prediction approach is brought forth. Specifically, the authors make a zero-mean Laplace prior distribution assumption on the residuals of the QoS prediction, which corresponds to a Lasso regression problem. To reduce the search range while improving the prediction accuracy; the approach uses the geo-localization of web services to handle the sparse representation of temporal QoS values.

The system proposed in [23] uses the linear regression to predict unknown QoS data from known QoS values. The work in [24] constructs a recommendation system by inferring the satisfaction probability of the user with respect to a given service. This inference is based on a Bayesian network.

To alleviate the limits of the neighborhood methods, the community has designed another type of approaches which is based on matrix factorization. In fact, this category reduces the sparsity of the invocation matrix by inferring a low dimension model for both services and users [6,25]. In [7] the authors propose three contributions for solving the recommendation problem. The first one combines the matrix factorization with the QoS data provided by the user's neighbors. This data is derived from the user's context (like, the latitude and the longitude of geographical position, and the IT infrastructure). The second one, combines the matrix factorization with the QoS data provided by the service's neighbors. This data is derived from the service context (such as the country, the autonomous system), we also notice that the matrix factorization is solved as an optimization problem with a regularization term. The third contribution combines both the matrix factorization, the user's context and the service context. The experimental results show that the third approach is more effective than the first two.

The work presented in [26], leverages both matrix factorization and service clustering, first of all, the authors build a set of service clusters through the use of context information (like the country and service provider) and the Pearson Correlation Similarity. This hybridization is mainly motivated by the fact that the services which belong to the same geographical region tend to have correlated ratings or QoS data. Therefore the authors add a neighborhood based term to the service latent model.

In [15], the authors develop an enhanced matrix factorization approach by identifying the users' or the web services' neighborhoods. The users' neighbors are selected by measuring the network map distance between them. It is empirically proven that the users with smaller distances are likely to have more similar QoS values on a common set of web services.

In the field of cloud services, the system presented in [3], considers all the software/hardware characteristics of the Cloud Computing architecture. The authors propose a cloud service QoS prediction approach based on Bayesian Networks. The entire process is divided into three steps: data collection and pretreatment, Bayesian model training and prediction of QoS values.

Compared to these works, our approach refines clustering approaches based on service neighborhood by considering a training step that uses a neural network. Thanks to cross-validation, this network, an auto-encoder, is customized with the code size (number of hidden layers) that minimizes the prediction error. The ultimate goal of our work is to solve problems that are complementary to those addressed by the previous works, like data sparsity and over-fitting.

6 Conclusion and Perspectives

We have presented an auto-encoder for predicting unknown QoS scores of Web services based on their history. To achieve the best scores of accuracy, we leveraged the country ID for dividing the whole data set of QoS scores into clusters. Thereafter we have learned the latent factors by using the auto-encoder neural network. In addition we have derived the best code size through the use of cross validation. The comparison results between this prediction system and the state-of-the-art systems, showed the effectiveness of the proposed model.

As future works, we aim to enhance the prediction accuracy by addressing two particular points. First, we plan to develop other clustering alternatives (such as Expectation-Maximization) on user or provider properties. Second, our project is to develop more elaborated learning models such as stacked auto-encoders or denoising auto-encoders.

References

1. Chen, S., Fan, Y., Tan, W., Zhang, J., Bai, B., Gao, Z.: Service recommendation based on separated time-aware collaborative poisson factorization. J. Web Eng. **16**(7–8), 595–618 (2017)
2. Yueshen, X., Yin, J., Li, Y.: A collaborative framework of web service recommendation with clustering-extended matrix factorisation. Int. J. Web Grid Serv. **12**(1), 1–25 (2016)
3. Zhang, P., Han, Q., Li, W., Leung, H., Song, W.: A novel QOS prediction approach for cloud service based on Bayesian networks model. In: 2016 IEEE International Conference on Mobile Services (MS), pp. 111–118 (2016)
4. Rong, W., Peng, B., Ouyang, Y., Liu, K., Xiong, Z.: Collaborative personal profiling for web service ranking and recommendation. Inf. Syst. Front. **17**(6), 1265–1282 (2015)
5. Yin, J., Yueshen, X.: Personalised QOS-based web service recommendation with service neighbourhood-enhanced matrix factorisation. Int. J. Web Grid Serv. **11**(1), 39–56 (2015)
6. Lo, W., Yin, J., Li, Y., Zhaohui, W.: Efficient web service QOS prediction using local neighborhood matrix factorization. Eng. Appl. Artif. Intell. **38**, 14–23 (2015)

7. Yueshen, X., Yin, J., Deng, S., Xiong, N.N., Huang, J.: Context-aware QOS prediction for web service recommendation and selection. Expert Syst. Appl. **53**, 75–86 (2016)
8. Koren, Y., Bell, R., Volinsky, C.: Matrix factorization techniques for recommender systems. Computer **42**(8), 30–37 (2009)
9. Wang, X., Zhu, J., Zheng, Z., Song, W., Shen, Y., Lyu, M.R.: A spatial-temporal QOS prediction approach for time-aware web service recommendation. ACM Trans. Web **10**(1), 7:1–7:25 (2016)
10. Rumelhart, D.E., Hinton, G.E., Williams, R.J.: Learning internal representations by error propagation. In: Rumelhart, D.E., McClelland, J.L., Corporate PDP Research Group (eds.): Parallel distributed processing: explorations in the microstructure of cognition, vol. 1, pp. 318–362 (1986)
11. Hinton, G.E., Salakhutdinov, R.R.: Reducing the dimensionality of data with neural networks. Science **313**(5786), 504–507 (2006)
12. Zhang, Y., Zheng, Z., Lyu, M.R.: WSPred: a time-aware personalized QOS prediction framework for web services. In: Proceedings of the IEEE 22nd International Symposium on Software Reliability Engineering (ISSRE 2011), pp. 210–219 (2011)
13. Vincent, P., Larochelle, H., Lajoie, I., Bengio, Y., Manzagol, P.-A.: Stacked denoising autoencoders: learning useful representations in a deep network with a local denoising criterion. J. Mach. Learn. Res. **11**, 3371–3408 (2010)
14. Golub, G.H., Reinsch, C.: Singular value decomposition and least squares solutions. In: Bauer, F.L., Householder, A.S., Olver, F.W.J., Rutishauser, H., Samelson, K., Stiefel, E. (eds.) Handbook for Automatic Computation, pp. 134–151. Springer, Heidelberg (1971) https://doi.org/10.1007/978-3-642-86940-2_10
15. Tang, M., Zheng, Z., Kang, G., Liu, J., Yang, Y., Zhang, T.: Collaborative web service quality prediction via exploiting matrix factorization and network map. IEEE Trans. Netw. Serv. Manage. **13**(1), 126–137 (2016)
16. Breese, J.S., Heckerman, D., Kadie, C.: Empirical analysis of predictive algorithms for collaborative filtering. In: Proceedings of the Fourteenth Conference on Uncertainty in Artificial Intelligence, pp. 43–52 (1998)
17. Sarwar, B., Karypis, G., Konstan, J., Riedl, J.: Item-based collaborative filtering recommendation algorithms. In: Proceedings of the 10th International Conference on World Wide Web, pp. 285–295. ACM (2001)
18. Zheng, Z., Ma, H., Lyu, M.R., King, I.: WSRec: a collaborative filtering based web service recommendation system. In: Web Services, 2009, ICWS 2009. IEEE International Conference on Web Services (ICWS 2009), pp. 437–444. IEEE Computer Society (2009)
19. Zheng, Z., Ma, H., Lyu, M., King, I.: QOS-aware web service recommendation by collaborative filtering. IEEE Trans. Serv. Comput. **4**(2), 140–152 (2011)
20. Godse, M., Bellur, U., Sonar, R.: Automating QOS based service selection. In: IEEE International Conference on Web Services (ICWS), pp. 534–541. IEEE (2010)
21. Blumer, A., Ehrenfeucht, A., Haussler, D., Warmuth, M.K.: Occam's razor. Inf. Process. Lett. **24**(6), 377–380 (1987)
22. Shao, L., Zhang, J., Wei, Y., Zhao, J., Xie, B., Mei, H.: Personalized QOS prediction for web services via collaborative filtering. In: Proceedings of the IEEE International Conference on Web Services (ICWS 2007), pp. 439–446 (2007)
23. Ma, Y., Wang, S., Hung, P.C.K., Hsu, C.H., Sun, Q., Yang, F.: A highly accurate prediction algorithm for unknown web service QOS values. IEEE Trans. Serv. Comput. **9**(4), 511–523 (2016)

24. Kuang, L., Xia, Y., Mao, Y.: Personalized services recommendation based on context-aware QOS prediction. In: Proceedings of the IEEE 19th International Conference on Web Services (ICWS 2012), pp. 400–406. IEEE Computer Society (2012)
25. Deng, S., Huang, L., Guandong, X.: Social network-based service recommendation with trust enhancement. Expert Syst. Appl. **41**(18), 8075–8084 (2014)
26. Chen, Z., Shen, L., Li, F.: Exploiting web service geographical neighborhood for collaborative QOS prediction. Future Gener. Comput. Syst. **68**, 248–259 (2017)

Trustworthy Detection and Arbitration of SLA Violations in the Cloud

Christian Schubert, Michael Borkowski$^{(\boxtimes)}$, and Stefan Schulte

Distributed Systems Group, TU Wien, Vienna, Austria
{c.schubert,m.borkowski,s.schulte}@infosys.tuwien.ac.at

Abstract. In cloud computing, detecting violations of Service Level Agreements (SLAs) is possible by measuring certain metrics, which can be done by both the provider and the consumer of a service. However, both parties have contradicting interests with regards to these measurements, which makes it difficult to reach consensus about whether SLA violations have occurred.

Within this paper, we present a solution for measuring and arbitrating SLA violations in a way that can be trusted by both parties. Furthermore, we show that this solution is not intrusive to the service and does not incur a significant overhead system load, but nevertheless provides high accuracy in detecting SLA violations.

1 Introduction

Cloud computing offers a significant increase in flexibility and scalability for businesses offering their services to customers [2]. While cloud computing enables features like elasticity and paradigms like Infrastructure as a Service (IaaS), Platform as a Service (PaaS) and Software as a Service (SaaS) [18], all of which have proven to be highly effective tools in both industry and research [2], it also features a high level of distribution. This means that software components and services created and operated by various providers need to inter-operate with each other. As software development moves towards adopting Service-Oriented Architectures (SOA) [25], quality and reliability of individual services become important aspects [11], and parallel to agreeing on the service provided and consumed, *Service Level Agreements* (SLAs) are negotiated [30].

SLAs play a major role in cloud computing [8], and find application in grid computing, SOA, or generic Web services [24]. SLAs, negotiated between the provider and the consumer of a service, specify the relationship between those two signing parties regarding functional and non-functional requirements, such as availability, response time or data throughput. A key aim of SLAs is to protect the service consumers, as penalties can be defined for non-compliance with agreed constrains. For instance, the consumer can be awarded with credits by the provider upon detection of SLA violations [4].

SLA violations can be detected by real-time monitoring of the provided services and their runtime environment [25]. While this allows the consumer to

K. Kritikos et al. (Eds.): ESOCC 2018, LNCS 11116, pp. 90–104, 2018.
https://doi.org/10.1007/978-3-319-99819-0_7

detect SLA violations and benefit from penalty payments, the provider can use monitoring to avoid resource over-provisioning and unnecessary cost [6,15].

However, a fundamental problem with SLA monitoring is that both signing parties have contradicting interests with regards to the outcome. For instance, the provider might want to conceal an increase in response time, while the consumer is interested in revealing this violation to benefit from a penalty charge. Therefore, the *trust* of both parties in the measurements, and the arbitration whether an SLA violation has occurred, must be preserved to reach consensus.

In this paper, we provide a solution to ensure trustworthy measurement and arbitration of metrics to detect SLA violations in the cloud. Our solution does not significantly impact the service performance for either party. It allows to monitor detailed application-level details instead of only generic system-level metrics. We propose a hybrid approach, combining dedicated measurement software (agents) with Aspect-Oriented Programming (AOP). Furthermore, we propose a Trusted Third Party (TTP) component which uses Complex Event Processing (CEP) to efficiently handle high-volume data and automatically transforms SLA requirements into CEP expressions to utilize the high scalability of CEP engines. The presented approach does not require modifications to underlying software or protocols.

In summary, this paper provides the following contributions:

- We present a solution for using a TTP component for reliable and transparent SLA arbitration. Our solution is a hybrid approach, using AOP as well as agent-based monitoring, and is transparent for the service as well as its consumer.
- We propose the usage of CEP, together with an automated SLA-to-CEP mapping, to detect SLA violations in an effective and scalable manner.
- We provide a reference implementation of our solution, and valuate its accuracy and performance impact in a testbed.

The remainder of this paper is structured as follows: In Sect. 2, we provide background later used in Sect. 3 to describe our approach. We then evaluate the approach and its implementation in Sect. 4. In Sect. 5, we discuss related work. Finally, we conclude and give an overview of future work in Sect. 6.

2 Background

SLAs, i.e., contracts between service providers and consumers [19], play a major role in cloud computing [8], and are also found in the field of grid computing [19]. Conceptually, SLAs are applicable to any kind of service provided from one stakeholder to another, where not only the functionality, but also non-functional agreements must be negotiated. While we describe our approach in the context of cloud services, the work presented in this paper is not limited to any specific service paradigm.

The design of SLAs is usually tightly coupled with service selection, since it is in the interest of the client to select the provider with the most favorable

SLAs while maintaining a moderate price, and at the same time, it is in the interest of the provider to avoid defining overly strict SLAs. Several approaches for SLA negotiation have been presented in literature [7,30]. Therefore, we do not consider this negotiation phase. Instead, we assume that there is consensus about the SLAs in effect between the two parties.

Furthermore, there is a gap between non-functional business requirements, which are often high-level specifications, possibly provided by non-technical staff, and low-level metrics, which can be directly monitored by software [10]. There exist several approaches in present literature [28] for performing a mapping between high-level specifications and low-level metrics. Again, we assume that this mapping has already been performed, and that the automated measurement of low-level metrics is sufficient to detect SLA violations.

There is a variety of concrete SLA metrics observed by various solutions. We refer to the OASIS Open Standard for Web Services Quality Factors (WS-Quality-Factors) [23], defining quality levels for Web services, e.g., business value quality, service level measurement quality, manageability quality or security quality. The service level measurement quality comprises quantitative, dynamically changing attributes which describe the Quality of Service (QoS) [20]. Consequently, these attributes are highly suitable for real-time SLA monitoring. These metrics are generally in line with metrics found in other literature [1,12]. Both metrics experienced by the client as well as metrics observable on the server are of interest. In detail, we monitor the response time, throughput, availability, successability, CPU and memory usage of cloud services, since these metrics are applied in many different cloud solutions in research and practice [17,21].

3   Trustworthy SLA Monitoring

As discussed in the previous sections, we aim to monitor and arbitrate SLAs in a way that does not require the two signing parties (provider and consumer of a service) to trust each other. In this section, we discuss the overall architecture as well as the individual components of our approach.

3.1   Architecture Overview

We present the architecture of our solution in Fig. 1. The *service provider* is responsible for providing a certain *service* to the *service consumer* running a *client* to access the service. To simplify the figure, we depict only the communication path between the service provider and one consumer. However, the service is not restricted to only one consumer. We use a common message broker to exchange information between all components in a unified and scalable way. We employ *AOP advices* on both sides, i.e., pieces of code injected into the application, responsible for detecting service requests and responses and transparently monitoring application-level metrics. Furthermore, an *agent* is used on the provider side to monitor system-level metrics. Finally, the *TTP* component is provided by an entity not associated with the signing parties, i.e., a *neutral*

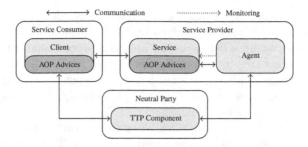

Fig. 1. Architecture overview of the proposed approach

party having no stake in the service and its SLAs. We do not define the process of determining such an entity, but assume that there is consensus between the two signing parties about the usage of a neutral party as a mediator.

Therefore, our solution consists of three main components, in addition to the pre-existing service and client: The agent, the AOP advices, and the TTP component. We describe these components in the following sections.

3.2 Agent

The agent is a stand-alone application hosted by the provider, and is independent of cloud services and other applications. It is responsible for the monitoring of metrics which are either impossible or not feasible to measure from within AOP advices, such as CPU or memory utilization during the execution. We also allow to extend the agent in a modular way by so-called *probes*. Probes act like additional monitoring services, running independently of the agent, but reporting to it. Such probes can be used to measure values from proprietary data sources, or to use other software already deployed. The interaction between the monitored services, the probes, the agent and the TTP is shown in Fig. 2.

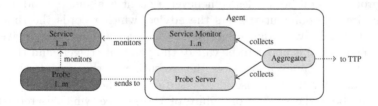

Fig. 2. Architecture of the agent component

The Agent uses Java bindings of the Sigar library[1] to retrieve CPU and memory metrics. Internally, it manages a list of Process Identifiers (PIDs) and

---

[1] Sigar is a software library to access native operation system and hardware activity information; cf. https://github.com/hyperic/sigar.

monitors their resource usage using Sigar. Furthermore, the agent keeps track of the tree of sub-processes possibly started by the monitored process. In contrast to other work [16], where a list is passed between processes and their children, we obtain the process tree by traversing the system process list, since this does not require changes in application code. Since our agent is aware of the SLA, it only monitors applications requiring the observation of CPU or memory usage, which reduces unnecessary overhead.

Note that it is not the agent's responsibility to interpret data or arbitrate SLA violations. It merely forwards the measurements to the TTP using the message broker. The messages consist of a timestamp, an identifier for the agent and the monitored application, a metric descriptor, and the measured value itself, and is signed using an SHA-256 Keyed-Hash Message Authentication Code (HMAC).

In order to prevent permanent network load and reduce the relative amount of overhead, we consolidate measurements into a queue. At an interval of 5 s, the agent sends the contents of the queue to the message broker. Furthermore, we do not send messages where the measured values diverge less than a certain level from the last transferred value. This is especially useful for processes having long periods of zero or near-zero CPU usage and reduces network traffic as well as computational load of both the agent and the TTP. In our experiments, we have found a threshold of 1% to be sufficient to avoid most of the unnecessary network load. This filtering and aggregation of messages is done in the *Aggregator* sub-component depicted in Fig. 2.

3.3 AOP Advices

In addition to the agent component, we use AOP advices on both the service and the client. AOP advices consist of code injected (*weaved*) into an application, which is executed at well-defined points in the code (*pointcuts*) and allows to transparently monitor software without modifying its source code, while still gaining measurements which would not be possible by the means of agent-based monitoring alone. As shown in Fig. 3, the AOP advices use pointcuts around the request procedures on both sides. Whenever a client is about to send a request to the service, the pointcut triggers the advice, which records the timestamp and request. Similarly, at the service side, whenever a request is received and the handling method is about to be called, the pointcut triggers and the service advice records the timestamp. After the execution of the service, this procedure is repeated for the response in reversed order. The response also contains information about the success or failure of the service, which is recorded by the advices. Finally, all advices independently report their measurements to the TTP component, which then matches the reported measurements, checks them for reasonability and decides whether an SLA violation has occurred.

The AOP advices only differ slightly for the provider and consumer sides. Advices on the consumer side must communicate with the message broker directly, while advices on the provider side are executed on the same machine as the agent, and can therefore report to this agent using local communication.

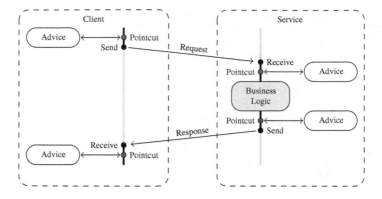

Fig. 3. Operation of AOP advices within Service and Client

3.4 TTP Component

The TTP component is the main unit responsible for detection and arbitration of SLA violations, and is hosted by a neutral party. Architecturally, the TTP component consists of the components shown in Fig. 4. Messages from agents and clients are received from the message broker using the *message receiver* component. They are fed into the *CEP engine* as events. In our implementation, we use the Esper[2] engine, which is used to process these events in an efficient and scalable way. For large-scale systems, this allows for easier outsourcing of this workload onto a distributed CEP system on its own [5]. In our implementation, we use the WSLA standard [12] to define SLAs. The negotiated SLA is read by the *WSLA reader* component. We then map this WSLA instance to CEP expressions in the *SLA-to-CEP mapper*. These CEP expressions are then fed to the *CEP engine*, which, together with the events from the *message receiver*, detects violations.

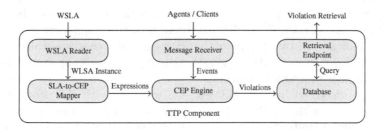

Fig. 4. Architecture of the TTP Component

We distinguish between simple SLA requirements, i.e., a direct mapping of SLA parameters to measured values, and complex SLA requirements, composed

---

[2] Esper is an open source event processing and correlation solution; cf. http://www.espertech.com/products/esper.php.

Listing 1.1. Extract of an Exemplary SLA Requirement

```
1  <Obligations>
2     <ServiceLevelObjective name="AverageResponseTimeSLO">
3        <Obliged>ServiceProvider</Obliged>
4        <Validity>
5           <Start>
6              2017-01-01T14:00:00.000-05:00
7           </Start>
8           <End>
9              2018-01-01T14:00:00.000-05:00
10          </End>
11       </Validity>
12       <Expression>
13          <Predicate xsi:type="LessEqual">
14             <SLAParameter>
15                AverageResponseTime
16             </SLAParameter>
17             <Value>2500</Value>
18          </Predicate>
19       </Expression>
20       <QualifiedAction>...</QualifiedAction>
21    </ServiceLevelObjective>
22    ...
23 </Obligations>
```

Listing 1.2. EPL Statement Generated by Mapper

```
1  SELECT AVG(responseTime) AS monitoredvalue,
2     'responseTime' AS metrictype,
3     'avg<=2500.0' AS requirementdesc, *
4     FROM ClientInfoMessage(responseTime >= 0)
5     GROUP BY serviceName
6     HAVING AVG(responseTime) > 2500.0 AND COUNT(*) >= MIN_QUANTITY
```

from several metrics, possibly applying additional aggregation functions. An example of a simple SLA requirement is "response time lower than 5 s". In contrast, "average response time lower than 5 s" is a complex SLA requirement. The WSLA language defines certain aggregation functions. Our implementation directly translates *Average*, *Median*, *Sum* and *Max* to equivalent expressions in the Event Processing Language (EPL) used by Esper.

As an example, an SLA requirement is shown in Listing 1.1, where the average response time is constrained to 2,500 ms. From this, the mapper creates the EPL expression shown in Listing 1.2. Note that certain sanity checks are already compiled into EPL expressions. For instance, the requirement `responseTime >= 0` filters out negative response durations.

Violations detected by the CEP engine, together with the proof, i.e., the involved events, are then persisted in a *database*, which enables accountability and traceability. Finally, the *retrieval endpoint* can be used to read violations and their information from the database.

4   Evaluation

In our evaluation scenario, a user can request image manipulation (resizing, rotating and flipping) of JPG, PNG and GIF images using a REST interface. The image manipulation service is cloud-based, and the user and provider of the service have agreed on a WSLA. We use this scenario for our evaluation since image manipulation requires a given computational complexity and is therefore a good placeholder for other possible cloud-based service tasks. For the evaluation experiments, the testbed environment, including the client, is controlled to allow automated repeated experiments with given parameters.

We present the testbed environment together with the image manipulation functionality in this section.

4.1 Testbed Environment

In our testbed, the configuration is provided as a pre-defined WSLA, and the detected violations are output as CSV logs in order to process the experiment results. In our experiment, the neutral party also fulfills the role of the component orchestrating the experiments, i.e., it is responsible for configuring both the provider and the consumer of the service while initiating the experiment.

The image manipulation service provided by the provider is capable of resizing, rotating and flipping JPG, PNG and GIF images using a REST interface. We use this service since this operation represents a given, well-defined computational complexity, and can therefore represent other computational workloads. We deploy the service on an Amazon Web Services (AWS) Elastic Compute Cloud (EC2) instance. EC2 is an IaaS service, which means that we are in control of the operating system and software. Note that since our approach does not require operating system-level operations on the client side, it can also be implemented using an PaaS or SaaS instance for the image service, where the latter requires that AOP advices are supported by the SaaS provider.

We use four image sizes in our experiments: small (640×426, 90 kB), medium (1280×898, 239 kB), large (1920×1280, 692 kB) and huge (4896×3264, 2,400 kB). Table 1 shows the employed infrastructure configuration.

Table 1. Testbed environment infrastructure configuration

Instance	OS	CPU (Core Count)	RAM
Provider	Ubuntu 16.04	Intel Xeon E5, 2.4 Ghz (1)	1 GB
Consumer	Windows 10	Intel Core i5, 3.4 GHz (4)	8 GB
TTP	Ubuntu 16.04	Intel Xeon E5, 2.4 Ghz (1)	1 GB

Figure 5 shows an example of an experiment execution by displaying the measured service response time in a series of 500 executions, demonstrating the general functionality of our testbed. We performed the experiment successfully for all metrics, and only show the response time results due to space constraints. The maximum response time is defined as 1,000 ms, and the observed average execution time is slightly higher than 200 ms. We injected deliberate delays of a random duration between 1,000 and 1,100 ms, all 12 of which were detected.

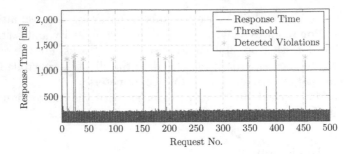

Fig. 5. Example of an experiment execution

For the following experiments, we used 600 experiment runs. Preliminary testing has shown that the system needs a certain amount of time to *settle*, i.e., to create reproducible results. This is most likely due to effects like the Java VM start-up and initial memory allocation. In order to avoid biasing our results with these implementation-dependent artifacts, in our statistical tests, we do not include all observations, but skip a fixed number of observations at the beginning of the experiment (7 for the experiments shown).

4.2   Accuracy: CPU and Memory Usage

We verify the accuracy of our measured CPU and memory usage. We perform t-tests (with a significance level of $\alpha = 0.05$) to verify significant equality of the baseline (see below) and results for the approaches presented in the work at hand. For both tests, the null hypothesis H_0 states equal means of both measurements (baseline and our result), while the alternative hypothesis H_1 states significant deviation between the data sets.

We use the Linux `top` tool in batch mode as a baseline. This tool displays CPU and memory-related information of running processes, which we log and compare to the measurements of our solution. We first measure the CPU usage using an interval of 1,000 ms, since this is the lowest resolution reliably supported by the baseline. We use a batch of 2,000 image resizing requests to create continuous load on our system. Figure 6 shows the overlay of the baseline measurement and the measurement provided by our solution. We also perform a paired t-test for 593 observations, with means of 9.177 and 9.156, and variances of 76.548 and 75.823. The results of the t-test supports our H_0 (p value 0.885 < 1.964).

From the same datasets, we verify our memory usage measurement. The results are shown in Fig. 7. A paired t-test for 593 observations, with means of 17.162 and 17.161, and variances of 1.484 and 1.485, results again in the support of H_0 (p value 0.693 < 1.964).

4.3   Successability

For verifying the successability, we inject failures into the service and observe the monitoring outcome. We use a likelihood of 3% of a failure injection, and

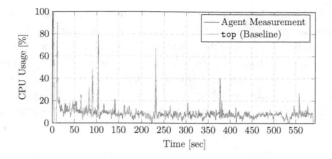

Fig. 6. CPU Usage: Baseline (Red) and Measurement (Blue) (Color figure online)

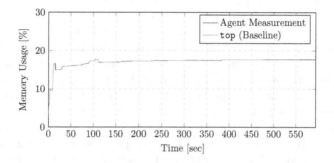

Fig. 7. Memory Usage: Baseline (Red) and Measurement (Blue) (Color figure online)

use 500 successive requests in this experiment. Figure 8 gives an overview of this experiment. The requests, together with their response times (shown on the left axis) are shown in red or green, depending on the outcome. The successability (shown on the right axis) is shown in blue. The effect of each failed request on the successability value can be observed. Also, the successability converges to a value of roughly 97%, corresponding to the 3% failure injection likelihood.

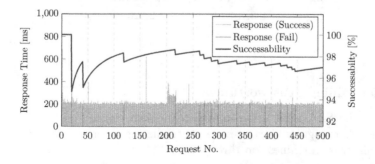

Fig. 8. Successability experiment (Color figure online)

Note that if the first few invocations happen to fail, the measured successability fluctuates subsequently due to the low number of measurements, and possibly incorrect SLA violation are reported. For instance, after around 30 observations, we measure a successability value of 95%, even though the actual baseline value is 97%. We conclude from this experiment that in practice, a lower bound should be set for the total number of observations. We therefore suggest the inclusion of an additional condition to the SLA to restrict the total observation number.

4.4 Performance Impact

Another key aspect, apart from measurement accuracy, is the impact of our monitoring solution on the performance of the service itself. We therefore perform experiments to measure the difference in response time experienced on the client, both with and without our monitoring approach enabled.

When performing the traditional t-tests used in the previous experiments, we encounter the problem that the network between our instances has a significant impact on the response time, seemingly much higher than the monitoring itself. This is indicated by the fact that the executed t-test yield varying results, even for experiment runs with the same configuration, and are therefore inconclusive.

For this experiment, we therefore use a purely local setup with all instances running on a single machine. We use a batch of 1,000 requests per image size and record response times. These results conclusively show that the impact of our monitoring on the response time is negligible. An overview is shown in Table 2. We see that the impact of our solution is well within the standard deviation σ, and never exceeds 3%.

Table 2. Comparison of response times in ms (σ in Brackets)

Workload	With Monitoring	Without Monitoring
Small	27.054 (4.375)	26.524 (3.524)
Medium	53.537 (18.943)	53.383 (17.664)
Big	97.540 (32.987)	95.732 (25.026)
Huge	483.707 (36.481)	482.326 (36.443)

4.5 Maintaining Trustworthiness

Trust into the SLA arbitration approach of both signing parties is crucial in situations where signing parties have contradicting interests. We consider how to maintain trustworthiness on three levels:

Trust in Measurement: The first element of trust is built on the aspect of the accuracy of the measurements. Our solution employs the software architecture described above, which provides reliable and accurate measurements according to the experiments shown in Sects. 4.1 through 4.4. Ensuring that no measurement is knowingly manipulated on-site can be achieved by using open-source software together with code signing (e.g., by the neutral party hosting the TTP component).

Trust in Communication: Messages exchanged between the components pose potential for deliberate or accidental manipulation. We use ActiveMQ, a well-established open-source broker [27]. In order to further strengthen the trust, we use HMACs to sign our measurement messages, which can be verified by the TTP.

Trust in Arbitration: Finally, both parties must trust the TTP to perform a neutral and fair arbitration. While this trust can be increased again by making the TTP software open-source and by using code signing, in our current implementation, we ultimately rely on the neutrality of the entity hosting the TTP.

5   Related Work

The topic of SLAs has been discussed extensively in existing work. We therefore provide a short overview of the most relevant literature, some of which presents concepts we have adapted in our solution, and conclude by discussing the differences between our work and the two approaches which come closest. We generally classify approaches by their measurement technique, and distinguish between agent-based, middleware-based, and AOP-based monitoring techniques.

A large body of work is found for the mapping of high-level SLA objectives to low-level system metrics. [16] provides an exhaustive overview of this topic, without focusing on the detection of SLA violations, and only takes into account provider-side metrics. Similarly, [22] proposes such a mapping, also taking into account SLA violation detection. The authors evaluate their work in private and public clouds. Again, they do not take into account measurements performed on the client side. Both of these solutions use agent-based monitoring. [13] extends this by using CEP for the detection of SLA violations, a concept we have adopted for our approach.

Instead of using agents, [26] uses a middleware on both sides of the connection. While this enables monitoring of client-side metrics, the authors do not discuss how to use these metrics to verify plausibility, leading to trust increase on both sides, like the checks for reasonable measurements performed by our TTP component. Also, their approach does not provide transparency (non-intrusiveness) to the client and service software. This transparency is provided, however, by works like [29], which provides agent-based monitoring on multiple levels, is extensible and uses a rule language. The authors evaluate their approach using public and private clouds and prove its scalability. [9] also uses agents for measurement, but focuses on predicting SLA violations in the cloud before they happen. [17] uses AOP instead of agents, and also provides transparency.

All of the mentioned approaches, however, do not take into account the trustworthiness of the resulting measurements. Adding a neutral party has been discussed by two approaches which, to the best of our knowledge, come closest to our solution. [3] suggests a third party similar to our TTP component. However, neither an implementation nor an evaluation is presented. Their solution is using a monitoring agent and is not transparent to the existing code. Furthermore, the solution is limited to the monitoring of communication data, and system resources are not taken into account. [14] also proposes an entity similar to our TTP component, but merely discusses a conceptual framework without providing an implementation or evaluation. Also, this approach is purely agent-based and as such, not transparent to existing code.

6   Conclusion and Future Work

In this paper, we have presented a solution allowing the provider and the consumer of a cloud service to detect violations of defined SLAs, and to allow mutual agreement on the outcome of this detection, without any of the two parties having to trust the other. For this, we have proposed the usage of a neutral third party, which is in charge of the collection of measured values, and the subsequent arbitration of SLA fulfillment.

The neutral third party is hosting the TTP component, which uses a hybrid of agent-based, as well as AOP-based data collection. The TTP component uses CEP to maintain scalability by evaluating the SLA fulfillment using CEP expressions automatically generated from the SLA requirements. Using experiments run in a testbed environment, we have shown that this solution does not only provide accurate measurements, but also does not significantly impact the performance of the service. We have also provided a discussion about various additional aspects of maintaining trust in such a multi-stakeholder scenario.

We currently assume the two parties to trust the neutral third party. In our future work, we plan an extension to our approach using signatures in the verdict of the TTP component, which, coupled with code signing, could remote this requirement and allow for completely trust-less operation. Instead of using a centralized third party, we are currently also observing the possibility of using decentralized consensus, e.g., a blockchain, to increase trust.

Acknowledgment. This work is partially funded by COMET K1, FFG – Austrian Research Promotion Agency, within the Austrian Center for Digital Production.

References

1. Ameller, D., Franch, X.: Service Level Agreement Monitor (SALMon). In: 7th International Conference on Composition-Based Software Systems (ICCBSS), pp. 224–227. IEEE (2008)
2. Armbrust, M., et al.: A view of cloud computing. Commun. ACM **53**(4), 50–58 (2010)
3. Balfagih, Z., Hassan, M.F.B.: Agent based monitoring framework for SOA applications quality. In: International Symposium on Information Technology (ITSim), vol. 3, pp. 1124–1129. IEEE (2010)

4. Baset, S.A.: Cloud SLAs: present and future. ACM SIGOPS Oper. Syst. Rev. **46**(2), 57–66 (2012)

5. Borkowski, M., Fdhila, W., Nardelli, M., Rinderle-Ma, S., Schulte, S.: Event-based failure prediction in distributed business processes. In: Information Systems (2018)

6. Borkowski, M., Hochreiner, C., Schulte, S.: Moderated resource elasticity for stream processing applications. In: Heras, D.B., Bougé, L. (eds.) Euro-Par 2017. LNCS, vol. 10659, pp. 5–16. Springer, Cham (2018). https://doi.org/10.1007/978-3-319-75178-8_1

7. Brandic, I., Music, D., Leitner, P., Dustdar, S.: *VieSLAF* framework: enabling adaptive and versatile SLA-management. In: Altmann, J., Buyya, R., Rana, O.F. (eds.) GECON 2009. LNCS, vol. 5745, pp. 60–73. Springer, Heidelberg (2009). https://doi.org/10.1007/978-3-642-03864-8_5

8. Buyya, R., Yeo, C.S., Venugopal, S., Broberg, J., Brandic, I.: Cloud computing and emerging IT platforms: vision, hype, and reality for delivering computing as the 5th utility. Future Gener. Comput. Syst. **25**(6), 599–616 (2009)

9. Emeakaroha, V.C., Ferreto, T.C., Netto, M.A.S., Brandic, I., Rose, C.A.F.D.: CASViD: application level monitoring for SLA violation detection in clouds. In: IEEE 36th Annual Computer Software and Applications Conference (COMPSAC), pp. 499–508. IEEE (2012)

10. Emeakaroha, V.C., Brandic, I., Maurer, M., Dustdar, S.: Low level metrics to high level SLAs-LoM2HiS framework: Bridging the gap between monitored metrics and SLA parameters in cloud environments. In: International Conference on High Performance Computing and Simulation (HPCS), pp. 48–54. IEEE (2010)

11. Islam, S., Lee, K., Fekete, A., Liu, A.: How a consumer can measure elasticity for cloud platforms. In: 3rd ACM/SPEC International Conference on Performance Engineering, pp. 85–96. ACM (2012)

12. Keller, A., Ludwig, H.: The WSLA framework: specifying and monitoring service level agreements for web services. J. Netw. Syst. Manag. **11**(1), 57–81 (2003)

13. Leitner, P., Inzinger, C., Hummer, W., Satzger, B., Dustdar, S.: Application-level performance monitoring of cloud services based on the complex event processing paradigm. In: International Conference on Service-Oriented Computing and Applications (SOCA), pp. 1–8. IEEE (2012)

14. Maarouf, A., Marzouk, A., Haqiq, A.: Towards a trusted third party based on multi-agent systems for automatic control of the quality of service contract in the cloud computing. In: International Conference on Electrical and Information Technologies, pp. 311–315. IEEE (2015)

15. Mao, M., Humphrey, M.: Auto-scaling to minimize cost and meet application deadlines in cloud workflows. In: International Conference for High Performance Computing, Networking, Storage and Analysis. Article number 49. ACM (2011)

16. Mastelic, T., Emeakaroha, V.C., Maurer, M., Brandic, I.: M4Cloud - generic application level monitoring for resource-shared cloud environments. In: International Conference on Cloud Computing and Services Science (CLOSER), pp. 522–532. Springer (2012)

17. Mdhaffar, A., Halima, R.B., Juhnke, E., Jmaiel, M., Freisleben, B.: AOP4CSM: an aspect-oriented programming approach for cloud service monitoring. In: IEEE 11th International Conference on Computer and Information Technology (ICCIT), pp. 363–370. IEEE (2011)

18. Mell, P., Grance, T.: The NIST definition of cloud computing recommendations of the national institute of standards and technology. In: National Institute of Standards and Technology, Information Technology Laboratory 145 (2011)

19. Menascé, D.A., Casalicchio, E.: QoS in grid computing. IEEE Internet Comput. 8(4), 85–87 (2004)
20. Michlmayr, A., Rosenberg, F., Leitner, P., Dustdar, S.: Comprehensive QoS monitoring of web services and event-based SLA violation detection. In: 4th International Workshop on Middleware for Service Oriented Computing, pp. 1–6. ACM (2009)
21. Mirobi, G.J., Arockiam, L.: Service level agreement in cloud computing: an overview. In: International Conference on Control, Instrumentation, Communication and Computational Technologies (ICCICCT), pp. 753–758 (2015)
22. Moustafa, S., Elgazzar, K., Martin, P., Elsayed, M.: SLAM: SLA monitoring framework for federated cloud services. In: International Conference on Utility and Cloud Computing (UCC), pp. 506–511. IEEE/ACM (2015)
23. OASIS Open. Web Services Quality Factors Version 1.0. Candidate OA- SIS Standard 01 (2012). http://docs.oasis-open.org/wsqm/WS-Quality-Factors/v1.0/WS-Quality-Factors-v1.0.html
24. Repp, N., Eckert, J., Schulte, S., Niemann, M., Berbner, R., Steinmetz, R.: Towards automated monitoring and alignment of service-based workflows. In: IEEE International Conference on Digital Ecosystems and Technologies (DEST), pp. 235–240. IEEE Computer Society, Washington, DC (2008)
25. Rosen, M., Lublinsky, B., Smith, K.T., Balcer, M.J.: Applied SOA: service-oriented architecture and design strategies. Wiley (2012)
26. Al-Shammari, S., Al-Yasiri, A.: MonSLAR: a middleware for monitoring SLA for RESTFUL services in cloud computing. In: IEEE International Symposium on the Maintenance and Evolution of Service-Oriented and Cloud-Based Environments (MESOCA), pp. 46–50. IEEE (2015)
27. Souto, E., Guimarães, G., Vasconcelos, G., Vieira, M., Rosa, N., Ferraz, C.: A message-oriented middleware for sensor networks. In: Workshop on Middleware for Pervasive and Ad-Hoc Computing, pp. 127–134. ACM (2004)
28. Theilmann, W., Yahyapour, R., Butler, J.: Multi-level SLA management for service-oriented infrastructures. In: Mähönen, P., Pohl, K., Priol, T. (eds.) ServiceWave 2008. LNCS, vol. 5377, pp. 324–335. Springer, Heidelberg (2008). https://doi.org/10.1007/978-3-540-89897-9_28
29. Trihinas, D., Pallis, G., Dikaiakos, M.D.: JCatascopia: monitoring elastically adaptive applications in the cloud. In: 14th IEEE/ACM International Symposium on Cluster, Cloud and Grid Computing (CCGrid), pp. 226–235. IEEE/ACM (2014)
30. Wu, L., Garg, S.K., Buyya, R., Chen, C., Versteeg, S.: Automated SLA negotiation framework for cloud computing. In: 13th IEEE/ACMInternational Symposium on Cluster, Cloud, and Grid Computing, pp. 235–244. IEEE/ACM, May 2013

Distributed Complex Event Processing in Multiclouds

Vassilis Stefanidis$^{(\boxtimes)}$, Yiannis Verginadis$^{(\boxtimes)}$,
Ioannis Patiniotakis$^{(\boxtimes)}$, and Gregoris Mentzas$^{(\boxtimes)}$

Institute of Communications and Computer Systems,
National Technical University of Athens, Zografou, Greece
{stefanidis, jverg, ipatini, gmentzas}@mail.ntua.gr

Abstract. The last few years, the generation of vast amounts of heterogeneous data with different velocity and veracity and the requirement to process them, has significantly challenged the computational capacity and efficiency of the modern infrastructural resources. The propagation of Big Data among different processing and storage architectures, has amplified the need for adequate and cost-efficient infrastructures to host them. An overabundance of cloud service offerings is currently available and is being rapidly adopted by small and medium enterprises based on its many benefits to traditional computing models. However, at the same time the Big Data computing requirements pose new research challenges that question the adoption of single cloud provider resources. Nowadays, we discuss the emerging data-intensive applications that necessitate the wide adoption of multicloud deployment models, in order to use all the advantages of cloud computing. A key tool for managing such multicloud applications and guarantying their quality of service, even in extreme scenarios of workload fluctuations, are adequate distributed monitoring mechanisms. In this work, we discuss a distributed complex event processing architecture that follows automatically the big data application deployment in order to efficiently monitor its health status and detect reconfiguration opportunities. This proposal is examined against an illustrative scenario and is preliminary evaluated for revealing its performance results.

Keywords: Distributed CEP · Cloud monitoring · Multiclouds
Big data

1 Introduction

Nowadays, we witness a constant increase of the connected devices and services that continuously produce data and transmit health status events. The generation of vast amounts of heterogeneous data and their propagation among different processing and storage architectures, has amplified the need for adequate and cost-efficient infrastructures to host them. The recent uptake of Cloud computing adoption could be considered as a remedy to this situation where the growing needs of the so-called Big-Data applications, are met by the vastly improving offerings of the cloud providers [1]. Such applications require to efficiently deal with the volume, variety, velocity, and veracity of the data, using any resources available in a cost-effective and efficient way.

© IFIP International Federation for Information Processing 2018
Published by Springer Nature Switzerland AG 2018. All Rights Reserved
K. Kritikos et al. (Eds.): ESOCC 2018, LNCS 11116, pp. 105–119, 2018.
https://doi.org/10.1007/978-3-319-99819-0_8

In recent years, Big-Data applications have been developed and used successfully over cloud infrastructures [2]. Such an adoption of the Cloud computing, theoretically satisfies unlimited hosting requirements, for storing and processing Big Data, in a reliable, fault-tolerant and scalable way. Cloud's ability comprises resources virtualization that requires minimum interaction with cloud service providers and enables users to access terabytes of storage, high processing power and high availability in a pay-as-you-go model [3]. As more enterprises started to trust the Cloud computing paradigm, they started outsourcing their workload to infrastructures, offered by single cloud providers. This led to vendor lock-in situations that didn't allow the use of the most optimal infrastructure (with respect to the processing location, efficiency, cost etc.) per each case and at each given time. Thus, the recent availability of a variety of public IaaS providers (e.g. Amazon, Google, HP, IBM, RackSpace) as well as private offerings (e.g. Openstack, VMware), still remains un-exploitable by the average cloud user [4–9]. In the majority of cloud applications, the cloud users seek to commit their entire processing stack over a single cloud provider, by considering only the planned or expected behaviour of the application. As a result, they neglect to consider flexible infrastructures able to mix and match platforms from multiple cloud providers, and meet, in such way, the dynamically changing requirements of their Big Data applications [10]. In other words, these users miss exploiting the benefits of the multicloud architectures.

Nevertheless, the use of multicloud offerings especially at the level of infrastructure in order to cope with the needs of big data applications still involves several challenges and open research questions. These mainly correspond to how data-intensive computing can be hosted in highly distributed and federated cloud environments by keeping the Quality of Service (QoS) guarantees. This generic challenge can be analysed into a number of fine-grained challenges that refer to scalability, resiliency, and security issues faced by big data and data-intensive applications on distributed platforms. The purpose of this paper is to address the applications' scalability and resiliency challenges when attempting to exploit the benefits of multiclouds. Such benefits become even more obvious, if the reader considers the new business and scientific needs for distributed data processing among various locations, for real time processing of data from various heterogeneous sources. Nevertheless, multicloud computing environments consist of many resources that are simultaneously accessed by several tenants, which means that often suffer from unanticipated behaviour such as performance degradations either for the infrastructure or the software parts, component failures and security threats. For these reasons, it is very important to constantly monitor and analyse multiclouds to detect situations that should lead to reconfigurations of the used processing topology (e.g. scale up or scale down according to the current workload). In a way, monitoring delivers the knowledge that is required to make appropriate decisions with respect to the way applications are deployed and hosted over multiclouds, thus answers the challenges mentioned above.

Monitoring and analysing Clouds correspond to challenging tasks that require sophisticated tools and methods. Event processing is a method of tracking and analysing streams of data about application-related occurrences that happen (i.e. events), and issuing some alerts based on them. Complex event processing (CEP), corresponds to event processing that combines data for inferring patterns of events that may suggest more complicated circumstances [11]. CEP systems [12] are valuable in digesting and processing a multitude of event streams. Their big advantage is the ability to collect information from various heterogeneous data sources and filter, aggregate or combine them over defined periods of time (i.e. time windows). The idea of using CEP for monitoring cloud applications has been applied with respect to two types of architectural approaches: centralized and distributed. The centralized CEP architecture is based on a single CEP engine which processes all monitored data and detects patterns by using rules. On the other hand, the distributed CEP architecture consists of a set of cooperating CEP engines that exchange messages and are able to more efficiently detect event patterns by considering rules that differ according to the proximity of the processing engine to the event source. In existing centralised CEP approaches [13–15] huge bandwidth and computational capabilities are required and usually they lack robustness and scalability because of the single point of failure when processing vast amounts of health status data. On the other hand, the distributed CEP architectures such as the parallel CEP processing architecture of Hirzel's [16] and the work of Ku et al. [17], present better performance in terms of data processing throughput, due to workload sharing across multiple CEP engines, and establish better scalability results without any risk of single point of failure. Nevertheless, all these cases are bound to the use of a single cloud vendor, a fact that limits, by default, the big data-intensive applications capacities.

In this paper, a distributed CEP system is presented, appropriate for applications deployed over multicloud resources, proposing a multi-level event processing architecture. The paper is organized as follows: Sect. 2 describes the related work, while in Sect. 3, the proposed conceptual architecture is discussed along with the relevant technological grounding details. In Sect. 4, an illustrative example is presented for better demonstrating the benefits of the proposed approach. In Sect. 5, a preliminary evaluation of the proposed system is given and in Sect. 6, we conclude by discussing the next steps of this work.

2 Related Work

CEP signifies a very important role in detecting and integrating events through pattern matching and using rules for issuing alerts, in cases where increasing amounts of data streams are present. Concerning the distribution of CEP, a few recent works focus on the technique of parallelization of pattern-matching processing in which pattern matching is seen as a stateful operator in a general purpose streaming system.

More specifically, Hirzel [16] by using the keys to partition the incoming events, proposes a pattern matching syntax and a way of translation based on the concept of partitions. Therefore, events with different keys can be processed in parallel. Hirzel exploits the partitioning constructs provided by the queries of the specific language he uses. In a similar work, Ku et al. [17] propose a distributed CEP architecture which splits various centralized CEP tasks load across multiple stations. The core of communication architecture is achieved by using a distributed message broker based on Apache River, a network of distributed systems in the form of modular co-operating services. The authors use a distributed complex event detection algorithm with a

Masters/Workers pattern. The innovation of this proposal can be found in geographical distribution of tasks for sub-detection using CEP engines in a Master/Slave flowchart concept. In the first work [16], the presented approach is adequate to be used only when the querying language's built-in partitioning constructs (i.e. data-structures with specific properties), satisfy the needs of specific processing scenarios that should be supported. The parallelism technique that the authors use, is either centralized in one machine or distributed in various machines from a single cloud vendor. In the second work [17], the technique that is used, presents an important communication overhead when the number of events to be processed is less than 500 events/sec. Both approaches miss the multicloud benefits that we propose in this paper, since the parallelism technique that the authors use, is distributed in various machines from a single cloud vendor without considering cross-cloud level deployments. Moreover, in the second work, the case of scaling-in or scaling-out the cluster of deployed CEP engines is not supported and a static architecture of a pre-considered number of deployed CEP engines is used.

Paraiso et al. [18] present a distributed CEP engine (DiCEPE) which is a platform that focuses on the integration of CEP engines in critical-case distributed systems. Appropriate communication protocols are used in order to integrate CEP engines easily and interconnect them across vast geographical areas. In a similar architecture, Flouris et al. [19] present the FERRARI which is a prototype that implements real-time CEP for large volume event data streams over distributed architectures by sharing the load over a set of streaming cloud platforms. In addition, an intra-cloud CEP is used where appropriate. In the [18] approach, despite the communication heterogeneity, adaptability and scalability of the proposed architecture, the introduction of Frascati [20] open source platform layer, induces an overhead due to the increased number of messages that should be exchanged. In the [19] approach the authors do not provide any dynamic publish/subscribe model for communicating among various CEP engines and they use instead push/pull techniques. Moreover, they do use only one CEP engine in each Cloud environment with partitioning (parallelism) in contrast to our approach that uses many CEP engines in each Cloud vendor. Neither of the two similar and interesting approaches use any Event Processing Network (EPN) which can be automatically deployed and configured on multiple cloud environments using various levels of event processing complexity. Especially, in the case of Flouris et al. work [18] a web-based authoring tool is used for manually building the EPN and performing the query optimization across the Cloud environments. A third approach that uses a distributed approach for event detection, called Next CEP is that of Schultz-Moller et al. [21]. As the previous both architectures, this approach uses an event query language for expressing event patterns in a distributed way but by using the same rules in all CEP engines without the option to provide dynamic rule adaptation. In our proposed architecture, a domain specific rule (for each CEP instance) can be changed and deployed at runtime as well as adapted according to the run-time monitoring needs.

Mdhaffar et al. [22] introduces a dynamic architecture for measuring cloud performance and analysing various situations based on a complex event processing either in a centralized or a distributed architecture. The specific paper demonstrates a system that is designed to dynamically switch between different centralized and distributed CEP engines, depending on the current machine load and network traffic conditions.

However, in this dynamic CEP system, no event processing takes place locally to each Virtual Machine concerning aggregation functions or processing query rules. The local processing is limited to outliers and anomaly detection. In our approach, local aggregation function operations take place and the aggregated data results are published to higher levels CEP processing nodes. Moreover, our approach does not face any latency or delay set up issues, originated from the need to switch between various architectures.

One additional interesting approach by Boubeta et al. [14], presented a centralized CEP architecture that combines technologies such as Mule ESB and ESPER engine, while using the Xively IoT platform. Data is gathered from various sources for Home Automation operations. In addition to this work, Leitner et al. [15] propose a centralized event-based approach for monitoring cloud applications by using a multi-step CEP-based event correlation schema which can be used for cloud applications with a large number of virtual resources. By this way, the application elasticity is increased. In another similar approach, CloudScale [23] framework uses the monitoring data to dynamically acquire and release cloud hosts. Nevertheless, the specific approach does not investigate the co-existence of low-level metrics such as CPU utilization, memory consumption etc. along with the application specific metrics i.e. responsiveness of a very critical application that controls i.e. a nuclear factory. The most important issue though is that these three approaches, neglect the benefits of multi-cloud environments and do not use any dynamic communication protocol suitable for event-driven architectures that dynamically may change their number of hosts.

Finally, a number of other approaches have been studied, which use data from events coming from heterogeneous environments on a cloud level and are based on service-oriented architectures (SOA). In [24] the authors introduce an architecture that uses a meta-model to describe the components of the cloud service-based application with a specific algorithm that discovers valid event patterns that signify specific SLO violations (e.g., storage violations). In addition, the authors in [25, 26] propose an event-driven SOA architecture that provides context awareness in the scope of Internet of Things. It provides the means for context handling from the reception to delivery of personalized context-aware services. The result is a scalable context-aware architecture which can be applied in a wide spectrum of domains but it uses a CEP engine in a more centralized and less distributed way to process the data. As can be seen, these three approaches seem to neglect the benefits of multi-cloud environments as they do not consider at all the option of two or more cloud vendors. Moreover, an approach with just one level of CEP is adopted on these architectures. On the contrary, in our proposed approach, a distributed multi-level cross-cloud CEP paradigm is used with a pub/sub communication concept which offers more flexibility, modularity, extensibility of the infrastructure and the option for adaptation to a dynamically changing environment of resources. What is also noteworthy in our approach is the fact that multiple events can be produced from different layers that can be correlated by using custom made functions that extend the event algebra processing capabilities, which is something not presented in previous works.

3 Distributed Complex Event Processing (DCEP) Architecture

3.1 Conceptual Architecture

In this section, we discuss our approach for a novel Event Processing Network (EPN) that can be efficiently distributed over several virtualized resources that may span multiple providers to monitor the deployment of multicloud applications. Such advanced monitoring capabilities are valuable for detecting reconfiguration opportunities that will safeguard the desired quality of service of the multicloud applications. An EPN is a conceptual model that refers to a set of Event Processing Agents (EPA), Event Producers and Event Consumers all connected by a set of Event Channels(EC) [11]. The event producers are resources that generate events while the event consumers are components that receive such events. In multiclouds, the event producers involve VMs that host parts of a multicloud application and transmit monitoring events with respect to the health status of the hosting resource and any application specific information. The EPAs act both as event consumers (subscribe for monitoring events) and as event producers since they are able to relay any detected complex event patterns to other parts of the EPN. Each EPA filters, match and derivate complex events according to specific rules, expressing patterns that reveal the multicloud application health status. In our approach, we consider the implementation of these EPAs by using interconnected Complex Event Processing (CEP) engines. The goal of CEP technique is to identify events and patterns with great importance such as opportunities or threats for the current multiclouds processing topology and respond to them as quickly as possible. The use of multiple EPAs in a distributed architecture brings about the advantage of multi-level complex event processing. Specifically, three distinct layers of CEP are considered (as seen in Fig. 1) for hierarchically detecting interesting complex events (e.g. average CPU > 80% for an application server instance, average CPU > 80% for all application server instances on Cloud X and average CPU > 80% for all application server instances on all Clouds used for a certain multicloud application). Each of these EPAs are integrated with an appropriate pub/sub system for message queueing and event propagation across the three event processing layers, constituting the DCEP agents. As depicted in Fig. 1, this network of DCEP agents is structured across three main layers: (i) the VM instance layer (1st Level Event Patterns Detection), (ii) the Cloud layer (2nd Level Event Patterns Detection) and (iii) the Global layer (3rd Level Event Patterns Detection). The first one corresponds to the installation and configuration of Event Processing Agents on each VM instance in order to focus on the aggregation, filtering and propagation of raw health status events. The second layer involves the use of one such agent per Cloud for extracting higher-level information on the placed data and cloud application. This allows for a valuable consolidated view of all the resources' and applications' statuses deployed per cloud provider based on the aggregation and processing of the output of "local" DCEP Agents that report from each VM. Consequently, the third layer involves the output aggregation of the "second level" Agents in order to allow for a global overview of the status of the whole processing topology.

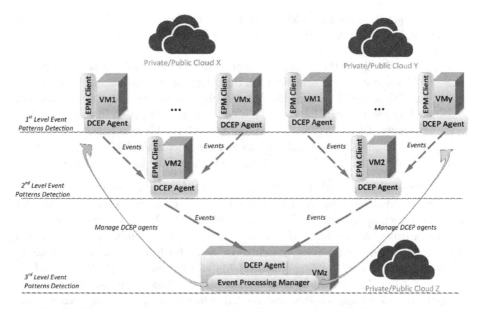

Fig. 1. Conceptual architecture of a DCEP for monitoring multicloud applications

Moreover, in a dynamic environment where the multicloud resources to be used for hosting an application are not static and predefined, a dedicated mechanism for setting up and maintaining the described EPN according to the requirements of the DevOps or the application developers, is a necessity. Thus, we introduce the so-called Event Processing Management (EPM) server and its EPM Clients which are responsible for the deployment, synchronization and orchestration of the DCEP Agents, hosted in various VMs and heterogeneous Cloud providers. Upon successful deployment of these agents, the Event Processing Management also undertakes the configuration or enhancement of all the appropriate complex event pattern rules that should be used by each EPA.

3.2 Deploying and Managing DCEP Agents Over Multiclouds

The EPM subsystem is responsible for deploying and managing the monitoring network of Event Processing Agents, and it uses a client-server architecture which comprises two distinct architectural components types:

i. The EPM clients, which are the DCEP controlling agents. They accompany the DCEP agents at each VM, on the first, second or third level of event pattern detection. They do not undertake monitoring tasks (in contrast to EPAs) but they are separate modules. These Clients contain configuration scripts for setting up and launching first level or second level DCEPs according to the instructions of the server (i.e. Event Processing Manager). They also contain information and credentials for connecting to server. EPM Clients are installed in a VM during VM initialization. An alternative approach would be that the server connects to each

VM and install clients after VM initialization. This approach requires that each VM offer an interactive SSH shell and the VM network address and administrator credentials are available to server.

ii. The server (i.e. Event Processing Manager) is the controller of clients. It is a part of the EPM subsystem and resides at the third level of the DCEP architecture (see Fig. 1). The server is responsible for installing clients to VMs (if they are not installed during VM initialization) and afterwards for instructing them to configure the respective DCEP Agents as first or second level event patterns detection. Moreover the server periodically checks whether clients and VMs are active and if one goes offline (e.g. if it crashes) it can reconfigure the EPN appropriately.

It is noteworthy to mention that before the multicloud application should start its operation the EPN must be in place and ready to capture and process monitoring events. Therefore, upon each VM boot, the installed EPM client attempts to connect to EPM server using SSH protocol. If it succeeds it sends VM identification information and the server assigns it a unique Id (which is stored for future sessions). The server will decide (using a specific strategy) which VMs will act as first level EPAs and which as second (or first and second level simultaneously). Subsequently the server signals clients about its decision, passing any needed information, and clients execute pre-configured setup scripts that prepare and launch the DCEP Agents. The EPM Client monitors the DCEP Agent launching and when it is ready the client updates the server. When the EPN is in place and operational, the server signals that the multicloud application may be deployed and start operating.

It is also important to mention that second level DCEP Agents are configured and launched before the first level DCEP Agents, since their network information must be passed to the subordinate first level DCEP Agents. First level DCEP Agents are configured and launched afterwards and forward their events to the designated second level DCEP Agent, resulting in a hierarchical network structure. Second level DCEP Agents are also configured to forward their events to the third level where EPM resides. The process of bootstrapping the EPN is depicted in Fig. 2.

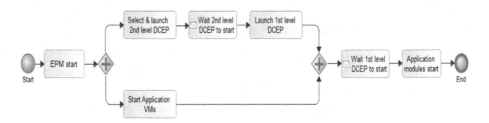

Fig. 2. Multi-cloud DCEP application bootstrap

3.3 DCEP Implementation

In this section, we ground the conceptual architecture presented in Sect. 3.1 and discuss the technologies used for each of the components of the proposed DCEP system. Based on the presented architecture, two basic functionalities should be supported. The first is related to the queueing and propagation (to subscribers) of monitoring events coming from multicloud resources, while the second corresponds to the complex event processing of these events. For the first functionality, the use of an Enterprise Service Bus (ESB) is in order while for the second basic functionality several instances of CEP engines have been adopted. The event producers perceived in this approach, refer to: (i) virtualized resources-related sensors that capture information related to infrastructural performance issues (e.g. VMs' RAM usage, CPU load etc.); application-related sensors which propagate the multicloud application's performance (e.g. Response Time) and (iii) the complex events produced by EPAs based on the previous two types of events. The data obtained from these event producers are published through the use of an ESB. An ESB instance is used in each VM employed for hosting the components of the multicloud application (e.g. DBs, application servers etc.). In parallel, a CEP engine instance is also installed per each VM used. This CEP engine uses event patterns (rules) that specify the conditions under which reconfiguration events are produced or specific aggregated events are propagated to a higher processing level.

In this work we have used and configured the MuleSoft open source software [27] for the implementation of ESB functionalities. MuleSoft ESB was evaluated by the Rademakers and Dirksentt [28] as the best-of-breed products currently available according to the following criteria: ESB core functionality, quality of documentation, market visibility, active development and support community, custom logic, transport protocols and connectivity options, integration capabilities with open source frameworks, and tool support. Due to the need for dynamic and adaptive deployments of various Virtual Machines among various Cloud environments, it is obvious that a flexible type of messaging protocol should be used to transfer the raw data coming from the data sources (hardware and software sensors) to the EPAs. Therefore, we have adopted the Advanced Message Queueing Protocol (AMQP) protocol to propagate monitoring events over the MuleSoft ESB, according to the Publish/Subscribe paradigm. Apache ActiveMQ [29] is one of the most popular and powerful open source messaging and Integration Patterns server. It is an open source message broker written in Java together with a full Java Message Service (JMS) client. Many features that it provides, fits our Cross-Cloud distributed CEP Architecture:

- ActiveMQ is standards-based in that it is a JMS 1.1 compliant. The JMS specification provides many benefits and guarantees including asynchronous message delivery, message durability for subscribers which are very crucial for the dynamic cross-cloud scaling architecture;
- ActiveMQ provides a wide range of connectivity options including support for protocols such as HTTP/S, multicast, TCP, SSL, and others. This gives a substantial flexibility for the implementation of communication among publishers and subscribers;
- Due to the proposed distributed architecture, the use of tightly coupled architectures for message brokering can be problematic. Loosely coupled architectures exhibit fewer dependencies which are very useful in a dynamically changing (by scaling in or out) event-driven architecture [29].

Moreover, ESPER [30] was used for the CEP capabilities required for this approach. ESPER is an open source engine that combines Event Stream Processing (ESP) and CEP capabilities. ESPER uses the Event Processing Language (EPL) and provides a highly scalable, memory-efficient data stream processing tool to detect event patterns and create alerts. EPL is used to express filtering, aggregation joins, and define patterns over multiple events streams. In Fig. 3, we provide a UML component diagram that conceptually depicts the detailed subcomponents of the proposed architecture per each layer and EPA. We note that grey color was used to denote newly developed subcomponents that augment the MuleSoft and Esper subcomponents that are offered as open-source software. The subcomponents include the:

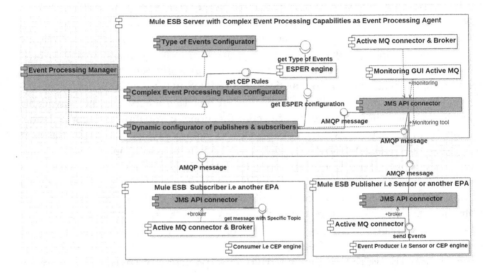

Fig. 3. Communication details between ESB and EPAs

- *Type of Events Configurator* - This is a subcomponent that provides to the ESPER engine the information about the type of events that the engine should process;
- *Complex Event Processing Rules Configurator* - This subcomponent injects to the ESPER engine the appropriate event patterns expressed in EPL for detecting complex event patterns at run-time.
- *ESPER Engine* - This corresponds to the core ESPER component re-used and spawned in multiple instances over the proposed distributed architecture for detecting complex event patterns;
- *Dynamic Configurator of publishers & subscribers* - This subcomponent can register any consumer to needs to subscribe to events according to a specific event topic that is defined via the JMS API of Active MQ service;
- *JMS API Connector* - This subcomponent is used as a software entity that propagates events to other subscribers hosted in several VMs;
- *Monitoring GUI Active MQ* - This subcomponent is used as a monitoring tool where valuable information is presented through a user interface concerning the

way that various events are forwarded according to pub/sub model through the Active MQ broker;

- *Active MQ Connector & Broker* - This subcomponent is an open source message broker written in JAVA providing an efficient Java Message Service;
- *Event Processing Manager* - This subcomponent, as described in the previous section, is responsible for the synchronization and orchestration of the deployment and reconfiguration of EPAs and ESB instances to be hosted in all the VMs that will accommodate aspects of a big data-intensive application.

4   An Illustrative Example

To illustrate the details of this approach, we use the case of a Vehicle Traffic Simulation application, which is a big data processing application due to its dynamic and demanding nature, requires deployment over a multi-cloud environment, thus continuous and efficient monitoring for optimisation purposes. In this example, the traffic system includes many heterogeneous agents (e.g., people, cars, public transport, and traffic signals) and depends on several factors (e.g., weather, mass events, road works etc.). Therefore, it involves big data-intensive scenarios, where the capability to detect multiple complex events, is a necessity to recognise and react on situations that may jeopardise the health of the deployment topology and eventually the quality of service of the target application. This involves the real-time analysis of huge amount of data coming from various sources that represented application fragments that undertake data intensive traffic simulations. To be more specific, our proposed framework can be used to run simulations with different input settings (e.g. traffic control settings) and produce output, such as congestion, travel times, average speeds and total waiting times. So, it may be used to evaluate a large number of traffic control settings, e.g. traffic signal settings or make decisions on the construction of new roads, bridges etc.

In this illustrative example, the complex event patterns deployed, use raw monitoring events coming from the traffic simulating sensors (i.e. RawExecutionTime, SimulationLeftNumber, RemainingSimulationTimeMetric and TotalCores events). The complex events patterns required for monitoring the application and making reconfiguration decision based on its current status, involve complex function such as the *percentile* and the *floor* functions which use specific time windows and specific output rates. To be more specific, time batch windows have been used, instead of simple sliding windows in order to be more efficient in resources consumption and offer a stable operation. These time batch windows buffer events and release them every specified time interval in one update. The complex event processing rules which have been used are the following:

- MinimumCores event expressed as: *Ceil(SimulationLeftNumber/floor(Remaining SimulationTimeMetric/ETPercentile))*
- SimulationNotFinishOnTime scaling event expressed as: *(ceil(SimulationLeft Number/TotalCores) * ETPercentile) - RemainingSimulatioTimeMetric*

5 Evaluation

The testbed used for the Vehicle Traffic Simulation scenario includes 3 VMs in a private cloud infrastructure (using Openstack) and a Windows 10 PC. Each of the VMs has 64-bit CPUs with 20 GB of disk and 4 GB of RAM and comes with Ubuntu 16 operating system. The following components were used for this evaluation: (1) an events generator capable to publish events in a configurable rate; (2) the DCEP Agent and (3) the evaluation monitoring tool. The event generator has been placed on the VM hosted in the Windows machine and corresponds to a specific Mule Application, developed based on the Quartz[1] module, which supports the scheduling of programmatic events.

For this evaluation scenario we have measured the RAM and CPU usage on the machines that hosted the DCEP agents for a number of incoming event rates. Specifically for our evaluation scenarios, we have used 500 events/sec and 1000 events/sec, corresponding to the RawExecutionTime events of the Vehicle Traffic Simulation scenario. The other events i.e. SimulationLeftNumber, RemainingSimulationTimeMetric and TotalCores generated by the Simulation Manager (the big data-intensive application) have smaller rates i.e. 100 events/sec etc. The measurements for the CPU and RAM usage are depicted in Fig. 4 for a period of 10 min.

Based on these results, we notice that our DCEP approach presents a stable memory consumption of around 30% which abides with what was discussed in the previous section for the use of time batch windows of rules, without any major fluctuations, while the CPU usage doesn't exceed 36%. The latter seems even more improved as the number of events per second increase, a fact that denotes good queuing capabilities. Peaks being observed during the first two minutes of operation, both in Memory usage and CPU usage graphs, are expectable since the JVM (used in Mule application) requires a (warm-up) period of execution to provide the best performance results. In our tests, this performance is usually achieved after about 5 min of operation. An important advantage of the implementation of the proposed DCEP system is the use of complex event processing technologies that enable the transparent join of two or more streams and the use of complex mathematical formulas that may result in (highly) complex event pattern rules. In the Vehicle Traffic Simulation scenario, several events of various topics were used and joined in order to detect and emit a final scaling event, called SimulationNotFinishOnTime. This has been achieved by utilizing user defined functions on the definition of patterns and calculation of complex formulas (e.g. percentile function).

6 Conclusions

In this paper, we presented a three level distributed architecture for monitoring big data intensive applications deployed over multicloud resources. The conceptual architectural design was discussed along with the implementation details and technological

---

[1] https://docs.mulesoft.com/mule-user-guide/v/3.6/quartz-connector.

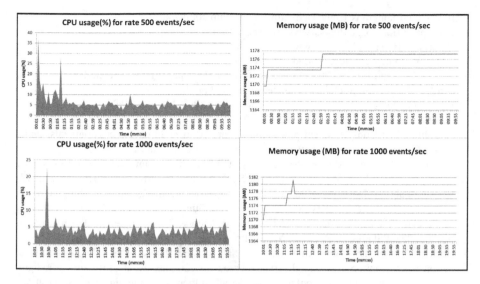

Fig. 4. Evaluation results

decisions. Furthermore, we used an illustrative scenario in order to present and evaluate the main benefits of this approach. The preliminary evaluation revealed adequate processing and memory consumptions levels that will be further compared, in the future, against other prominent complex event processing solutions. In addition, this work will continue in terms of integrating such an approach with a holistic platform that will be able to manage the complete lifecycle of multicloud applications and their processed data. The role of this solution will be to adequately monitor the health status of the application, in order to maintain a constantly optimised deployment of all the application components, over heterogeneous VMs that span the boundaries of several cloud providers.

Acknowledgements. The research leading to these results has received funding from the European Union's Horizon 2020 research and innovation programme under grant agreement No. 731664. The authors would like to thank the partners of the MELODIC project (http://www.melodic.cloud/) for their valuable advices and comments.

References

1. Zanoon, N., Al-Haj, A., Khwaldeh, S.: Cloud computing and big data is there a relation between the two: a study. Int. J. Appl. Eng. Res. **12**(17), 6970–6982 (2017)
2. Hashema, I., Yaqoob, I., Anuar, N., Gani, A., Khan, S.: The rise of "big data" on cloud computing: review and open research issues. J. Inf. Syst. **47**, 98–115 (2015)
3. Martinez, G., Bote, M., Gómez-Sánchez, E., Cano-Parra, R.: Cloud computing and education. J. Comput. Educ. **80**(C), 132–151 (2015)
4. Amazon Web Services Homepage. https://aws.amazon.com/
5. Hewllet Packard Homepage. https://www.hpe.com/emea_europe/en/solutions/cloud.html

6. IBM Cloud Solutions Homepage. https://www.ibm.com/cloud/
7. Rackspace Homepage. https://www.rackspace.com/
8. Openstack Homepage. https://www.openstack.org/
9. VMware Homepage. https://cloud.vmware.com/
10. The Multi-Cloud Future: Challenges and Benefits Homepage. https://technodrone.blogspot.com/2014/03/the-multi-cloud-future-challenges-and.html
11. Etzion, O., Niblett, P.: Event Processing in Action (20). Manning Publications Company, Greenwich (2010)
12. Higashino, W.: Complex event processing as service in multi-clouds environments. Ph.D. thesis. Univerity of Western Ontario, Department of ECE, Canada (2016)
13. Cugola, G., Margara, Al.: Processing flows of information: from data stream to complex event processing. J. ACM Comput. Surv. (CSUR) **44**(issue 3, article 15), 15:1–15:62 (2012)
14. Boubeta-Puig, J., Ortiz, G., Medina-Bulo, I.: Approaching the Internet of Things through Integrating SOA and complex event processing. In: Sun, Z., Yearwood, J. (eds.) Handbook of Research on Demand-Driven Web Services: Theory, Technologies, and Applications, pp. 304–323. IGI Global, Hershey (2014). https://doi.org/10.4018/978-1-4666-5884-4.ch014
15. Leitner, P., Inzinger, C., Hummer, W., Satzger, B., Dustdar, S.: Application-level performance monitoring of cloud services based on complex event processing paradigm. In: 5th IEEE International Conference on Service-Oriented Computing and Applications (SOCA) (2012)
16. Hirzel, M.: Partition and compose: parallel complex event processing. In: DEBS 2012 - Proceedings of the 6th ACM International Conference on Distributed Event-Based Systems, Berlin, Germany, pp. 191–200. ACM (2012)
17. Ku, T., Long-Zhu, Y., Yuan-Hu, K.: A novel distributed complex event processing for RFID application. In: 2008 Third International Conference on Convergence and Hybrid Information Technology, Busan, South Korea (2008)
18. Paraiso, F., Hermosillo, G., Rouvoy, R., Seinturier, L.: A middleware platform to federate complex event processing. In: 2012 IEEE 16th International Enterprise Distributed Object Computing Conference (EDOC), Beijing, China, pp. 113–122 (2012)
19. Flouris, I., et al.: FERARI: a prototype for complex event processing over streaming multi-cloud platforms. In: DEBS 2016 Proceedings of the 10th ACM International Conference on Distributed and Event-based Systems, Irvine, CA, USA, pp. 348–349 (2016)
20. Seinturier, L., Merle, P., Rouvoy, R., Romero, D., Schiavoni, V., Stefani, J.-B.: A component-based middleware platform for reconfigurable service-oriented architectures. J. Softw. Pract. Exp. (SPE) **42**(5), 559–583 (2012)
21. Schultz-Møller, N., Migliavacca, M., Pietzuch, P.: Distributed complex event processing with query rewriting. In: Proceedings of the Third ACM International Conference on Distributed Event-Based Systems, DEBS 2009, Nashville, Tennessee, USA (2009)
22. Mdhaffar, A., Halima, R., Jmaiel, M., Freisleben, B.: A dynamic complex event processing architecture for cloud monitoring and analysis. In: 2013 IEEE 5th International Conference on Cloud Computing Technology and Science, Bristol, UK (2013)
23. Leitner, P., Hummer, W., Satzger, B., Inzinger, C., Dustdar, S.: CloudScale- a novel middleware for building transparently scaling cloud applications. In: Proceedings of the 27th Annual ACM Symposium on Applied Computing, Trento, Italy, pp. 434–440. ACM (2012)
24. Zeginis, C., Kritikos, K., Plexoudakis, D.: Event pattern discovery for cross-layer adaptation of multi-cloud applications. Int. J. Syst. Serv.-Oriented Eng. 78–103 (2015)
25. Garcia de Prado, A., Ortiz, G., Boubeta-Puig, J.: CARED-SOA: a context-aware event-driven service oriented architecture. IEEE Access J. **5**, 4646–4663 (2017)

26. Garcia de Prado, A., Ortiz, G., Boubeta-Puig, J.: COLLECT: collaborative context-aware service oriented architecture for intelligent decision-making in the Internet of Things. J. Expert Syst. Appl. **85**, 231–248 (2017)
27. Mule Soft Homepage. www.mulesoft.com
28. Rademakers, T., Dirksentt, J.: Open-Source ESBs in Action, 1st edn. Manning, Greenwich (2009)
29. Apache Active MQ Homepage. http://activemq.apache.org/
30. Esper CEP engine Homepage. http://www.espertech.com/esper/

A Multi-level Policy Engine to Manage Identities and Control Accesses in Cloud Computing Environment

Faraz Fatemi Moghaddam[1,2(✉)] ⓘ, Süleyman Berk Çemberci[3],
Philipp Wieder[1], and Ramin Yahyapour[1,2]

[1] Gesellschaft für wissenschaftliche Datenverarbeitung mbH Göttingen
(GWDG), Göttingen, Germany
{faraz.fatemi-moghaddam,philipp.wieder,ramin.
yahyapour}@gwdg.de
[2] Institute of Informatics, Georg-August-Universität, Göttingen, Germany
[3] Systeme, Anwendungen und Produkte in der Datenverarbeitung (SAP),
Walldorf, Germany
suleyman.berk.cemberci@sap.com

Abstract. Security challenges are the most important obstacles for the advancement of IT-based on-demand services and cloud computing as an emerging technology. Lack of coincidence in identity management models based on defined policies and various security levels in different cloud servers is one of the most challenging issues in clouds. In this paper, a policy-based user authentication model has been presented to provide a reliable and scalable identity management and to map cloud users' access requests with defined polices of cloud servers. In the proposed schema several components are provided to define access policies by cloud servers, to apply policies based on a structural and reliable ontology, to manage user identities and to semantically map access requests by cloud users with defined polices.

Keywords: Cloud computing · Security · Policy management
Identity management · Access control

1 Introduction

Cloud security issues are mainly classified to three major categories [1]: data protection in cloud-based data centers, isolated and secure resource provisioning and reliable access control by identity management and authentication procedures [2]. These concerns are the most apparent reasons why most of individuals and businesses still have doubt to delegate management of their sensitive data to cloud service providers as third party collaborates [3]. One of the most challenging security issues in clouds that has led to the appearance of several researches and solutions is to ensure reliable accesses to different cloud servers based on various policies in each server. In fact, service providers needs to manage access requests and map them to resources according to defined policies from cloud customers or service providers [4].

K. Kritikos et al. (Eds.): ESOCC 2018, LNCS 11116, pp. 120–129, 2018.
https://doi.org/10.1007/978-3-319-99819-0_9

Using a federated identity management schema is the most popular solution for managing accesses to different cloud servers with single identity. In recent years most cloud services have adopted OpenID [5] or Shibboleth [6] as the most independent and flexible authentication and identity management models in cloud-based platforms. The proliferation of these identity federations has allowed cloud users belonging to one network (known as home organization) to access the services provided by other networks (known as remote organizations), all members of the same federation [7]. Therefore, there isn't any necessity for cloud users to re-introduce their credentials for each access in different cloud servers. The most important characteristic of identity management models is to provide a framework with fast-authentication mechanisms [8], low access time and reduced authentication data exchanges between different service access requests [9]. Although the establishment of multiple security mechanisms in each node enhance the security of resources and reduces considerable processing power for manipulating sensitive and also non-sensitive data [10], the authentication data exchange and access time for cloud users in identity management models are also affected. In particular, two important concerns in cloud-based identity management models are still challenging:

- Managing defined policies in different virtualized nodes according to capabilities of service providers, requirements of resource owner and constraints.
- Mapping access requests to cloud-servers based on established security mechanisms and defined policies of each node.

In this paper, a policy-based user authentication model is presented to provide a reliable identity management mechanism for establishing multiple access policies in different virtualized nodes and mapping access requests to defined policies accordingly capabilities of cloud servers and requirements of resources.

2   Problem Description

As described in previous section, the main aim of proposed model is to manage identities based on defined policies in cloud servers. Each virtualized node in cloud-based data center is associated with set of policies. These polices are classified in several protocols according to Protection Ontology [11]. The classification of security policies are based on three main parts: Resource Protection (including cryptography and key management policies), Confidential Transport (including signature and transport policies) and Identity Management (including authentication and access control policies). The latter, which is the focus of this work, refers to the capabilities that are provided to ensure the reliable access mapping between requests and policies by managing identities based on capabilities of service provider and requirements of cloud users.

Assume that there are N virtualized node (server) in the cloud-based data center, denoted as $\{S_1, S_2, \ldots, S_N\}$, and the current authentication policy set of node S_n with $s \in \{1, 2, \ldots, N\}$ is $P(S_n) = \{p_1, p_2, \ldots, p_M\}$. Given I registered users' access requests waiting to be processed, denoted as $\{U_1, U_2, \ldots, U_I\}$, and each U_i is associated with specific identity set (authentication and authorization set):

$$AA(U_i) = \left\{ \begin{array}{l} ID_i, h(PW_i), (h(ID_i) \oplus h(PW_i)), (AP_1, h(AR_1), (h(AP_1) \oplus h(AR_1)))_i, \ldots, \\ (AP_j, h(AR_j), (h(AP_j) \oplus h(AR_j)))_i \end{array} \right\}$$

where ID, PW, AP and AR are user ID, user basic password, access policy and access response respectively. There are several authentication and authorization (access) policies that are defined for each node to enhance the security level of the node in comparison between other nodes. The authentication policies are focus on confidentiality and integrity of resources, while the authorization policies are based on privacy and access management features of cloud resources. To provide a semantic mapping between requests and policies, each of authentication and authorization policies of a specific node need to be evaluated according to the characteristic of cloud user. The objective of suggested model is to map elements of the policy set for each node to appointed access responses for cloud users to provide decisive access permit. For instance, consider a cloud provider with different services (*e.g.* storage, platform, software, *etc.*) and each service has dedicated security policies (*e.g.* two factor authentication for storage and one-time single pass for software). The main problem is to address the process of mapping security requirements of these cloud services to defined authentication and authorization capabilities of the cloud user in identity set. Overall, the access request of specific node is granted if and only if the following equation is applied to the request:

$$\forall p_i \in P(S_n) : (\exists (AP_j, AR_j)_i : \{(p_i = (AP_j)_i) \wedge ((AR_j)_i = true)\}) \tag{1}$$

In fact, cloud user needs to provide additional authorization and authentication capabilities for nodes with higher security policies. The proposed model tries to manage access requests and map between access policies and authentication capabilities of cloud users.

3   Proposed Schema

Using an agent-based authentication model [12] to send access requests, to search on policy queues and to match access requests to a specific defined policy may seem like a plausible solution for achieving the goal. However, this agent-based authentication process in not scalable and takes lots of processing power to map between requirements and capabilities. Thus, the design of our proposed model is based on a different manner. Our schema uses a framework with several components to define, store, check and match policies with identity details. Figure 1 shows the overall architecture of our model.

3.1   Policy Engine

The main duty of Policy Engine is to define and generate authentication and authorization policies based on the structural Protection Ontology [10] for cloud customers according to security requirements. Protection Ontology is a policy language based on

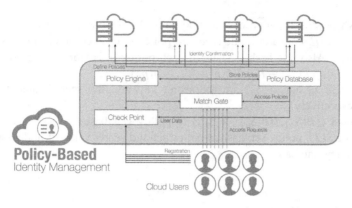

Fig. 1. Architecture of policy-based identity management

WS-Policy [13] as a recommended W3C [23] language for defining various security levels in cloud-based environments. Protection ontology classifies security algorithms to three main levels: Protocol, Mechanism and Algorithm. In the proposed model authentication and authorization capabilities of service provider are offered according to this classification. This structural classification helps to apply different security mechanisms to virtualized nodes and creates security levels based on requirements of cloud users and sensitivity of resources. Each of the offered algorithms is associated to a structural semantic resource for security level establishment according to the concepts of WS-Policy and Protection Ontology. A security-based SLA is the output of security ring (level) establishment and is defined as Security Level Certificate (SLC).

As described the main duty of policy engine is to define and generate authentication and authorization policies for different virtualized nodes according to the sensitivity of nodes and capabilities of service provider. The process of policy application is done by policy engine based on generated SLC as follows:

Step 1.   Policy engine sends SLC ID to node n to apply policies of SLC to the node.
Step 2.   According to the associated SLC, node n calls semantic resources of SLC to create $P(S_n)$.

$$for \left(i = 0 \ to \ \sum_{\alpha=0}^{R} (rdf : Algorithm)_\alpha \right)$$

$$\left\{ \begin{array}{c} p_i = (p_i \ \| \ add(SP_\mu)) \\ X(p_i) = h(p_i) \\ HP(S_n) = add(X(p_i)) \end{array} \right\}$$

where R is the total of semantic algorithm resources and $\mu = \sum_{\varepsilon=0}^{Count(HLSP)}$ $(rdf : HLSP)_\varepsilon$ are the defined sub-policies for each algorithm based on the SLC. Also, the hashed value of each policy p_i is stored in the set $HP(S_n)$.

Step 3. $X(S_n) = h(x_n) \oplus h(p_1) \oplus h(p_2)\ldots \oplus h(p_n)$
where x_n and $X(S_n)$ are the secret key and the secret value for node n respectively.

Step 4.   Send $\{(P(S_n), HP(S_n)), X(S_n)\}$ to Policy Database.
The SLC, policy set, hashed policy set and secret value of node n are sent to policy database.

3.2   Policy Check-Point

The check point component creates, updates and manages identities for accessing to different nodes. Identities are defined in registration phase, updated in checking phase and managed in access control phase. In recent years, two types of registration progresses are performed in web-based models:

- Normal Registration: The creation of personal identity within cloud provider with User ID, Password and other personal details.
- 3rd-Party Registration: Using identities in social media or other providers.

During the registration phase by each of these models, an Identity set (Authentication and Authorization) object $AA(U_i)$ is created from identity set class for user U_i. The basic identity set with the lowest identity details is associated with the ID and password:

$$I(U_i) = \{ID_i, h(PW_i), (h(ID_i) \oplus h(PW_i))\}$$

By the basic identity set, cloud users can access to the nodes with the lowest security level in cloud environment. However, three types of authentication and authorization access policies need to be defined and added to the identity set based on polices and capabilities of service provider:

- User Access Policies (UAP): These types of policies are defined by cloud users according to capabilities of cloud provider. For instance, cloud user can establish second password with an authenticator application or email.
- Cloud Access Policies (CAP): These types of policies are awarded to cloud users by the provider or admin after an identity validation (e.g. RBAC in a university).
- Temporary Access Policies (TAP): These types of policies are based on dynamic parameters such as location, hardware and time.

An access policy is defined in identity set according to the characteristics of policy by a triplex set as follows:

$$\left(AP_j, h(AR_j), \left(h(AP_j) \oplus h(AR_j)\right)\right)_i$$

where AP_j and AR_j refer to semantic resource access policy (*e.g.* two factor authentication by Email) and access responses (*e.g.* confirmed email address) respectively. Therefore, the authentication set for U_i are updated based on defined UAP, CAP and TAPs as:

$$AA(U_i) = \left\{ \begin{array}{c} ID_i, h(PW_i), (h(ID_i) \oplus h(PW_i)), (AP_1, h(AR_1), (h(AP_1) \oplus h(AR_1)))_i, \ldots, \\ (AP_j, h(AR_j), (h(AP_j) \oplus h(AR_j)))_i \end{array} \right\}$$

3.3 Policy Match-Gate

The proposed identity management model for mapping accesses requests to defined policies is based on the performance of policy match gate. Given I registered users' access requests waiting to be processed, denoted as $\{U_1, U_2, \ldots, U_I\}$, and each U_i is associated with a specific authentication set $AA(U_i)$. The main aim of Match Gate is to process access requests and to map between these requests and defined polices for each node according to the identity set. To provide an efficient policy mapping algorithm, a session class is defined by policy match gate for creation of access session objects according to the capabilities of cloud users. The objects from this class (*AccessSession* class) use several security functions and parameters to ensure about the reliable mapping between capabilities and security policies. After the registration phase in the check point component, cloud users are able to sign in to cloud computing environment by their basic internal or external login information. A successful basic login lets the policy match gate to create a session object from the access session class for basic or additional security checking. The process of using this object for identity management is in number of steps as follows:

Step 1. An object is created from *AccessSession* class with basic parameters.

$$AccessSession\, ASU_i = new\, AccessSession(ID_i, h(PW_i), TS, (h(ID_i) \oplus h(PW_i)), TK_i, e)$$

where TK_i is a basic token for U_i and is valid if login details are matched with $A(U_i)$ and e is a Boolean property that shows the status of TK_i whether is enabled or disabled.

Step 2. The basic value of TK_i after the first login lets the cloud user to access basic nodes with lowest security level. In this level policy match gate checks if ΔTS and e are still valid, the access of cloud user to the root nodes are granted. The basic value of TK_i is calculated as follows:

$$TK_i = (h(h(ID_i \parallel TS) \oplus h(PW_i)))$$

Step 3. When the cloud user requests for accessing to basic nodes, the match gate calculates Node Access Request (*NAR*) as follows:

$$if\ ((e = true) \wedge (\Delta TS = Valid))\ then\ \{NAR_{(i,n)} = (TK_i, Enc(TK_i, x_n))\}$$

where *Enc* is AES-256 func. with the secret key for node *n*. The checking phase confirms the user identity and the value of *NAR* is sent from match gate to requested node.

Step 4. Server *n* receives the request from Match Gate and access is granted if the difference between timestamps and the following equation is valid:

$$if\ ((\Delta TS = Valid) \wedge (TK_i = Dec(TK_i, x_n)))\ then\ Access\ is\ Granted$$

This calculation helps to check if the secret key of node *n* is still valid or not. In fact, the validated identity from match gate can access to request node if the secret value of node is valid. If the validity of the equation is not confirmed, Match Gate should update the secret key of server *n* in database.

Step 5. If the cloud user requests for accessing to nodes with the defined security policies and higher privacy levels, further identity details are requested from Match Gate based on the defined policies. Thus, Match Gate checks $P(S_n)$ from policy database and asks U_i if UAP or TAP policies are needed for authentication and authorization checking. Also, the user database is checked by Match Gate for CAP policies for only authorization checking if needed. Each of the requested access details should be provided by the cloud user (*i.e.* UAP and TAP) or the user database (*i.e.* CAP) and ASU_i is updated according to the provided details:

$$ASU_i.AddAccessCapability(AP_1, h(AR_1), (h(AP_1) \oplus h(AR_1)), AST_1);$$
$$ASU_i.AddAccessCapability(AP_2, h(AR_2), (h(AP_2) \oplus h(AR_2)), AST_2);$$
$$\vdots$$
$$ASU_i.AddAccessCapability(AP_j, h(AR_j), (h(AP_j) \oplus h(AR_j)), AST_j);$$

where *AST* is the Algorithm Session Time that shows the maximum validity of confirmed access response. For instance, the valid time for confirmed second password is longer that 1-time password. By each of the additional identity details the value of TK_i is updated as follows:

$$TK_i = TK_i \oplus (h(AP_j \| TS) \oplus h(AR_j))$$

Step 6. After updating the value of Tk_i and confirming the identity of cloud user by additional identity request and according to the capabilities of user, the match gate sends server access requests to the requested node as follows:

$$X'(S_n) = (h(x_n) \oplus h(AP_1) \oplus h(AP_2)\ldots \oplus h(AP_j))$$

$$if \ ((e = true) \wedge (\Delta TS = Valid)) \ then \ \{NAR_{(i,n)} = (TK_i, Enc(TK_i, x_n), h(X'(S_n)), TS')\}$$

Step 7. Server n receives the request from Match Gate and access is granted if the ΔTS and the following equations are valid:

$$if \ ((\Delta TS = Valid)) \wedge (TK_i = Dec(TK_i, x_n)) \wedge (h(X(S_n)) = h(X'(S_n)))) \ then \ Access \ is \ Granted$$

This calculation checks the validity of timestamp, the validity of secret key and finally the confirmed application and mapping process of defined policies by checking the validity of secret value.

Step 8. If the user requests to access to a node with common policies that were confirmed by match gate before and the Algorithm Session Time for the access response is still valid for the policy, just un-checked policies are evaluated and the is no necessity to re-check previous policies. In fact, every functions and properties of ASU_i are confirmed and stay reusable until the algorithm session time for that authentication or authorization algorithm is still valid. For instance, the session time for double authentication is less than single authentication and U_i needs to be double-authenticated again after the session time for double authentication is over while the session time for basic authentication is still valid. Also, re-authentication for some authorization access policies (*e.g.* Geographical or Software authenticators) or One-Time passwords need to be checked periodically or continuously. These valid session times are defined as sub-policies in the ring establishment stage based on Protection Ontology [11].

4 Discussion and Conclusion

In order to incarnate the superiorities of this schema in cloud-based environments, we give a performance analysis of the proposed model in this section. In this experiment the performance of match gate in different types of workloads was evaluated. Accordingly, the total process time for processing 500 access requests to VMs with high secure VMs with more authentication and authorization policies was examined in the first step. The aim of this case study is to examine the effects of static, continuously changing, dramatic increase and predictable increase workloads on the performance of match gate task management. The experiment was in 6 rounds based on different types of workloads. Figure 2 shows the results in details. In the static workload, the number of user accesses was same in all rounds. However, the total processing time was decreased slightly due to the common policies in different VMs. Thus, there was not any necessity to re-check common policies. As expected, in the dramatic increase of users requests, the total processing time was risen dramatically and in the respective rounds the total processing time was reduced considerably to the normal range. This change was less in predictable change due to the predictable scheduling in associated task processing. Finally, the rate of change in continuously increase of requests is significantly slight. That was because two different effects: increase due to the number of requests and decrease due to the common policies in different VMs. Overall, the results show the performance of match gate task management for semantic mapping of access polices to request was scalable enough in different types of workloads.

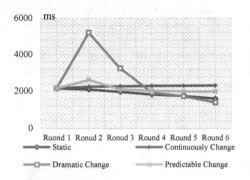 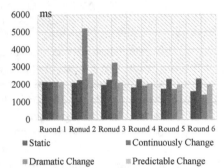

Fig. 2. Effects of different workload on the performance of match gate task management

Acknowledgement. This research has been supported by CleanSky project (No. 607584) funded by the Marie-Curie-Actions within the 7th Framework Program of the European Union (EU FP7).

References

1. Fatemi Moghaddam, F., Ahmadi, M., Sarvari, S., Eslami, M., Golkar, A.: Cloud computing challenges and opportunities: a survey. In: 1st International Conference on Telematics and Future Generation Networks (TAFGEN), pp. 34–38 (2015)
2. Sadiku, M.N.O., Musa, S.M., Momoh, O.D.: Cloud computing: opportunities and challenges. IEEE Potentials **33**(1), 34–36 (2014)
3. Wang, C., Ren, K., Lou, W., Li, J.: Toward publicly auditable secure cloud data storage services. IEEE Netw. **24**(4), 19–24 (2010)
4. Coppolino, L., D'Antonio, S., Mazzeo, G., Romano, L.: Cloud security: emerging threats and current solutions. Comput. Electr. Eng. **59**, 126–140 (2017)
5. Recordon, D., Reed, D.: OpenID 2.0: a platform for user-centric identity management. In: Proceedings of the Second ACM Workshop on Digital Identity Management - DIM 2006, p. 11 (2006)
6. Morgan, R.L., Cantor, S., Carmody, S., Hoehn, W., Klingenstein, K.: Federated security: the Shibboleth approach. Educ. Q. **27**(4), 12–17 (2004)
7. Pérez Méndez, A., Marín López, R., López Millán, G.: Providing efficient SSO to cloud service access in AAA-based identity federations. Futur. Gener. Comput. Syst. **58**, 13–28 (2016)
8. de Carvalho, C.A.B., de Castro Andrade, R.M., de Castro, M.F., Coutinho, E.F., Agoulmine, N.: State of the art and challenges of security SLA for cloud computing. Comput. Electr. Eng. **59**, 141–152 (2017)
9. Liu, Z., Yan, H., Li, Z.: Server-aided anonymous attribute-based authentication in cloud computing. Futur. Gener. Comput. Syst. **52**, 61–66 (2015)

10. Fatemi Moghaddam, F., Wieder, P., Yahyapour, R.: Policy Engine as a Service (PEaaS): an approach to a reliable policy management framework in cloud computing environments. In: IEEE 4th International Conference on Future Internet of Things and Cloud (FiCloud), pp. 137–144 (2016)
11. Fatemi Moghaddam, F.: Multi-layered policy generation and management in clouds. University of Göttingen (2018)
12. Hajivali, M., Fatemi Moghaddam, F., Alrashdan, M.T., Alothmani, A.Z.M.: Applying an agent-based user authentication and access control model for cloud servers. In: International Conference on ICT Convergence (ICTC), pp. 807–812 (2013)
13. Bajaj, S., Box, D., Chappell, D., Curbera, F., Daniels, G., Hallam-Baker, P., Hondo, M., Kaler, C., Langworthy, D., Malhotra, A.: Web Services Policy Framework (WS-Policy). Specif. IBM, BEA, Microsoft, SAP AG, Sonic Software, VeriSign (2004)

A Practical Approach to Services Composition Through Light Semantic Descriptions

Marco Cremaschi[✉] and Flavio De Paoli

Department of Informatics, Systems and Communication,
University of Milan - Bicocca, Viale Sarca 336/14, Milan, Italy
{cremaschi,depaoli}@disco.unimib.it

Abstract. Services composition has been much investigated over the last decade without reaching shared and consolidated results mainly for the lack of interoperable descriptions of services and the consequent need of extensive user intervention. In this paper, we propose a light and practical approach to create machine-readable descriptions of output data that can be merged or used (as-is or adapted) as input data to other services. The solution relies on the popular and standard OpenAPI descriptions augmented with annotations based on JSON-LD format. Services descriptions are created by table annotations techniques applied on sets of given or retrieved output values. The approach has been implemented in a tool and validated with a set of real services.

1 Introduction

In the last decade, we have witnessed the evolution of web services models from the WSDL/SOAP to the REST. This change is tangibly visible, for example, by searching ProgrammableWeb[1], perhaps the largest repository of web descriptions. One of the reasons for this evolution is the need to simplify the service reference model to enhance comprehensibility and standardisation, and therefore provide the bases for automatic management of descriptions and composition. A similar evolution is needed in the realm of semantic web services. As a matter of facts, well-defined proposals that deliver machine-readable descriptions, such as OWL-S: Semantic Markup for Web Services [10], Semantic Annotation for WSDL and XML Schema (SA-WSDL) [7], Micro Web Service Model Ontology (MicroWSMO) [6] and Semantic Annotations for REST (SA-REST) [5], failed to become widely used mainly for their complexity that requires the involvement of experts.

The work presented in this paper has been partially supported by the EU H2020 project EW-Shopp - Supporting Event and Weather-based Data Analytics and Marketing along the Shopper Journey - Grant n. 732590.

[1] https://www.programmableweb.com/apis/directory.

Current description models address services accessible through API REST, and provide meta-languages to describe services as documents based on *property-value* pairs. OpenAPI Specification[2], also known as Swagger[3], API Blueprint[4] and RAML[5] are the most representative. However, these models do not support semantic annotations to make *property-value* pairs interoperable. In this paper, we discuss an extension of the popular OpenAPI model to add semantic annotations on input parameters and output properties of services. Such annotations are compliant with the JSON-LD[6] format to follow the REST philosophy in order to minimise the user involvement in many practical situations.

The availability of semantic descriptions of APIs enables the development of automatic techniques and tools to support services composition [13]. A general definition states that a process of composition is defined as the aggregation of different Web services into a single compound service to perform more complex functions [14]. In this context, we refer to information services and the mash-up of *results* got from independent services to deliver comprehensive answers to users' requests, or to prepare data coming from a set of services to invoke another service. We call the former *merge composition* and the latter *sequence composition*. Merge composition involves more services that are invoked in parallel with the same input data, whose answers are then composed. Sequence composition involves a service which is invoked with input data coming from the composition of answers from one (adaptation) or more (mash-up) services. This work roots and extends the one presented in [3,8] by proposing a formalised model to create semantic descriptions for Web APIs, and a set of composition rules based on semantic annotations inside the descriptions. Moreover, we implemented the AutomAPIc tool to support users in the creation and composition of semantic descriptions.

Services composition may occur at design time or at runtime. At design time, the ability of automatic processing of descriptions enables actors (users or machines) to discover, select and compose services. If semantic descriptions are not available, actors can rely on techniques, such as table interpretation and NLP techniques, to build such missing descriptions. At runtime, composition supports adaptation and substitution of services to ensure contextualization and accomplishment of tasks.

In the next section, we discuss services description and composition to motivate the work. Then, Sect. 3 describes the proposed extension of the OpenAPI model to include semantic annotations. Section 4 discusses the composition techniques in the split and sequence cases. Section 5 presents the tool that provides full support to users to manage the process of building descriptions and composing services. Section 6 validates the approach by addressing a set of real services. Finally, Sect. 7 draws some conclusions.

---

[2] https://www.openapis.org.
[3] http://swagger.io.
[4] https://apiblueprint.org.
[5] http://raml.org.
[6] https://json-ld.org.

2   Services Description and Composition

In the last decade, the composition of services has been widely investigated without getting to effective results for many reasons. Among others, the most relevant are the use of different architectural styles, the unexpected evolution of services, and the use of different description languages and different conceptual models [12]. Moreover, composition may occur at the design stage, leading to *static* compositions, or at runtime, leading to *dynamic* composition. The latter is best suited to address the issues in real environments that change continuously and requires automatic tools to search for, select and compose Web services automatically. The main issue affecting automatic composition is the limited number of available machine-readable descriptions associated with services.

A traditional way to compose services is the use of orchestration languages, such as BPEL (Business Process Execution Language) [16] or OWL-S (Ontology Web Language for Services) [10], which support the manual definition of abstract processes that can be implemented by actual services. On the other side, dynamic composition in *automatic* way can be achieved by exploiting the semantic Web and the planning techniques. However, the realisation of a completely automatic composition process is complex and presents several issues [14]. The main problems are the missing of semantics associated with services, and the capability of understanding the semantics even when present.

The most popular syntactic description model is WSDL 2.0 (Web Services Description Language) [1], which defines an XML format for describing Web services by separating the abstract functionality offered by a service from concrete details such as how and where that functionality is offered. Although it supports descriptions of both SOAP-based services, and REST/API services, it is the de-facto standard for the former but is rarely adopted for the latter. The Web Application Description Language (WADL) is a machine-readable XML format that was explicitly proposed for API services. WADL was also proposed for standardisation, but there was no follow-up.

Recently, *user-friendly* and *easy-to-use* metadata formats have been introduced, along with editors to support developers in the creation of descriptions for REST APIs. Among others, popular description formats are the Open API Specification, which provides human-readable API descriptions based on YAML and JSON. RAML is a YAML-based language for describing RESTful APIs. API Blueprint is a documentation-oriented web API description language, which provides a set of semantic assumptions laid on top of the Markdown syntax. The Hydra specification, which is currently under massive development, aims to enrich current web APIs with tools and techniques from the semantic web area.

Table 1 is an extension of the one presented in [15] to compare the number of questions posed in Stack Overflow and the number of Git stars (showing appreciation to a project) received by the four description models under study. The increasing number of available descriptions highlights the growing popularity of descriptions, and the relevance of tools that support the creation, publication, use and maintenance of service descriptions. The common limitation of such models is the lack of semantic descriptions, which motivated our previous

Table 1. Comparison of API description models (at May 27, 2018).

Detail/Model		API Blueprint	RAML	WADL	OpenAPI Spec
Format		Markdown	YAML	XML	YAML, JSON
Licence		MIT	ASL2.0	Sun	ASL 2.0
Version		Format 1A revision 9	1.0.1	31 August 2009	3.0.1
Initial commit		Apr 2013	Sep 2013	Nov 2006	Jul 2011
Pricing plan		Yes	Yes	No	No
StackOverflow Questions	2015	88	153	86	13
	2016	61	168	84	166
	2017	40	174	74	319
	2018	15	56	33	218
Github Starsub Stars	2015	1,819	1,058	N/A	2,459
	2016	X	X		X
	2017	5,390	2,735		6,360
	2018	6566	3060		9836
Google Search		985K	1M	486K	8M

paper [3]. In order to be effective, we extended the most popular model, Ope-nAPI, to support semantic-enabled tools for describing, discovering, and then compose APIs.

3 A Light Semantic Web API Description Model

The OpenAPI is the most promising description model since it defines a simple format to specify descriptions supported by a broad set of vendor-neutral API tools, whose development involves a massive community of active users. Such tools provide significant support to almost every modern programming languages to create and test APIs. Moreover, the OpenAPI Initiative is an open source project sustained by relevant stakeholders, including Google, IBM, Microsoft and PayPal. There are several repositories collecting API REST described using OpenAPI, such as *SmartAPI*[7] and *APIs.guru*[8].

An OpenAPI description is a YAML or JSON document that contains a list of resources and a list of operations that can be applied to those resources. An example is provided in Listing 1.1, which describes the Google Books API. Notice that the API is described by *name:value* pairs of strings without any semantics.

We propose to extend such descriptions by inserting annotations (i.e., links to ontology classes and ontology properties) through the use of the JSON-LD[9] format. JSON-LD provides (i) a universal identification mechanism for JSON objects through the use of Internationalized Resource Identifiers (IRIs); (ii) a way to disambiguate shared keys between different JSON documents through IRIs mapping and context; (iii) the possibility to annotate the strings with indications

---

[7] http://smart-api.info/registry.

[8] https://apis.guru/openapi-directory/.

[9] https://json-ld.org/spec/latest/json-ld/#basic-concepts.

on the used language; and (iv) a way to associate data types with values (e.g., dates, times, etc.).

Listing 1.1. OpenAPI description of the Google Books API.

```
1   "paths": {
2   "/volumes": {
3       "get": {
4           "parameters": [{
5               "name": "title", [...]
6           }],
7       },
8       "responses": {
9           "200": {
10              "schema": {
11                  "title": "result",
12                  "type": "object",
13                  "properties": {
14                      "isbn": { "type": "string"},
15                      "author": { "type": "string" },
16                      "title": { "type": "string" }, [...]
```

The marriage between JSON-LD and OpenAPI descriptions occurs through the introduction of the *semanticAnnotations* property (e.g., Listing 1.2, line 8 and 27), which is composed of two parts: the definition of a context, by the keyword *@context* (e.g., line 9 and 28), to set short names for the reference ontologies used throughout the description; and a list of annotations for parameters (input values) and responses (output values). Each annotation is a pair to annotate the *name*, introduced by the keyword *@id* (e.g., line 14 and 33), and the *value*, introduced by the keyword *@type* (e.g., line 15 and 34). Annotations are IRIs that uniquely identify elements.

Listing 1.2. Semantic OpenAPI description of the Google Books API.

```
1   "basePath": "/books/v1",
2   "paths": {
3   "/volumes": {
4       "get": {
5           "parameters": [{
6               "name": "title", [...]
7           }],
8           "semanticAnnotations": {  /** Input semantics **/
9               "@context": {{
10                  "dbp": "http://dbpedia.org/property/",
11                  "xsd": "http://www.w3.org/2001/XMLSchema#"
12              },
13              "title": {
14                  "@id": "dbp:title",
15                  "@type": "xsd:string"
16              }
17          },
18          "responses": {
19              "200": {
20                  "schema": {
21                      "type": "object",
22                      "properties": {
23                          "isbn": { "type": "string" },
24                          "author": { "type": "string" },
25                          "title": { "type": "string" }
26                      },
27                      "semanticAnnotations":{  /** Output semantics **/
28                          "@context": {
29                              "dbp": "http://dbpedia.org/property/",
30                              "xsd": "http://www.w3.org/2001/XMLSchema#"
31                          },
32                          "isbn": {
33                              "@id": "dbp:isbn",
34                              "@type": "xsd:integer"
35                          },
36                          "author": {
37                              "@id": "dbp:author",
38                              "@type": "xsd:string"
```

```
39        },
40        "title": {
41            "@id": "dbp:title",
42            "@type": "xsd:string"
43        }, [...]
```

4   Composition Types and Rules

In this context, we consider the composition of information services and interested in mashing up results from independent services to deliver a comprehensive answer to users' requests, or to prepare data coming from a set of services to invoke another service. We call the former *merge composition* and the latter *sequence composition*. Merge composition involves more services that are invoked in parallel with the same input data, and the results are composed [11]; while sequence composition involves a service which is invoked with input data that are coming from one (data adaptation) or more (data mash-up) services.

Dealing with automatic *sequence composition*, semantic compatibility needs to be verified. In this context, semantic compatibility occurs when a semantic relationship holds between the semantic classes[10] of output properties of an API and input parameters of another API. In such cases, output properties can be used as input parameters, possibly after some transformations (Fig. 1).

Fig. 1. Schema of sequence composition.

To evaluate semantic compatibility, we can define four rules:

Rule 1: single ontology, same concepts. If annotations refer to the same ontology, and name/value pairs refer to the same concept, or two concepts in relation *owl:sameAs*, then the composition is straightforward since they are compatible (see Fig. 2(1)).

Rule 2: different ontologies, same concepts. If annotations refer to different ontologies (see Fig. 2(2)), we need to verify if the annotations of involved name/value pairs are *equivalent* (i.e., they refer to the same ontology concepts or property). For example, some ontologies such as DBPedia[11] and Wikidata[12] provide the properties *owl:equivalentProperty* and *owl:equivalentClass* to address the issue. These properties, however, are not supported by all ontologies, therefore some *Ontology matching* [4] techniques may need to be exploited to check for compatibility.

---

[10] https://www.w3.org/TR/owl2-syntax/#Classes.
[11] https://dbpedia.org.
[12] https://www.wikidata.org.

Rule 3: single ontology, different concepts in relation to each other.
If annotations refer to the same ontology, and name/value pairs refer to different ontology concepts or properties, then values' compatibility need to be checked. If between the involved concepts relations such as *subclass* and *subproperty* hold, then they may be compatible and the composition may occur. An example is shown in Figure see Fig. 2(3), where the annotation *@type: dbp:zipCode* refers to a subproperty of *dbp:postalCode*. Therefore, API 1 and API 2 are compatible.

Rule 4: different concepts not related to each other. If annotations of the name/value pairs refer to different ontology concepts or properties in the same ontology or different ontologies, and among these elements none of the above rules apply, compatibility may occur after a transformation (e.g., by invoking a third-party service). For example (see Fig. 2(4)), if API 1 returns a mail address, and API 2 requires latitude and longitude values as input parameters, then a third API is needed to perform the conversion.

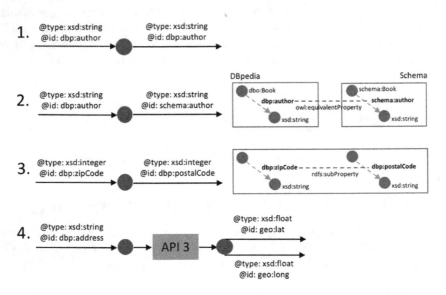

Fig. 2. Sequence composition: examples of the four compatibility cases.

Let's consider a use case to discuss the composition rules described above. Assume we seek an application that helps students to retrieve information to access textbooks. The application should provide information about different options: bookshops or e-commerce purchase, library consultation, or free download. The composition related to this use case is shown in Fig. 3: we consider a process that starts with Google Books API, which gets a title in input and delivers a full report about accessing the requested book in output.

Fig. 3. Example of a process of composition of the use case.

A first example of *sequence* composition type, is the service that collects information about a book from Google Books API[13] and calls Amazon Market API[14] to check if it is available. The Semantic OpenAPI Description of Amazon Market API is in Listing 1.3. The semantic annotation in line 6 finds a correspondence in the description of the Google Books API, in line 33 of Listing 1.2; in both descriptions the concept of *ISBN* is described with the same semantic annotation. Therefore, the services can be composed (rule 1).

Listing 1.3. The input part of the description of the Amazon Market API.

```
1   "get": {
2       "parameters": [{
3           "name": "IsbnItem", [...]
4       }],
5       "semanticAnnotations": {
6           "IsbnItem": {
7               "@id": "dbp:isbn",
8               "@type": "xsd:integer"
9           }, [...]
```

A second example is the sequence composition of the Google Books API, the Library API, and the Google Transit API: first the Library API is invoked to check the presence and availability of the book, and then the Google Transit API is invoked to check the existence of public transport to reach the library.

The composition of Google Books API and the Library API can be performed according to rule 1, and rule 3. The annotations on line 8 and line 16 of Listing 1.4 are compatible with the annotations in line 8 and 16 of Listing 1.2 (rule 1). The parameter on line 12 of Listing 1.4 is compatible with the property present in line 36 of Listing 1.2 since the relation *rdfs:SubPropertyOf* holds between them (rule 3).

Listing 1.4. Extract from the description of the Library API.

```
1   "get": {
2       "parameters": [
3           { "name": "Isbn" },
4           { "name": "author" },
5           { "name": "title" }
6       ],
7       "semanticAnnotations": {
8           "Isbn": {
9               "@id": "dbp:isbn",
10              "@type": "xsd:integer"
11          },
12          "author": {
13              "@id": "dbp:writen",
14              "@type": "xsd:string"
15          },
```

---

[13] https://developers.google.com/books/.

[14] https://developer.amazonservices.it/gp/mws/docs.html.

```
16        "title": {
17            "@id": "dbp:title",
18            "@type": "xsd:string"
19        }, [...]
```

The composition between the Library API and the Google Transit API cannot be performed directly because the first API returns the mail address of a library in text format, while the Google Transit API gets geographic coordinates as input. For this reason, between the two compositions a third API (Google Maps geocoding API) is used to perform geocoding (rule 4). Listing 1.5 shows the annotations of the Google geocoding API.

Listing 1.5. Extract from the description of Google geocoding API.

```
1  "get": {
2      "parameters": [
3          { "name": "address" }
4      ],
5      "semanticAnnotations": {
6          "address": {
7              "@id": "dbp:address",
8              "@type": "xsd:string"
9          },
10     }
11 },
12 "responses": {
13     "200": {
14         "location": {
15             "properties": {
16                 "lat": { "type": "number" },
17                 "long": { "type": "number" }
18             },
19             "semanticAnnotations": {
20                 "lat": {
21                     "@id": "dbp:latitude",
22                     "@type": "xsd:float"
23                 },
24                 "long": {
25                     "@id": "dbp:longitude",
26                     "@type": "xsd:float"
27                 }, [...]
```

Now that all the information on the different ways to get access to the textbook have been collected, we can compose the results to deliver the requested report to the user.

Dealing with *merge composition*, we need to verify the semantic compatibility of at least two different outputs (Fig. 4).

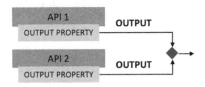

Fig. 4. Schema of merge composition.

To evaluate semantic compatibility in the merge composition, we can define an additional rule:

Rule 5: concepts as unique identifiers. If two or more descriptions share compatible concepts (i.e., they are linked by properties like *owl:sameAs*, *owl:equivalentClass*, *rdfs:subClassOf*, or *rdfs:subPropertyOf*), and these concepts uniquely identify the represented resources (e.g., ISBN for a book, VAT ID for a company, BARCODE for a products), then the outputs of the APIs can be merged.

The Listing 1.6 is a fragment of the Archive.org API[15] description; as shown in line 10, 14, 18, respectively the annotation of the output properties, ISBN, title, author; it is possible to observe how these properties are compatible with the response of Google Books API (Listing 1.1). According to rule 5, the merge composition can occur if compatible properties allow us to conclude that outputs refer to the same resources. In the use case, the *ISBN* can be adopted as unique identifier for books, thus allowing composition of outputs into the final comprehensive report.

Listing 1.6. Extract from the output part of the description of the Archive API.

```
1   "200": {
2       "Book": {
3           "type": "object",
4           "properties": {
5               "ISBN": { "type": "string" },
6               "title": { "type": "string" },
7               "author": { "type": "string" }, [...]
8           },
9           "semanticAnnotations": {
10              "ISBN": {
11                  "@id": "dbp:isbn",
12                  "@type": "xsd:integer"
13              },
14              "title": {
15                  "@id": "dbp:title",
16                  "@type": "xsd:string"
17              },
18              "author": {
19                  "@id": "dbp:author",
20                  "@type": "xsd:string"
21              }, [...]
```

5   AutomAPIc: Composition of REST APIs

AutomAPIc is a comprehensive tool to manage semantic descriptions and input/output composition of services. In this paper, we concentrate on the the description editor, which supports semi-automatic creation of semantic descriptions, and automatic composer, which supports compatibility matching. AutomAPIc is available via Git repository[16]. The Fig. 5 shows the architecture of the tool.

It is possible to identify 6 main components: (i) Description Editor, for the definition and management of API descriptions in OpenAPI format; (ii) Description Annotator, for adding semantic annotations; (iii) Composition Editor, which allows for the selection of a set of composable APIs by the user; (iv) API Connector, component for automatic identification of the composable APIs in relation

---

[15] http://blog.archive.org/developers/.

[16] https://bitbucket.org/disco_unimib/automapic-tool/.

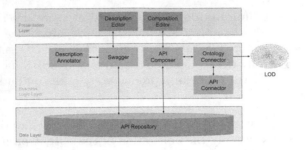

Fig. 5. Architecture of AutomAPIc tool.

to the composition rules described above; (v) Ontology Connector, component to extract semantic relations by queries to the LOD Cloud[17] with SPARQL query; (vi) Composer API, for the execution of the composition previously defined by the user.

5.1 Getting OpenAPI Descriptions

The description process is semi-automatically managed by augmenting existing API descriptions, which can be retrieved from existing repositories (e.g., ApisGuru, SmartAPI), or created manually using the Description Editor. These descriptions are represented in JSON or YAML format, and include all relevant information such as available HTTP operations, the list of input parameters and output responses for each operation. The process of creating a description is detailed in Algorithm 1.

Algorithm 1. Retrieve or create API description.

Result: API description

1 **if** *description is available* **then**
2 | retrieve description from existing repositories and registries of services;
3 **else**
4   ⌊   create it manually using the Description Editor;

5.2 Adding Semantic Annotation

If semantic annotations are missing, we need to annotate input and output data. To annotate output data, AutomAPIc provides users with a service that collects a set of output values of GET calls into a table and applie Semantic Table Interpretation [17] techniques to *understand* such values and identify the annotations to be added.

Table interpretation consists of associating data with semantic concepts in an ontological structure, within the LOD Cloud, which aims to represent the knowledge of a certain domain through the connections that exist between these same elements. The GET method is mainly considered since it is the most frequent.

---

[17] http://lod-cloud.net.

In this way API's parameters and properties can be managed by a computer. The code related to the Table Interpretation technique used in this proposal is available through a Git repository[18].

The input parameters are annotated differently because it is not possible to transform the parameters into a table. AutomAPIc provides a service based on *Natural Language Processing* [2] techniques. In particular the *Stanford CoreNLP* tools[19] [9] has been adopted. These tools provide several libraries that allow for the extraction of entities from API descriptions, which will then be associated with concepts. The application of these techniques on hundred descriptions from the repository *APIs.guru* led to the correct identification of entities and properties for 93% of the cases. Algorithm 2 defines the process to insert semantic annotations in API descriptions. This algorithm revises and extends the one presented in [3].

Algorithm 2. Create and add semantic annotation to API descriptions.

Data: API description
Result: API description with semantic annotations

1 Detect all resources' end-point;
2 **foreach** *end-point* **do**
    // collect data
3   **repeat**
4   generate input parameters following the API description;
5   generate semantic annotation of the input parameters using NLP technique;
6   insert semantic annotation of the input parameters in API description;
7   **if** *input parameters cannot be generated* **then**
8   take input parameters from the user
9   invoke API with input parameters;
10   collect results;
11   **until** *at least N results are collected*;   /* default N=10 */
    // create tables
12   **foreach** *results* **do**
13   create a header row with API properties;
14   fill content-cells with values from inputs and responses;

    // add semantic annotations
15 **foreach** *tables* **do**
16   apply table interpretation technique;
17   show table to the user;
18   **if** *table annotation is not complete* **then**
19   show related vocabularies and/or alternatives to the user;
20   ask the user to manually add links;

21   **if** *the user wants to review the annotations* **then**
22   show related vocabularies to the user;
23   let the user confirm or modify the links;

24   insert semantic annotation of properties in API description;

5.3 Performing Automatic Composition

The presence of semantic annotations allows the automatic identification of the composable APIs given a starting API. The API composer component automatically shows the compatible APIs. The possible combinations have been

---

[18] https://bitbucket.org/disco_unimib/mantistable-tool/.
[19] https://stanfordnlp.github.io/CoreNLP/index.html.

previously calculated by the API connector, through the use of SPARQL queries, in order to apply the compatibility rules (Algorithm 3).

Algorithm 3. Identification of compatibility between the APIs.

Result: Composed APIs

1 inserting a new API into the system;
2 parsing of the description;
3 extraction of semantic annotations;
4 **foreach** *APIs* **do**
5 $\quad$ creation and execution of SPARQL queries to identify the relationships between the annotations of the APIs;
6 $\quad$ update the graph of possible compositions;

---

6   Validation

To verify the validity of the proposed composition approach, we collected a set of APIs (Table 2) for the creation of a *benchmark* with characteristics that cover all possible cases. The chosen APIs comes from various domains, including public transport, films, books, music and events.

In a second phase the descriptions and their annotations were analyzed, to identify the possible compositions. Through the combinatorial calculation it is possible to calculate the maximum number of combinations. In particular, given 20 APIS, using provisions without repetitions (since an API cannot be composed with itself), the maximum number of compositions is 380.

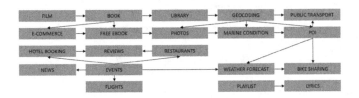

Fig. 6. List of the possible compositions.

As shown in Fig. 6, depending on parameters and annotations, the actual combinations are twenty four. AutomAPIc was able to identify the 85% of them. Table 3 reports the *confusion matrix* of the results, where attributes are: (i) TP: number of correctly composed APIs, (ii) FP: number of APIs that were composed but which should not be composed, (iii) FN: number of APIs that were not composed but that had to be composed, (iv) TN: number of APIs that were not to be composed and were not composed. The *accuracy* of the system is $(TP+TN)/Total = 0.99$. Going into detail, the combinations that led to composition failures are mainly three: weak support to manage concepts connected by the *owl:subProperty* relation, incomplete relationships between ontologies (e.g., DBpedia and KBpedia), and inaccurate semantic annotations of parameters returned by table interpretation techniques. A discussion on the quality of results of table interpretation techniques is out of scope of this paper, however interested readers can refer to [17] for details.

Table 2. Validation dataset.

API	Description	Source
GEOCODING	Converts an address into latitude and longitude	Google Maps
MARINE CONDITION	Forecast of marine conditions	World Weather Online
WEATHER FORECAST	Weather forecasts	Weather Underground
PHOTOS	Photos geolocated in a specific position	Flickr
NEWS	List of news	NewsAPI
BOOK	List of information about a book	Google
MOVIE	List of information about a film	OMDb API
POI	Points of interest of a city	Sygic API
LIBRARY	List of information about the availability of a book	Opac Unimib
E-COMMERCE	Information regarding the price of a product	Amazon Market
FREE EBOOK	Information on the presence of a free eBook	Archive.org
PLAYLIST	List of songs contained in a playlist	Spotify
LYRICS	Text of a song	Musixmatch API
FLIGHTS	Airport information	Ryanair API
BIKE SHARING	List of bicycles available	City Bike
EVENTS	List of events in a city	EventiFul
HOTEL BOOKING	List of hotels available on a specific date on a certain day	HotelsCombined API
REVIEWS	List of reviews of places and events	TripAdvisor Content API
PUBLIC TRANSPORT	List of information about public transport in a particular place	Google Transit
RESTAURANTS	List of restaurants in a specific city	Zomato API

Table 3. Confusion matrix.

Tot. $= 380$	Composed	Not - Composed
Composed	**TP $= 17$**	**FP $= 0$**
Not - Composed	**FN $= 3$**	**TN $= 360$**

7   Conclusions and Future Work

The work presented in this paper aims to propose an extension of the OpenAPI specification to support the semantic annotations of services descriptions and the automatic composition of services. The goal is to support users without specific skills to manage semantics annotations, thus encouraging the delivery of semantically annotated descriptions. For this reason, two solutions have been proposed. For the annotation of input parameters, the use of Natural Language Processing (NLP) techniques has been proposed, while for the annotation of output properties, a reviewed Table Interpretation approach has been developed. The validation of the proposal through a subset of real APIs has underlined how the use of semantic annotations and the definition of a set of composition rules lead to an effective support to the composition of APIs, even if further development is necessary to improve both precision and recall. Future work will go in that direction to consolidate the AutomAPIC tool, along with fully integration with the Swagger interface. Moreover, further investigations will be conducted to verify the quality of the table interpretation outputs, which play an important role in our composition approach. In addition, a user-centric evaluation is planned in order to verify the ability of users to manage this new type of descriptions with semantic annotations. Finally, to enhance the automation of the entire process, we will study how to capture and model the user requirements.

References

1. Chinnici, R., Moreau, J.J., Ryman, A., Weerawarana, S.: Web services description language (WSDL) version 2.0 Part 1: Core language. W3C Recommendation 26, 19 (2007)
2. Chowdhury, G.G.: Natural language processing. Ann. Rev. Inf. Sci. Technol. **37**(1), 51–89 (2003)
3. Cremaschi, M., De Paoli, F.: Toward automatic semantic API descriptions to support services composition. In: De Paoli, F., Schulte, S., Broch Johnsen, E. (eds.) ESOCC 2017. LNCS, vol. 10465, pp. 159–167. Springer, Cham (2017). https://doi.org/10.1007/978-3-319-67262-5_12
4. Euzenat, J., Shvaiko, P.: Ontology Matching. Springer, Heidelberg (2007). https://doi.org/10.1007/978-3-540-49612-0
5. Gomadam, K., Ranabahu, A., Sheth, A.: SA-REST: semantic annotation of web resources. W3C Member Submission 5, 52 (2010)
6. Kopecký, J., Vitvar, T., Fensel, D., Gomadam, K.: hRESTS & MicroWSMO. Technical report, STI International (2009)
7. Lausen, H., Farrell, J.: Semantic annotations for WSDL and XML schema. W3C Recommendation, W3C 69 (2007)
8. Lucky, M.N., Cremaschi, M., Lodigiani, B., Menolascina, A., De Paoli, F.: Enriching API descriptions by adding API profiles through semantic annotation. In: Sheng, Q.Z., Stroulia, E., Tata, S., Bhiri, S. (eds.) ICSOC 2016. LNCS, vol. 9936, pp. 780–794. Springer, Cham (2016). https://doi.org/10.1007/978-3-319-46295-0_55

9. Manning, C., Surdeanu, M., Bauer, J., Finkel, J., Bethard, S., McClosky, D.: The Stanford CoreNLP natural language processing toolkit. In: Proceedings of 52nd Annual Meeting of the Association for Computational Linguistics: System Demonstrations, pp. 55–60. Association for Computational Linguistics (2014)
10. Martin, D., et al.: OWL-S: semantic markup for web services. W3C Member Submission 22, 2007–04 (2004)
11. Paulraj, D., Swamynathan, S., Madhaiyan, M.: Process model-based atomic service discovery and composition of composite semantic web services using web ontology language for services (OWL-S). Enterp. Inf. Syst. 6(4), 445–471 (2012)
12. Rao, J., Su, X.: A survey of automated web service composition methods. In: Cardoso, J., Sheth, A. (eds.) SWSWPC 2004. LNCS, vol. 3387, pp. 43–54. Springer, Heidelberg (2005). https://doi.org/10.1007/978-3-540-30581-1_5
13. Roman, D., Kopeck, J., Vitvar, T., Domingue, J., Fensel, D.: WSMO-lite and hRESTS: lightweight semantic annotations for web services and restful APIs. Web Semant. Sci. Serv. Agents World Wide Web 31, 39–58 (2015)
14. Sheng, Q.Z., Qiao, X., Vasilakos, A.V., Szabo, C., Bourne, S., Xu, X.: Web services composition: a decades overview. Inf. Sci. 280, 218–238 (2014)
15. Tsouroplis, R., Petychakis, M., Alvertis, I., Biliri, E., Lampathaki, F., Askounis, D.: Community-based API builder to manage APIs and their connections with cloud-based services. In: CAiSE Forum (2015)
16. Weerawarana, S., Curbera, F., Leymann, F., Storey, T., Ferguson, D.F.: Web Services Platform Architecture: SOAP, WSDL, WS-Policy, WS-Addressing, WS-BPEL, WS-Reliable Messaging and More. Prentice Hall PTR, Upper Saddle River (2005)
17. Zhang, Z.: Effective and efficient semantic table interpretation using TableMiner+. Semant. Web 8(6), 921–957 (2017)

Using a Microbenchmark to Compare Function as a Service Solutions

Timon Back and Vasilios Andrikopoulos(✉)(iD)

University of Groningen, Groningen, The Netherlands
t.back@student.rug.nl, v.andrikopoulos@rug.nl

Abstract. The Function as a Service (FaaS) subtype of serverless computing provides the means for abstracting away from servers on which developed software is meant to be executed. It essentially offers an event-driven and scalable environment in which billing is based on the invocation of functions and not on the provisioning of resources. This makes it very attractive for many classes of applications with bursty workload. However, the terms under which FaaS services are structured and offered to consumers uses mechanisms like GB–seconds (that is, X GigaBytes of memory used for Y seconds of execution) that differ from the usual models for compute resources in cloud computing. Aiming to clarify these terms, in this work we develop a microbenchmark that we use to evaluate the performance and cost model of popular FaaS solutions using well known algorithmic tasks. The results of this process show a field still very much under development, and justify the need for further extensive benchmarking of these services.

Keywords: Function as a Service (FaaS) · Microbenchmark
Performance evaluation · Cost evaluation

1 Introduction

The wide adoption of cloud-native enabling technologies and architectural concepts like containers and microservices in the recent years has created an increasing interest in *serverless computing* as a programming model and architecture. In this model, code is executed in the cloud without any control of the resources on which the code runs [1]. Serverless encompasses a wide range of technologies, that following the discussion in [13] can be grouped into two areas: *Back-end as a Service (BaaS)* and *Function as a Service (FaaS)*. BaaS is especially relevant for mobile application development and is closely related to the SaaS delivery model, allowing the replacement of server-side components with third party services. Google's Firebase[1] is an example of such a service. FaaS, on the other hand is closer to the PaaS model, allowing individual business operations to be built and deployed on a FaaS platform. The key difference between FaaS and

---

[1] Firebase https://firebase.google.com/.

K. Kritikos et al. (Eds.): ESOCC 2018, LNCS 11116, pp. 146–160, 2018.
https://doi.org/10.1007/978-3-319-99819-0_11

PaaS is the scaling scope as discussed by Mike Roberts[2]: in PaaS the developer is still concerned with scaling an application up and down as a whole, while FaaS provides complete transparency to the scaling of functions, since this is handled by the platform itself.

There are a number of claimed benefits of serverless computing, and by extension also of FaaS, identified for example by [13]. More importantly, scaling becomes the responsibility of the platform provider and the application owner is charged only for how long a function is running as a response to its invocation (within a billable time unit—BTU). This is a big departure from the "traditional" model of cloud computing so far, at least when compared to other compute–oriented solutions like VM– and Container as a Service, where the owner is charged for provisioning these resources irrespective of their utilization. As a result, FaaS is perceived as the means to achieve significant cost savings, especially in the case of bursty, compute-intensive workloads [1] such as the ones generated by IoT applications.

At the same time, however, the pricing model of FaaS solutions can be difficult to decipher and surprisingly complex to model [2]. FaaS users are typically charged based on two components: *number of function invocations* across all functions belonging to the user, and *function execution duration* measured, confusingly enough, in *GB–seconds* per billing cycle. The first metric is relatively straightforward but potentially extremely dangerous in the case of decomposing application functionality into too many fine–grained functions that result into ever expanding cumulative costs. The second one is based on the practice of most FaaS providers, as discussed in the following section, of requiring the user to define a fixed memory amount to be allocated for each function execution. Users are then charged for the BTUs (in seconds) for which a function executed, multiplied by the allocated (or peak in the case of one provider) amount of memory in GB, times the per GB–seconds cost defined by the provider. FaaS adoption essentially also means loss of control over the performance of the functions themselves, since their execution is hidden under multiple layers of virtualization and abstraction by the platform providers, resulting into inconsistent performance results even for the same service and configuration [13].

With the aim of investigating and clarifying these two phenomena and their impact on FaaS adopters, this paper discusses the use of a *microbenchmark* in order to study how different FaaS solutions, and especially ones in the public cloud deployment model, behave in terms of performance and cost. More specifically, Sect. 2 presents the FaaS solutions that we will consider for the rest of this work and discusses related work. Section 3 incorporates a small set of algorithmic tasks with known computational and memory requirements in a microbenchmark of our design and implementation. Section 4 presents the results of executing the benchmark in a time window and discusses our findings while evaluating the selected FaaS solutions. Based on these findings we provide a series of lessons that we learned and that we believe are relevant for FaaS adopters in Sect. 5. Finally, Sect. 6 concludes this work with a short summary and future work.

---

[2] For more on the subject, see https://martinfowler.com/articles/serverless.html.

2   Background and Related Work

Since the introduction of Amazon Web Services Lambda[3] back in 2014 all major cloud providers have developed their own FaaS solution. Table 1 summarizes and compares the offerings of the most popular public Cloud providers [12]. More specifically, and in alphabetical order:

- *AWS Lambda* was the first FaaS public offering. At the time of writing, it offers memory usage to be specified in the [128, 3008] MB interval in increments of 64 MB. It offers the most flexibility in terms of configuration options, and is the more mature of implementations from the offerings investigated by this work.
- *Google Cloud Functions*[4] is in beta status since its launch in February 2016. While the least flexible in terms of configuration options, Cloud Functions is the only of the FaaS solutions that clearly defines the amount of allocated CPU cycles per memory allocation option in its documentation.
- *IBM Cloud* (formerly known as IBM Bluemix) *Functions*[5] is based on the Apache OpenWhisk[6] FaaS platform implementation, allowing for easy hybrid deployment. It requires all functions to run as Docker containers, which allows for function development in any language.
- *Microsoft Azure Functions*[7], also launched in 2016, differs significantly from the other solutions in the sense that it does not expect the user to specify a fixed amount of memory to be used by the function in advance. The service bills only for the used memory per invocation, rounded up to the nearest 128 MB step, using at the same time the smallest billable time unit (1 ms).

In terms of related work, and considering how recently serverless computing was introduced, existing literature on the subject is relatively limited. Van Eyk et al. [3] for example identify the need for community consensus on what constitutes FaaS, and set the goal of developing an objective benchmark of FaaS platforms as a target for future work. The approaches presented by [8,15] investigate the cost of FaaS solutions as an infrastructural platform for the hosting of microservices. Their interest is in evaluating alternative deployment scenarios involving FaaS services and not with the performance of FaaS solutions themselves. The Costradamus approach [6] aims to measure the computation waste in FaaS usage accrued by monitoring function calls duration and contrasting them to billed BTUs. Both [5,14] use microbenchmarking of FaaS solutions in order to compare providers and calibrate their proposed systems, but for these works the comparison of providers is incidental and not the main focus. These works are therefore relevant but not directly related to the goals set for this work.

From more related works, [7,10] set out to explicitly benchmark and compare FaaS solutions in terms of performance and cost. While useful and insightful in

---

[3] AWS Lambda: https://aws.amazon.com/lambda/.
[4] Google Cloud Functions: https://cloud.google.com/functions/.
[5] IBM Cloud: https://console.bluemix.net/openwhisk/.
[6] Apache OpenWhisk: https://openwhisk.apache.org/.
[7] Microsoft Azure Functions: https://azure.microsoft.com/services/functions/.

Table 1. Comparison of the offerings by the major Cloud Service Providers (May 2018)

	Amazon WS Lambda	Google Cloud Functions	IBM Cloud Functions/Apache Open-Whisk	Microsoft Azure Functions
Memory Min	128 MB	128 MB	128 MB	128 MB
Memory Max	3008 MB	2048 MB	512 MB	1536 MB
Timeout Max	5 min	9 min	5 min	10 min
Billing Interval	100 ms	100 ms	100 ms	1 ms
Memory Allocation	Fixed	Fixed	Fixed	Dynamic
Natively Supported Languages	C# Go Java Node.js Python	Node.js	Java Node.js PHP Python Swift ...	C# F# Node.js
HTTP Invocation	✓	✓	✓	✓
HTTP plus Authentication	✓	—	✓	✓
Free Tier (One time/Periodical)	✓/✓	✓/✓	✓/✓	✓/✓

their own right, both works use much more coarse–grained tasks for their evaluation, focusing on concurrency and latency, respectively. The work by Malawski et al. [11] provides similar conclusions to ones discussed by this work, and in some ways supplements our findings with further insights; however it only discusses performance issues with FaaS solutions and does not investigate their impact on cost.

With this work, we focus on investigating the differences between the FaaS solutions presented above with respect to their compute/memory allocation policies, and their consequent effect on the cost model of cloud functions running on them.

3   Microbenchmark Design

As discussed in the previous section, and given the current lack of a FaaS benchmark, it becomes a common and necessary practice to use a microbenchmark for performance evaluation purposes. We chose a microbenchmark for this purpose since we aim to measure a basic feature of FaaS services (compute/memory allocation) for which a simple program should suffice, and because microbenchmarking is quite popular for cloud services evaluation [9]. The faas-μbenchmark is available online[8] and it actually contains more functions than the ones we explain in the following. In the interest of space, we limit the presentation of results to only three major functions from the microbenchmark.

---

[8] faas-μbenchmark: https://github.com/timonback/faas-mubenchmark.

Functions

The following functions were selected for inclusion in the faas-μbenchmark based on their characteristics with respect to their computational and memory requirements:

- Fast Fourier Transformation (FFT): performs an FFT computation using the Cooley-Tukey method as implemented by the fft-js library of Node.js (version 0.0.11)[9] for an increasing amount of discrete signals $k = 2^i, i \in \mathbb{N}^+$. The Cooley-Tukey method has computational complexity $O(NlogN)$ and is therefore representative of a moderate load to the system.
- Matrix Multiplication (MM): multiply square matrices of increasing size without any optimization (i.e. with complexity $O(n^3)$); the length of the matrices is defined as $n = i \times 100, i \in \mathbb{N}^+$, i.e. it increases by a step of 100 starting from 100.
- Sleep (S): sleep for $t = 2^i, i \in \mathbb{N}^+$ ms. This function is selected for evaluating the sensitivity of the FaaS offering to its invocation. Measured execution durations should in principle be equal to the specified parameter t, plus some initialization time.

Table 2 summarizes the characterization of the selected functions:

Table 2. Relative resource requirements for the benchmarking functions

Function	Computational	Memory
Fast Fourier Transformation (FFT)	Moderate	Moderate
Matrix Multiplication (MM)	High	High
Sleep (S)	Minimum	Minimum

The microbenchmark itself is highly configurable, allowing for subsetting or extending the parameter values for each function as desired by the user. All functions are implemented on top of the Node.js JavaScript runtime, since it is the execution environment that is common across all FaaS offerings (see Table 1).

Instrumentation

In order to reduce the complexity of the deployment process of the defined functions across different providers we decided to use the *Serverless framework*[10], as also adopted by [11]. This framework allows for the deployment of code to the majority of FaaS/serverless solutions by a simple command, assuming of course that an account has been created with the respective provider and the necessary authentication credentials have been provided to it. Since FaaS providers expect

---

[9] https://www.npmjs.com/package/fft-js.
[10] Serverless: https://serverless.com/.

different bindings for functions executed in their platform we created a custom minimal wrapper for each provider which reads the passed-in parameters, calls the appropriate function, and returns the result. The called algorithm is the same for every provider. The wrapper function is provided together with the rest of the microbenchmark as discussed above.

4 Services Evaluation

In the following we discuss how we use the faas-μbenchmark to compare the FaaS solutions presented in Sect. 2.

4.1 Evaluation Setup

Apache OpenWhisk is used as the baseline for the comparison between solutions. The February 2018 version from the OpenWhisk GitHub repository was deployed inside a VirtualBox machine (version 5.2.8) running Ubuntu Linux 14.04 LTS with 4 GB of memory allocated to it, on a notebook with a quad–core Intel i7–6700HQ (@2.6 GHz) and 8 GB of memory in total. The three functions discussed in the previous section (i.e. FFT, MM and S) are deployed on it, and on the FaaS solutions offered in the public cloud deployment model using the Serverless framework. Five configurations for each FaaS service are selected for comparison purposes by setting the allocated memory to 128, 256, 512, 1024 and 2048 MB, and the functions are deployed in all of these configurations.

Looking at the comparison in Table 1, we need to clarify that IBM Cloud Functions/Apache OpenWhisk has a maximum allocation limit of 512 MB per function. However by building on Docker's memory management, more memory is addressable for function execution without terminating due to insufficient memory. As we will show in the following, this works quite well for most of the experiments we performed.

Moving on, in order to avoid potential differences among regions we try to keep the location of the deployments comparable (more specifically, AWS Lambda: us-east-1, Google Cloud Functions: us-central-1, Microsoft Azure Functions: Central US) with the exception of IBM Cloud Functions that were deployed in the United Kingdom region since this could not be changed for the free tier version that we are using for all experiments. The functions are invoked by a local machine at the University of Groningen using simply the curl command on the Linux OS; as we will discuss in the following, the location of the invoker does not affect any measurements, and it can therefore be placed anywhere it is deemed more convenient. Timeout is set for all solutions and configurations at 300 s (i.e. 5 min) except in the case of Google Cloud Functions where it is set to 540 s (9 min).

The microbenchmark was executed across 3 consecutive working days in the end of April 2018, resulting in three measurements per function and parameter for each service configuration. For each microbenchmark run we execute all three functions in Table 2 sequentially with their parameters ranging over the following intervals ($i \in \mathbb{N}^+$ in all cases):

1. S: $t = 2^i, i \in [1, 13]$
2. MM: $n = i \times 100, i \in [1, 10]$
3. FFT: $k = 2^i, i \in [13; 21]$

For each invocation we are measuring the execution duration as reported by the FaaS provider (i.e. without network latency affecting the measurements), the execution status (i.e. success or reported type of error), the billed duration, and the incurred cost for the function execution. All measurements are collected from the respective logs of each service and are aggregated as CSV files for each function for further processing. The measurements we report and analyze in the following are also available in the faas-μbenchmark repository under /results/.

4.2 Microbenchmark Results and Findings

Note: for the rest of this discussion we will be using the convention FunM, as a shorthand for function Fun $\in$ {FFT,MM,S} executed on a service configuration with M MBs of allocated memory, where M $\in$ {128, 256, 512, 1024, 2048}, across all providers of interest. MM1024, for example, refers to the execution of the matrix multiplication function in configurations with 1024 MB of allocated memory in all providers, for all parameter values $n = [100, 1000]$ with step 100. For purposes of space saving, in the following we are also using only the provider's name instead of the full name of the FaaS solution, with the exception of Apache OpenWhisk which is simply shortened to OpenWhisk.

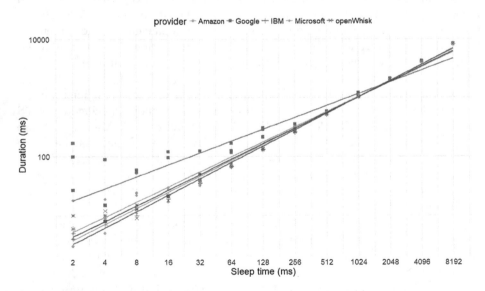

Fig. 1. Measured durations for S128 across all providers (log2–log plot). The straight lines show the fitted linear models to the observed data per provider.

Table 3. Mean Square Error (MSE) for linear regression to the observed data of S per provider for the different memory configurations.

Configuration	Provider				
	Amazon	Google	IBM	Microsoft	OpenWhisk
S128	265.82	2597.61	1.63	22.4	6.18
S256	62.46	1589.33	12.4	57.72	24.1
S512	41.96	726.93	1.79	20.04	12.06
S1024	31.62	757.52	2.03	14.63	15.96
S2048	12.31	851.3	2.4	18.75	5.72
mean (MSE)	81.03	1304.54	4.05	26.71	12.8

Sleep: With respect to function S, Fig. 1 shows the measured execution durations for S128. As it can be seen in the figure, the benchmarked FaaS solutions behave for the most part as expected, with a linear relation between execution time and sleep parameter t. This holds true however only after a sufficient large value of t—64 ms in our measurements—which is also around half of the BTU for all providers (except Microsoft, see Table 1). The solution that delays the most to converge into a linear relation with t, and at the same time exhibits the most variance, is actually the one by Google. This phenomenon appears also in the rest of the memory allocation configurations of this provider, as summarized by Table 3 which presents the mean square error (MSE) for the fitting of the measurements to a linear model with parameter t. The lm function of the R programming language (version 3.4.3) is used for the model fitting in Table 3. While the error in most configurations can be deemed acceptable, in the case of S128 as illustrated in Fig. 1 it is roughly ± 51 ms for the 128 MB configuration of Google Cloud Functions—that is, 50% of the service's BTU—and still an order or two magnitudes larger than the other ones in Table 3.

Matrix Multiplication: For MM we discuss our findings for the largest configurations (i.e. 1024 and 2048 MB), since we know that this function is the heaviest, at least in theory, of the functions that we include in the microbenchmark. Similar findings, but with the observed phenomena proportionally exaggerated are also concluded from the measurements in smaller configurations.

Figure 2 illustrates the collected measurements for progressively increasing matrix size n. Since we are in the normal–normal scale and we expect $O(n^3)$ complexity, we use the loess method of R for local polynomial regression fitting instead of the linear one. Looking at the measurements, it appears that the policy of Microsoft Azure Functions to assign memory dynamically instead of allocating it in advance is resulting in the relative worse among providers performance for this function as n grows. Further investigations in the effect of memory allocation in such calculations is necessary. On the other end of the spectrum, the OpenWhisk and consequently the IBM Cloud Functions solutions appear to be better able to handle the memory and computational requirements of this task

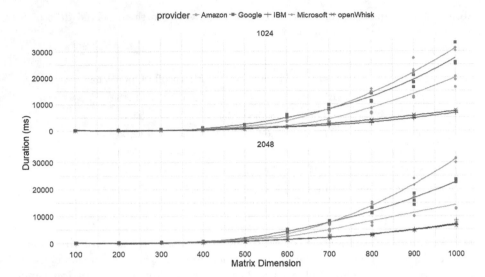

Fig. 2. Execution of MM1024 & MM2048 across all providers (norm–norm plots).

when compared to the other providers. It also seems that adding more memory to Amazon and Google's solutions results in better performance. Using only $n = 1000$ as a reference, the average execution times in these two solutions improve by 31.5% and 17.4%, respectively, when comparing the two configurations. We are going to use FFT to investigate this improvement in more depth in the following.

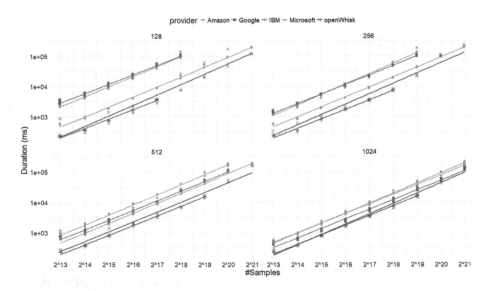

Fig. 3. Measured durations of successful executions of FFT128–FFT1024 across all providers (log2–log plots).

Table 4. Successful executions of FFT across all configurations per parameter k value.

k	Provider				
	Amazon	Google	IBM	Microsoft	OpenWhisk
$[8192; 131072]$	15	15	15	15	15
262144	15	15	12	15	15
524288	12	12	9	15	15
1048576	9	9	0	15	15
2097152	6	6	0	15	13
Total	$\sim86.7\%$	$\sim86.7\%$	$\sim71.1\%$	100%	$\sim98.5\%$

FFT: Figure 3 shows the reported execution durations of FFT across the first four memory configurations for comparison purposes, omitting any error responses. As it can be seen better in Table 4, only the dynamic memory allocation scheme of Microsoft Azure Functions allows for all values of parameter k to be calculated successfully. OpenWhisk is able to get additional memory from the local VM in order to calculate the FFT for k in most of the higher values, at the clear expense of speed however, as shown in Fig. 3. The figure also shows that for the rest of the providers, allocating more memory to the function results in more successful executions as k grows.

Zooming in on the interval of k values for which all FaaS solutions are able to successfully execute FFT, that is $k \in [8192; 131072]$ as shown in Table 4, we can study better the effect of memory allocation to the overall performance of each solution.

More specifically, as shown in Fig. 4, the solutions are separated into two groups. In the first group, the FaaS implementations by Microsoft and IBM/Apache do not meaningfully benefit from faster execution times by allocating more memory—in the former case because memory is actually allocated dynamically anyway, and in the latter because of the way OpenWhisk allows for partially dynamic memory allocation through its interaction with Docker. As shown in Table 4, however, the latter case can only cope with additional load so far before it starts producing error responses. In the second group, Amazon and Google's implementations clearly benefit from additional allocated memory, not only in terms of more successful executions, but also in terms of performance.

Focusing now on the cost incurred by the execution of FFT, Table 5 summarizes the cost calculation for all studied solutions[11] as *cumulative total (sum) cost* including all function invocations and consequent executions, and *mean cumulative cost* across configurations of 128 to 1024 MB per provider. While normalizing the cost per invocation may seem a more attractive option, the use

---

[11] OpenWhisk is deployed in a local VM, and therefore execution costs are not directly relevant; however for illustrative purposes we use the GB–seconds cost of IBM Cloud Functions for cost calculations. This makes the comparison between the private and public, in essence, deployment of OpenWhisk particularly interesting.

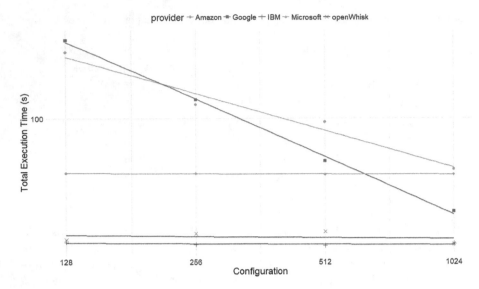

Fig. 4. Total duration per configuration and provider for FFT in seconds using only successful executions, i.e. $k \in [8192; 131072]$ (log2–log plot).

Table 5. Cumulative total and average costs per provider across all configurations for FFT in USD cents (April 2018 prices), respectively. See Footnote 11 for the cost calculation of OpenWhisk.

	Provider				
	Amazon	Google	IBM	Microsoft	OpenWhisk*
sum (cost)	2.832	1.941	0.258	3.305	2.228
mean (cost)	0.708	0.485	0.065	0.826	0.557

of cumulative costs fits better the interest of the consumer on the total cost of the FaaS service usage, especially given the observed variance we discussed in the previous.

As it can be seen from Table 5 and further reinforced by Fig. 5, when considering only successful function executions, IBM Cloud Functions is the most cost effective solution. Its high error rate due to its inability to deal with larger values of k has, however, to be taken seriously into consideration. Following on, Google's solution produces the next best solution in terms of cost, at the expense of high variability in its performance. Microsoft's solution on the other hand seems to be the most expensive and slow option, but at the time the one being able to scale better with k. Given the above, AWS Lambda seems to offer a good trade–off between performance, cost, and ability to cope with the requirements of the FFT function—but only if enough memory has been allocated per function.

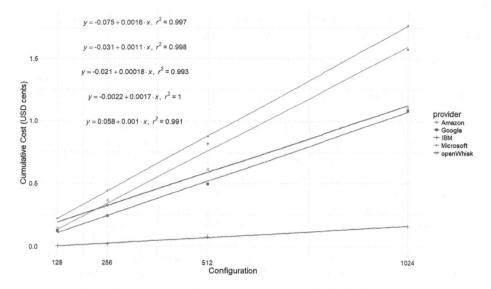

Fig. 5. Cumulative cost per provider and configuration for FFT in USD cents (April 2018 prices) with regression formulas (norm–norm scale).

5   Discussion and Lessons Learned

Before proceeding further, we have to identify the main threats to the validity of this work:

1. Not sufficient data points were collected during the microbenchmark execution to ensure the robustness of the findings. This is a known issue with this work and we plan to run it again for a longer period. Nevertheless, we can claim that anecdotally, the reported behavior of the FaaS solutions is consistent with any measurements we took outside of the reported ones in different days of April and May 2018. We are therefore confident in their validity, at least at this point in time.
2. Function implementation was done exclusively on Node.js; in principle, result replication is necessary in other programming languages but in the interest of time this is left as future work. In any case, as shown in Table 1, Node.js is the only common platform across all examined solutions. Comparing across programming languages could potentially only dilute the findings.
3. All measurements reported in the previous were taken on the free tier model offered by platform providers. We do not expect significant deviations when using the paid model, as the free tier seems to be a discount to have people try out (new) products. However, further experimentation is necessary in order to test this hypothesis.
4. The effect of the use of the Serverless framework for cross-provider deployment was not controlled; however we have no evidence of it affecting the validity of our measurements.

With respect to the lessons learned by the comparison of the various FaaS solutions, they can be summarized by the following:

1. The maturity of the examined FaaS solutions varies significantly when considering their observed performance. Especially Google's Cloud Functions seems to justify its label of beta state based on our measurements (see both Figs. 1 and 2).
2. There is a three–way trade–off between performance, cost, and ability to gracefully scale with each function's load before running out of memory or maximum execution time (see Figs. 2 and 3). Notice that there was no measurement with concurrent requests, so it is not possible to comment on the scaling of each solution with the overall load.
3. Adding more allocated memory only has a significant effect for some of the providers in terms of performance improvement (Fig. 4) and this has also been shown by [11]; however if the reliability of a function is important to the application developer then more memory is definitely recommended.
4. However, in addition to the above, it needs to be taken into account that while the relation between memory and cost appears to be linear, there is a significant difference between the coefficients of the cost functions per solution (see Fig. 5).
5. More extensive benchmarking of FaaS solutions is necessary in order to get a clearer picture of the state of play in FaaS solutions. As with the related works discussed in Sect. 2, this can extend beyond compute/memory evaluation to e.g. network and I/O parameters.

6   Conclusions and Future Work

In the previous sections we developed and used a microbenchmark in order to investigate two aspects of the Function as a Service (FaaS) sub–type of serverless computing: the differences in observable behavior with respect to the computer/memory relation of each FaaS implementation by the providers, and the complex pricing models currently being in use. For this purpose, we chose to include to our faas-μbenchmark three very common algorithmic tasks (Fast Fourier Transformation, matrix multiplication, and a simple sleep as a baseline), and implement them on top of the Node.js environment as the common denominator across the FaaS solutions under consideration. Executing the microbenchmark itself produced some unforeseen results with respect to the maturity of the offered solutions, and provided insights into the relation between performance and cost for software that is running in this cloud delivery model.

Future work is aimed at addressing the concerns discussed in the previous section. This entails proceeding with extensive benchmarking of the FaaS solutions across a longer period, considering also additional functions that impose different computational or memory constraints, and endeavor to clarify further the relation between memory and CPU cycle allocation. Potential differences between the perceived performance when functions are being executed in a free tier or not are also to be investigated. Furthermore, we also plan to expand the evaluation to OpenLambda [4], which is explicitly positioned as a research–oriented, non production–ready environment. The comparison with OpenWhisk as the only other open source solution would be particularly interesting. Finally, we aim to take the lessons learned by this work and put them into practice by developing instrumentation that allows application developers to route load across serverless or "traditional" IaaS resources in order to maximize their cost efficiency based on the characteristics of the application load.

References

1. Baldini, I., et al.: Serverless computing: current trends and open problems. In: Chaudhary, S., Somani, G., Buyya, R. (eds.) Research Advances in Cloud Computing, pp. 1–20. Springer, Singapore (2017). https://doi.org/10.1007/978-981-10-5026-8_1
2. Eivy, A.: Be wary of the economics of "serverless" cloud computing. IEEE Cloud Comput. **4**(2), 6–12 (2017)
3. van Eyk, E., Iosup, A., Seif, S., Thömmes, M.: The SPEC cloud group's research vision on FaaS and serverless architectures. In: Proceedings of the 2nd International Workshop on Serverless Computing, pp. 1–4. ACM (2017)
4. Hendrickson, S., Sturdevant, S., Harter, T., Venkataramani, V., Arpaci-Dusseau, A.C., Arpaci-Dusseau, R.H.: Serverless computation with OpenLambda. Elastic **60**, 80 (2016)
5. Jonas, E., Pu, Q., Venkataraman, S., Stoica, I., Recht, B.: Occupy the cloud: distributed computing for the 99%. In: Proceedings of the 2017 Symposium on Cloud Computing, pp. 445–451. ACM (2017)
6. Kuhlenkamp, J., Klems, M.: Costradamus: a cost-tracing system for cloud-based software services. In: Maximilien, M., Vallecillo, A., Wang, J., Oriol, M. (eds.) ICSOC 2017. LNCS, vol. 10601, pp. 657–672. Springer, Cham (2017). https://doi.org/10.1007/978-3-319-69035-3_48
7. Lee, H., Satyam, K., Fox, G.: Evaluation of production serverless computing environments. Technical report, April 2018. https://doi.org/10.13140/RG.2.2.28642.84165
8. Leitner, P., Cito, J., Stckli, E.: Modelling and managing deployment costs of microservice-based cloud applications. In: Proceedings of IEEE/ACM 9th International Conference on Utility and Cloud Computing (UCC), pp. 165–174, December 2016
9. Li, Z., Zhang, H., O'Brien, L., Cai, R., Flint, S.: On evaluating commercial cloud services: a systematic review. J. Syst. Softw. **86**(9), 2371–2393 (2013)
10. Lloyd, W., Ramesh, S., Chinthalapati, S., Ly, L., Pallickara, S.: Serverless computing: an investigation of factors influencing microservice performance. In: Proceedings of the IEEE International Conference on Cloud Engineering (IC2E 2018). IEEE (2018)
11. Malawski, M., Figiela, K., Gajek, A., Zima, A.: Benchmarking heterogeneous cloud functions. In: Heras, D.B., Bougé, L. (eds.) Euro-Par 2017. LNCS, vol. 10659, pp. 415–426. Springer, Cham (2018). https://doi.org/10.1007/978-3-319-75178-8_34
12. RightScale: RightScale 2018 State of the Cloud Report (2018). https://www.rightscale.com/lp/state-of-the-cloud

13. Roberts, M., Chapin, J.: What is Serverless? O'Reilly Media, Sebastopol (2017)
14. Spillner, J.: Exploiting the cloud control plane for fun and profit. arXiv preprint arXiv:1701.05945 (2017)
15. Villamizar, M., et al.: Infrastructure cost comparison of running web applications in the cloud using aws lambda and monolithic and microservice architectures. In: Proceedings of 16th IEEE/ACM International Symposium on Cluster Cloud and Grid Computing (CCGrid 2016), pp. 179–182, May 2016. https://doi.org/10.1109/CCGrid.2016.37

APIComposer: Data-Driven Composition of REST APIs

Hamza Ed-douibi[1]([✉])(iD), Javier Luis Cánovas Izquierdo[1](iD),
and Jordi Cabot[1,2](iD)

[1] Internet Interdisciplinary Institute (IN3),
Universitat Oberta de Catalunya (UOC), Barcelona, Spain
{hed-douibi,jcanovasi}@uoc.edu
[2] ICREA, Barcelona, Spain
jordi.cabot@icrea.cat

Abstract. More and more companies and governmental organizations
are publishing data on the Web via REST APIs. The increasing number
of REST APIs has promoted the creation of specialized applications aiming to combine and reuse different data sources to generate and deduce
new information. However, creating such applications is a tedious and
error-prone process since developers must invest much time in discovering the data model behind each candidate REST API, define the composition strategy, and manually implement such strategy. To facilitate this
process, we propose an approach to automatically compose and orchestrate data-oriented REST APIs. For an initial set of REST APIs, we
discover the data models, identify matching concepts, obtain a global
model, and make the latter available on the Web as a global REST API.
A prototype tool relying on OpenAPI for describing APIs and on OData
for querying them is also provided.

Keywords: REST API · Modeling · OData · OpenAPI
API Composition

1 Introduction

More and more individuals and organizations are sharing their data on the Web,
including governments and research initiatives. Web APIs have been increasingly
used to make these data available on the Web and allow third parties to infer
new information not visible at first glance. In particular, the REpresentational
State Transfer (REST) has become the prominent architectural style mainly due
to its adaptability to the Web, as it allows creating Web APIs by relying only
on URIs and HTTP messages.

This work has been supported by the Spanish government (TIN2016-75944-R
project).

K. Kritikos et al. (Eds.): ESOCC 2018, LNCS 11116, pp. 161–169, 2018.
https://doi.org/10.1007/978-3-319-99819-0_12

By enabling a programmatic access to data sources, REST APIs promote the creation of specialized data-driven applications that combine data from different sources to offer user-oriented value-added APIs. Creating such applications requires API discovery/understanding/composition and coding. Such tasks are not easy since developers should [2,11]: (i) know the operations and data models of the APIs to compose; (ii) define the composition strategy; and (iii) implement an application (usually another Web API) realizing such strategy.

While automatic Web API composition has been heavily studied for the classical WSDL/SOAP style [20], REST API composition is of broad and current interest specially after the emergence of new REST API specifications such as the OpenAPI specification[1] and OData[2]. OpenAPI is a vendor neutral, portable, and open specification initially based on Swagger[3] which allows defining the resources and operations of a REST API, either in JSON or YAML. The OpenAPI specification has become the choice of reference to describe REST APIs. As a result, OpenAPI is at the core of many research initiatives to, for instance, discover OpenAPI definitions [6,9], provide semantic descriptions for OpenAPI definitions [7,14], identify candidate REST APIs for selection [3], and allow semantic integration of REST APIs [19]. On the other hand, OData is an open protocol especially useful to expose and consume data sources as REST APIs.

In this paper we propose a lightweight model-based approach to automatically compose data-oriented REST APIs given an initial set of OpenAPI definitions (potentially inferred when not explicitly available). As a result of the composition, we obtain a global API that hides the complexity of the composition process to the user. Indeed, a user queries the global API and, in a completely transparent way, the global queries triggers a fully automatic process that accesses the individual APIs and combines their data to generate a single response.

To facilitate the consumption of the global API, we expose it as an OData service. OData allows creating resources which are defined according an *Entity Data Model (EDM)* and can be queried by Web clients using a URL-based query language in an SQL-like style. In our approach, this EDM corresponds to the data schema behind the global API, which is generated during the composition process based on the discovery of matches between the individual data schema of each single API. All these schemas are represented as models and their manipulation (e.g., concept matching or composition) are implemented as model transformations. Working at the model level helps us focus on the domain concepts while abstracting from the low level technical details [18].

The rest of the paper is organized as follows. Section 2 describes our approach, while Sects. 3 and 4 explain its main steps. Section 5 illustrates our approach using an example. Section 6 presents our tool support. Section 7 discusses some related works. Finally, Sect. 8 concludes the paper and presents some future work.

---

[1] www.openapis.org.

[2] www.odata.org.

[3] https://swagger.io.

2   Our Approach

We propose a model-based approach to compose data-driven REST APIs. From a set of initial REST APIs, our approach creates a global API exposing a unified data model merging the data models of the initial APIs. The global model is exposed as an OData service, thus allowing end-users to use the OData query language to get the information they need in an easy and standard way.

Figure 1 shows an overview of our approach. APIComposer takes as input the OpenAPI definitions of the REST APIs to be composed. Such definitions may be (i) supplied by the API provider, (ii) generated using tools such as APIDiscoverer [9] or AutoREST [6], which are able to infer OpenAPI definitions from API call examples or API documentation pages, respectively. (iii) or derived from other API definition formats (e.g., API Blueprint or RAML) using tools such as API Transformer[4].

Our approach includes two components, namely: (i) API importer, in charge of integrating a new REST API to the global API; and (ii) Requests resolver, responsible for processing the user requests and returning the queried data. We explain each component in the following sections.

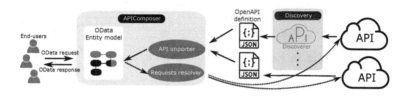

Fig. 1. Overview of our approach.

3   API Importer

Figure 2 shows the API importer process. For each input OpenAPI definition, the API importer first generates an equivalent model conforming to our OpenAPI metamodel (see step 1 in Fig. 2). We previously introduced this metamodel alongside the discovery process [9]. The generation of the OpenAPI model is rather straightforward since the OpenAPI metamodel conforms to the OpenAPI specification and only special attention had to be paid to resolve JSON references.

The second step of the process (see step 2 in Fig. 2) performs a model-to-model transformation to generate a UML model, which emphasizes the data schema of the input API to facilitate the matching process later on. This process consists on iterating over the data structures in the OpenAPI model (i.e., the *schema* elements) to generate the adequate UML elements (i.e. classes, properties and associations elements). This process relies on our tool OpenAPItoUML[5] which generates UML models from OpenAPI definitions [10].

---

[4] http://apimatic.io/transformer.
[5] http://hdl.handle.net/20.500.12004/1/A/O2U/001.

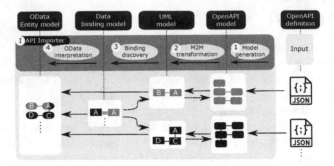

Fig. 2. Composition process.

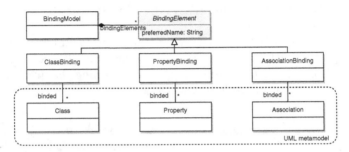

Fig. 3. Excerpt of the binding metamodel.

The third step (see step 3 in Fig. 2) analyzes the UML models to discover matching elements and creates bindings to express the matches between them. The binding model conforms to the binding metamodel which allows creating traceability and binding elements for the data elements in the UML models. Figure 3 shows an excerpt of the binding metamodel. The `BindingModel` element is the root element of the binding metamodel and includes a set of binding elements (i.e., `bindingElements` reference). The `ClassBinding`, `PropertyBinding`, and `AssociationBinding` elements allow defining bindings to `Class`, `Property`, and `Association` elements in a UML model, respectively. Each element includes a preferred name (i.e., the `preferredName` attribute inherited from the `BindingElement` element) and a set of binded elements (i.e., the `binded` references). We currently support a simple two-step matching strategy to define the bindings between elements. The first step finds matching candidates based on their names and types. Then, the second step validates the matches by calling the REST APIs and comparing data related to each candidate. Our experience showed that such strategy is sufficient for APIs coming from the same provider/domain, which share the same concept names across their APIs. However, our approach can be extended in order to support more advanced matching strategies specially for cross-domain composition by relying on, for instance, database schema integration approaches [4] or the new approaches to add semantic descriptions to OpenAPI [7,14]. Also, a designer can manually curate the initial automatic result.

Finally, the last step creates an OData metadata document from: (i) the generated UML models, and (ii) the binding model. This document includes an OData entity model created by merging all the data models of the input REST APIs and resolving the bindings between them. Thus, the creation process iterates over all the data elements in the UML models and creates a new element in the entity model if there is not a binding linking such element to another element, or merging both elements otherwise. The OData metadata document is the standard way OData provides to let end-users know how to query data using the OData query language.

4   Requests Resolver

The Requests resolver is an OData service exposing the created data model, and in charge of processing the end-user queries and building the query response based on the bindings and extended OpenAPI models generated during the import phase. Such process involves two steps, namely: query resolution and response resolution.

The query resolver interprets first the OData query in order to determine the target resource to retrieve (i.e., a collection of entities, a single entity or a property) and the options associated with the query (e.g., filter or ordering). The resolver transforms then the query into a set of API calls by tracing back the origin of each element thanks to the binding model. From the binding model we navigate first to the UML models then to the OpenAPI models. These OpenAPI models contain all the necessary details to generate the actual calls[6] as they contain the same information as the original OpenAPI definitions.

On the other hand, the response resolver is in charge of providing the result to the end-user by combining the different API answers in a single response conforming to the OData entity model defined in the OData metadata document.

5   Illustrative Example

To illustrate our approach, we consider the following REST APIs: BATTUTA[7], which allows retrieving the regions and cities of a country; and RESTCOUNTRIES[8], which allows getting general information about countries such as their languages, currencies and population. Our goal is to create a global API combining both APIs. Thanks to the global API, users will be able to query both kinds of country information (either geographical, general or both) in a transparent way, (i.e., without having to specify in each query what API/s the query

---

[6] We created a set of heuristics which map operations to entity elements. More information can be found at our repository.

[7] https://battuta.medunes.net/.

[8] https://restcountries.eu/.

should read from). As a preliminary step, we generated the OpenAPI definitions describing BATTUTA and RESTCOUNTRIES APIs using APIDiscoverer [9]. We used the resulting definitions as inputs for our approach.

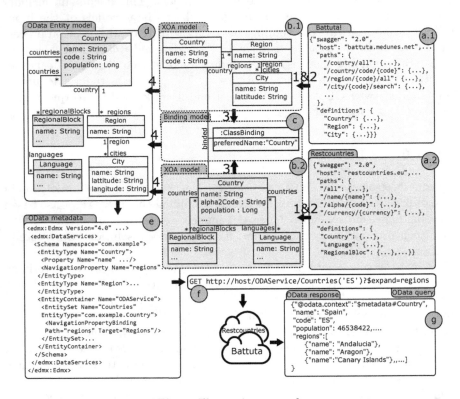

Fig. 4. Illustrative example.

Figure 4 illustrates the results of applying our composition mechanism on these APIs. Figures 4a.1 and a.2 show parts of the OpenAPI definitions of BATTUTA and RESTCOUNTRIES APIs, respectively. As explained in the previous section, the first step of the process generates an OpenAPI model describing the input definition, while the second step generates UML model where the data aspects have been refined and highlighted. Figure 4b.1 and b.2 show the generated UML models for BATTUTA and RESTCOUNTRIES APIs, respectively. As can be seen, the data model for the BATTUTA API includes the classes *Country*, *Region* and *City*, while the model for the RESTCOUNTRIES API includes the classes *Country*, *RegionalBlock*, and *Currency*. Figure 4c shows the binding model including a *ClassBinding* element for the *Country* entities of both data models, identified as a valid matching concept.

Figure 4d shows the OData Entity model created by joining the elements of both data models and resolving the match between the *Country* entities. As can be seen, the *Country* class is shared between both APIs and includes properties and relationships coming from both APIs. Figure 4e shows an excerpt of the Metadata document of the OData Entity model. This document can be retrieved by appending $metadata to the URL of the OData application and allows end-users to understand how to query the data.

OData defines a URL-based query language sharing some similarities with SQL that allows users to query the data described in the metadata document [16]. Figure 4f shows an example of an OData request to retrieve the details of *Spain* and its regions using the query option $expand[9]. This request relies on the concept binding for Country, which allows process the request using REST-COUNTRIES API (mainly for information about the country) and BATTUTA API (for information about the regions). Thus, the request is traced back to both RESTCOUNTRIES and BATTUTA APIs (i.e., the operations /alpha/{code} and /region/{code}/all, respectively), which are therefore queried. Figure 4g shows the response in OData format. More query examples can be found in our repository [1].

6   Tool Support

We created a proof-of-concept tool implementing our approach which we made available as an Open Source application [1]. Our tool has been implemented as a Java web application which can be deployed in any Servlet container (e.g., Apache Tomcat). The application relies on JavaServer Faces (JSF), a server-side technology for developing Web applications; and Primefaces[10], a UI framework for JSF applications; to implement a wizard guiding the user through the steps of the API importer and displaying the different models. The OpenAPI metamodel, the extended OpenAPI metamodel, and the binding metamodel have been implemented using the Eclipse Modeling Framework (EMF). OData implementation relies on Apache Olingo[11] to provide support for OData entity model, OData query language, and serialization.

7   Related Work

Most of the previous works on REST APIs composition are tight to specific API description languages [12]. For instance, some of them relied on WADL (Web Architecture Description Language) and hREST (HTML for RESTful Services) to describe the behavior of REST APIs, and WSMO (Web Service Modeling Ontology) and SA-REST (Semantic Annotation of Web Resources) to add semantic annotations (e.g., [8,13,15]). However, none of them gained a broad support mainly because those languages were not successfully adopted [12]. We decided to rely on the OpenAPI specification, which can be seen as a reference

---

[9] $expand specifies that the related resources have to be included in line with retrieved one.
[10] http://www.primefaces.org.
[11] http://olingo.apache.org/.

solution for REST APIs. The emergence of OpenAPI definitions has motivated initiatives to annotate OpenAPI definitions with semantic descriptions [7,14] and identify APIs for selection [3]. Our approach differs from these works by putting OpenAPI specification at the core of the composition strategy, but we can profit in the future from them (e.g., by considering semantic descriptions for concept matching).

Our approach focuses on the composition of data-oriented APIs, which allows us to rely on the family of approaches proposed for JSON data [5] and in the database world for schema matching and merging [4,17]. To the best of our knowledge, only the work by Serrano et al. [19] proposes a similar approach to ours but theirs require annotating REST APIs with Linked-Data ontologies and uses SPARQL to query to composed APIs.

8   Conclusion

We have presented a model-based approach to automatically compose and orchestrate data-driven REST APIs. Our approach parses OpenAPI definitions to extract data models, expressed as UML models, which are combined following a pragmatic matching strategy to create a global data model representing the union of all the data for the input APIs. The global model is exposed as an OData service, thus allowing users to easily perform queries using the OData query language. Queries on the global model are automatically translated into queries on the underlying individual APIs. In case users are not familiar with OData, OpenAPI definitions could also be easily derived from OData services[12]. Also, note that we illustrated our composition using OData but a similar approach could be followed to generate GraphQL APIs instead.

As future work we are interested in considering semantic descriptions for improving the matching strategy and non-functional aspects (like Quality-of-Service, QoS, or price) in the generation of the global model when alternative APIs have a high degree of overlapping. The latter would allow users to choose different resolution paths for the same query based on their preferences (e.g., by using free APIs when possible). We would like to extend our approach in order to support not only data retrieval but also data modification (i.e., support all CRUD operations). We are also interested in improving the maintainability of our approach by allowing the update of the composed APIs as they evolve.

References

1. APIComposer. http://hdl.handle.net/20.500.12004/1/A/APIC/001
2. Aué, J., Aniche, M., Lobbezoo, M., van Deursen, A.: An exploratory study on faults in web API integration in a large-scale payment company. In: International Conference on Software Engineering: Software Engineering in Practice, pp. 13–22 (2018)

---

[12] https://github.com/oasis-tcs/odata-openapi.

3. Baresi, L., Garriga, M., De Renzis, A.: Microservices identification through interface analysis. In: European Conference on Service-Oriented and Cloud Computing, pp. 19–33 (2017)
4. Boronat, A., Carsí, J.Á., Ramos, I., Letelier, P.: Formal model merging applied to class diagram integration. Electron. Notes Theoret. Comput. Sci. **166**, 5–26 (2007)
5. Cánovas Izquierdo, J., Cabot, J.: Composing JSON-based web APIs. In: International Conference on Web Engineering, pp. 390–399 (2014)
6. Cao, H., Falleri, J.-R., Blanc, X.: Automated generation of REST API specification from plain HTML documentation. In: Maximilien, M., Vallecillo, A., Wang, J., Oriol, M. (eds.) ICSOC 2017. LNCS, vol. 10601, pp. 453–461. Springer, Cham (2017). https://doi.org/10.1007/978-3-319-69035-3_32
7. Cremaschi, M., De Paoli, F.: Toward automatic semantic API descriptions to support services composition. In: European Conference on Service-Oriented and Cloud Computing, pp. 159–167 (2017)
8. De Giorgio, T., Ripa, G., Zuccalà, M.: An approach to enable replacement of SOAP services and REST services in lightweight processes. In: International Conference on Web Engineering, pp. 338–346 (2010)
9. Ed-Douibi, H., Cánovas Izquierdo, J.L., Cabot, J.: Example-driven Web API Specification Discovery. In: European Conference on Modelling Foundations and Applications (2017)
10. Ed-Douibi, H., Cánovas Izquierdo, J.L., Cabot, J.: OpenAPItoUML: a Tool to Generate UML Models from OpenAPI definitions. In: International Conference on Web Engineering (2018)
11. Espinha, T., Zaidman, A., Gross, H.G.: Web API growing pains: Stories from client developers and their code. In: International Conference on Software Maintenance, Reengineering and Reverse Engineering, pp. 84–93 (2014)
12. Garriga, M., Mateos, C., Flores, A., Cechich, A., Zunino, A.: Restful service composition at a glance: A survey. J. Netw. Comput. Appl. **60**, 32–53 (2016)
13. Lanthaler, M., Gütl, C.: Towards a RESTful service ecosystem. In: International Conference on Digital Ecosystems and Technologies, pp. 209–214 (2010)
14. Musyaffa, F.A., Halilaj, L., Siebes, R., Orlandi, F., Auer, S.: Minimally invasive semantification of light weight service descriptions. In: International Conference on Web Services, pp. 672–677 (2016)
15. Pautasso, C.: RESTful Web service composition with BPEL for REST. Data Knowl. Eng. **68**(9), 851–866 (2009)
16. Pizzo, M., Handl, R., Zurmuehl, M.: OData version 4.0 part 2: URL Conventions. Technical report, OASIS (2014)
17. Rahm, E., Bernstein, P.A.: A survey of approaches to automatic schema matching. VLDB J. **10**(4), 334–350 (2001)
18. Selic, B.: The pragmatics of model-driven development. IEEE Softw. **20**(5), 19–25 (2003)
19. Serrano, D., Stroulia, E., Lau, D., Ng, T.: Linked REST APIs: a middleware for semantic REST API integration. In: International Conference on Web Services, pp. 138–145 (2017)
20. Sheng, Q.Z., Qiao, X., Vasilakos, A.V., Szabo, C., Bourne, S., Xu, X.: Web services composition: a decade's overview. Inf. Sci. **280**, 218–238 (2014)

IaaS Service Selection Revisited

Kyriakos Kritikos[1(✉)] and Geir Horn[2]

[1] ICS-FORTH, Crete, Greece
kritikos@ics.forth.gr
[2] University of Oslo, Oslo, Norway
geir.horn@mn.uio.no

Abstract. Cloud computing is a paradigm that has revolutionized the way service-based applications are developed and provisioned due to the main benefits that it introduces, including more flexible pricing and resource management. The most widely used kind of cloud service is the Infrastructure-as-a-Service (IaaS) one. In this service kind, an infrastructure in the form of a VM is offered over which users can create the suitable environment for provisioning their application components. By following the micro-service paradigm, not just one but multiple cloud services are required to provision an application. This leads to requiring to solve an optimisation problem for selecting the right IaaS services according to the user requirements. The current techniques employed to solve this problem are either exhaustive, so not scalable, or adopt heuristics, sacrificing optimality with a reduced solving time. In this respect, this paper proposes a novel technique which involves the modelling of an optimisation problem in a different form than the most common one. In particular, this form enables the use of exhaustive techniques, like constraint programming (CP), such that both an optimal solution is delivered in a much more scalable manner. The main benefits of this technique are highlighted through conducting an experimental evaluation against a classical CP-based exhaustive approach.

1 Introduction

Cloud computing is a new computing paradigm that has revolutionized the way applications can be built and provisioned. Its high adoption is due to the main benefits that it delivers, which include flexible pricing and resource management as well as reduction of costs due to the outsourcing of infrastructure management.

This computing paradigm includes the potential delivery and exploitation of different service models, which include Infrastructure-as-a-Service (IaaS), Platform-as-a-Service (PaaS) and Software-as-a-Service (SaaS), with a gradual release of management control from the requester to the provider. The most widely used and researched model is the IaaS one. In this model, an infrastructure in the form of a Virtual Machine (VM) is offered to requesters to enable them to create an execution environment for their application components. Apart from this infrastructure, suitable tools are also supplied to requesters to enable them to better exploit this cloud service kind, including suitable restful management APIs.

K. Kritikos et al. (Eds.): ESOCC 2018, LNCS 11116, pp. 170–184, 2018.
https://doi.org/10.1007/978-3-319-99819-0_13

Once cloud computing has been set and evolved, it has also led to the rise of a new application design and provisioning model based on micro-services. This model caters for a better separation and reuse of business functionalities while enables a more flexible adaptation of the micro-service application. In this model, an application is functionally split into a set of services, which are deployed individually in containers in different VMs. As such, to better manage such an application's provisioning, there is a need to cover the selection and adaptation of the underlying IaaS services. This means that an initial set of IaaS services needs to be selected according to the application requirements, while the application can be reconfigured at runtime by either migrating micro-services from one IaaS service to another or creating new instances of the micro-services, e.g., to handle the additional, unexpected workload that might arrive.

Focusing on IaaS selection, various approaches have been proposed [1] which differ along the optimisation solving techniques that they adopt and the optimisation objective kinds that they can handle. This differentiation also impacts the capabilities of each approach with respect to the well-known solving time-to-optimality trade-off. For example, exhaustive approaches, like those adopting techniques like Constraint Programming (CP), are more suitable for delivering optimal results but in the expense of increased solving time. On the other hand, heuristic approaches more rapidly deliver near-optimal results.

In any case, current approaches follow a classical way to model the optimisation problem, where variables are mainly used to denote decisions that need to be taken with respect to which service component should be mapped to which IaaS offerings from those that satisfy its local (e.g., hardware or location) requirements. However, this classical way cannot scale in sight of the plethora of IaaS services available on the market. Just focusing on one big cloud provider like Amazon, one has to select among tens of thousands of IaaS offerings. Even if multiple local constraints are being supplied per service component, this can reduce the offering number to hundreds just for one cloud provider. However, by considering the combinational nature of the optimisation problem to solve, this can lead to a huge solution space that cannot be handled by any exhaustive approach, while the results provided by any heuristic approach would be just non-optimal, as a very small part of the solution space can be examined.

In our opinion, this inherent difficulty in the IaaS service selection problem has not been well and appropriately addressed in the literature. In this respect, this paper goes one step forward by proposing a novel technique which can enable the use of an exhaustive approach to a modified modelling of the optimisation problem in such a way that the main benefits of optimality are supplied in a much more scalable manner. In particular, in this modelling, the decision space is regulated by variables which map the service components to respective VM attributes. As the number of VM attributes is usually quite limited while the size of their value domain is small, this leads to the production of an optimisation problem which is less complex and leads to a quite reduced solution space.

While this modelling is more suitable, it comes also with a certain flaw. In particular, a solution mapping to a value for all these variables might not be associated with a real IaaS offering. This then required our approach to adopt a smart method to alleviate this. This method involves three main parts: (a) the derivation of the dependencies between the offering cost with respect to the values of the other VM variables in the form of a linear function; (b) the supply of if-then-else conditional statements which enable to reflect other dependencies between the different VM variables so as to further filter irrelevant combinations; (c) the post-processing of the produced solution to map it to a real one which has the least distance to the current, possibly virtual one.

The main benefits of our work are highlighted via an experimental evaluation assessing how well the IaaS selection problem is solved in the context of the Amazon cloud provider. The evaluation results show that our approach scales much better than a classical, exhaustive one and can deliver results of almost the same quality. Once the scalability limits are reached for the classical approach, the proposed one is also able to deliver results of even better quality.

The rest of the paper is structured as follows. The next section reviews the related work and provides important background knowledge. Section 3 analyses the proposed IaaS selection technique. Section 4 reports and discusses the main evaluation results. Finally, the last section concludes the paper and draws directions for further research.

2   Background

2.1   Related Work Analysis

Many approaches [2–4] have been proposed for VM consolidation in data centres. Such approaches tend to solve a similar problem, where instead of mapping application components to VMs, they associate VMs to respective hosts. As such, such approaches could be utilised only in the context of resource management internally within a cloud provider's data centre. However, their techniques are similar or equivalent to those used for solving the IaaS selection problem.

The IaaS selection approaches [1] either focus on local IaaS selection restricted to the context of one application component or on global IaaS selection where the selection concerns all components of a respective application. As this paper focuses over the second and more advanced form of the IaaS selection problem, the analysis is restrained over this form.

The global IaaS selection approaches differ [1] with respect to the solving technique adopted as well as in the number and kind of objectives optimised. Classically, depending on the solving technique used, there can be a trade-off between solving time and optimality. Exhaustive techniques like CP [5] or Linear Programming (LP) [6] attempt to explore the whole solution space so as to derive the most optimal solution. However, this exploration is costly with respect to solving time. In this respect, heuristic approaches have been adopted [7], such as nature-inspired ones, which tend to produce rapidly a sub-optimal solution.

Cost [8] is the dominant optimisation objective that is usually optimised [1]. However, there exist other approaches that also attempt to optimise resource-specific metrics [9], like the number of cores (mapping to the computational power to be devoted to a micro-service component). Others focus on reducing network latency [10] to guarantee a more suitable service execution time. There is also an approach which attempts to cover multiple levels [11] by being able to map resource-specific metrics to service-specific ones. Such an approach is then able to optimise metrics which reside at the service/application level.

To reduce the solving time by still adopting an exhaustive technique, some approaches attempt to learn from the application execution history. Such a learning enables then to fix some parts of the problem and thus accelerate its solving. Learning-based approaches adopt different ways to conduct this learning. In [12], a combined stochastic programming and learning approach is proposed which attempts to remember bad solutions and to discard them when re-solving the same optimisation problem. On the other hand, the approach in [13] employs a rule-based method to derive the best deployments for both the current application and its components from the application execution history.

The latter kind of approaches is complementary to our work. Such approaches could be employed for further reducing the solving time. However, the main advancement of the state-of-the-art lies on the capability to not require any prior knowledge about the application execution but rely on smart techniques that better and more rapidly explore the solution space by still employing an exhaustive technique to guarantee optimality. In this respect, a better trade-off between optimality and solving time is reached with respect to the state-of-the-art which is the main subject of research here. Further, our work is more scalable with respect to the others due to its capability to rely on a constant solution space when then number of VM offerings is increased.

2.2 IaaS Allocation Problem

The classical IaaS allocation problem attempts to optimise one or more objectives at the IaaS resource level. Let $x_{i,j} \in \{0,1\}$ be a binary decision variable indicating that application component type $i \in \mathbb{I}$ can be hosted on IaaS offering $j \in \mathbb{J}$. It is noted that there are $|\mathbb{I}| \cdot |\mathbb{J}|$ binary decision variables regarding the assignment of all application component types. Furthermore, there are $|\mathbb{I}|$ decision variables $n_i \in \mathbb{n}_i \subset \mathbb{N}_0$ representing the number of instances of application component type i.

The allocation problem has given Q "quality" dimensions for which the goodness of an allocation is measured; e.g., cost- or performance-related dimensions. Let

$$v_q\left(\mathbf{X}, \mathbf{n} \mid \boldsymbol{\theta}\right) : \{0,1\}^{|\mathbb{I}| \cdot |\mathbb{J}|} \times |\mathbb{I}| \mapsto \mathbb{D}_q \tag{1}$$

be the value function in dimension $q \in \{1, \ldots, Q\}$ given the matrix of the binary allocations $\mathbf{X} = [x_{i,j}]$ and the vector of instance counts $\mathbf{n} = [n_1, \ldots, |\mathbb{I}|]^T$. The vector $\boldsymbol{\theta}$ represents the context parameters for the allocation. The context parameters can be related to cost, performance or any other value that can be considered constant for the allocation problem. As an example, consider the situation where a quality dimension d represents the overall cost of an allocation and θ_j is the cost of IaaS offer j. Then, the value function takes the form $v_d\left(\mathbf{X}, \mathbf{n} \mid \boldsymbol{\theta}\right) = \sum_i \sum_j n_i \cdot x_{i,j} \cdot \theta_j$.

For each quality dimension value there is a utility function indicating how good this value is on a normalised scale, i.e. $u_q \left(v_q \left(\mathbf{X}, \mathbf{n} \,|\, \boldsymbol{\theta} \right) \right) : \mathbb{D}_q \mapsto [0, 1]$. The utility function is defined as the normalised value with respect to the extreme values of the domain.

$$u_q \left(v_q \left(\mathbf{X}, \mathbf{n} \,|\, \boldsymbol{\theta} \right) \right) = \frac{\sup \mathbb{D}_q - v_q \left(\mathbf{X}, \mathbf{n} \,|\, \boldsymbol{\theta} \right)}{\sup \mathbb{D}_q - \inf \mathbb{D}_q} \tag{2}$$

Two kind of constraints are involved in the problem modelling. The first kind involves component specific constraints that restrict the domain of respective decision variables. For each service component only one IaaS offering must be selected, which implies the following set of constraints

$$\sum_j x_{i,j} = 1 \quad \text{for all } i \tag{3}$$

The second kind of constraints attempts to reflect user requirements posed at the global level. For instance, if we consider the resource level, then we could have constraints for, e.g., VM offering characteristics like the cost and the number of cores. In general, the constraints of this kind can take the following form

$$g \left(\mathbf{X}, \mathbf{n} \,|\, \boldsymbol{\theta} \right) \le a \tag{4}$$

Additional constraints might also be posed to express further user requirements, like component co-location constraints. The interested reader can find more details about such constraints in [11].

Given that the utility is normalised in all dimensions, each of them is a simple unit less number in the interval $[0, 1]$, and the overall allocation utility can be computed as an affine combination of the utility dimensions, also known as the Simple Additive Weighting (SAW) [14] technique. The weights $w_q \in [0, 1]$ can be usually calculated by following the Analytic Hierarchy Process (AHP) [15]. The overall utility to be maximised is then given as

$$U \left(\mathbf{X}, \mathbf{n} \,|\, \boldsymbol{\theta} \right) = \sum_{q=1}^{Q} w_q \cdot u_q \left(v_q \left(\mathbf{X}, \mathbf{n} \,|\, \boldsymbol{\theta} \right) \right) \tag{5}$$

subject to the constraints (3)–(4).

The main issue with the above problem formulation lies on the huge solution space as can be seen from the Cartesian product in (1). By considering just one cloud provider (Amazon) and that common hardware constraints (over core number, memory, and storage size) are imposed at the local level which lead to around 400 Amazon cloud offerings matching each application component, this means that for an application with just 3 components, the number of combinations could be at least 3^{400}. Thus, such a solution space is already quite large. So, imagine what would be the case for applications with a greater size. The use of an exhaustive solver would be out of the question, while heuristic techniques would just supply non-optimal solutions as it will be impossible for them to check a great part of the solution space. This actually requires the proposal of a technique that more smartly explores or even filters the solution space. Such a technique is actually proposed in this paper and will be analysed in the following section.

3 Technique

In order to find a better trade-off between solving time and optimality, our technique attempts to modify the way the IaaS selection problem is modelled. The main rationale is that by changing the solution space and making it much smaller, we could still have the ability to exploit an exhaustive technique.

Indeed, this was the main idea that has been followed. Instead of mapping each service component to all the IaaS offerings that match it, we now associate it with the respective features of an IaaS offering, like the number of cores, the main memory size and so on. This new mapping has the advantage that the number of IaaS offering features is small and the value domain for that features is also small. Further, the problem now becomes independent on the number of IaaS offerings and thus more scalable.

However, this mapping comes with the penalty that the solution that is produced, mapping each service component to a value from the domain of each IaaS offering feature, might be virtual. This is actually quite probable as the offering space of any single provider is smaller than the solution space formulated by the cartesian product of the value domains of its IaaS offering features. In order to cope with this major issue, we have employed two main measures.

First, on the modelling side, we have introduced smart constraints that enable to further reduce the solution space, as it might be initially big, as well as guide the solution process towards picking more suitable combinations of values for the IaaS features.

Second, once a solution has been produced, we employ a post-processing logic aiming at making all IaaS offerings that have been mapped to the application components real. Such logic will be shown to employ a distance measure in order to guide the exploration for the finding of the most suitable, real IaaS offerings.

Both measures are now analysed in the following two sub-sections while the last one attempts to provide the complete modelling of the optimisation problem.

3.1 Smart Constraints

To reduce the solution space of a problem, one kind of measure would be to introduce special constraints which attempt to formulate dependencies between the main problem variables. Such constraints through the respective constraint propagation mechanism enable to restrict the solution space in a great extent.

As indicated in Sect. 2.1, one of the major factors always attempted to be optimised is cost. As such, we got the idea that we could introduce a respective constraint in the optimisation problem which correlates application component cost with the rest of the IaaS feature-based parameters. Such a constraint could be easily formulated if the exact cost model of an IaaS provider was known. However, even if such a cost model was available, it could be quite complex and might require formulating a great number of logical constraints of the form: **if** $(f_2 == v_{f_2} \wedge f_3 == v_{f_3} \ldots \wedge f_m == v_{f_m})$ **then** $(f_1 = 0.1)$, where f_k represents IaaS feature k and f_1 is the feature representing the cost. Unfortunately, logical constraints are difficult to handle in any kind of mathematical programming paradigm. They also create major scalability issues when their number is large.

In this respect, another idea came to our mind. Instead of attempting to formulate all possible logical constraint combinations, we could introduce just a single function enabling to model the needed correlation. This then led us to resort to linear regression techniques which have exactly this goal: to map one parameter or variable to a set of other variables. Thus, in the end, we could express *cost* as a function of the IaaS features for each cloud provider. This could then take the following constraint form: $f_1 = R_p(f_2, f_3, \ldots f_m)$, where $R_p(\cdot)$ is the regression function for IaaS provider p.

We could employ non-linear regression techniques instead but this did not seem to be actually needed as we were able to produce a relative accurate linear cost function for two of the most major IaaS providers, i.e., Amazon and Google.

However, the derived function does not exactly and completely solve the current issue. It provides a mapping that enables us to become independent of cost and be able to derive it through the rest of the variables. However, as IaaS offering cost maps to a quite large value domain, this action enabled us to significantly reduce the initial solution space.

To still follow the idea of formulating dependencies, the next clever development that has been performed was to introduce a restricted form of logical constraints for a widely used feature with a quite small domain. Such logical constraints will not thus be great in number and could be still easily handled by an exhaustive technique like Constraint Programming (CP).

This led us to focus on the *number of cores* feature which happens to have the smallest value domain among the most widely used IaaS features while also plays an important role in influencing IaaS offering cost. As such, we just processed the whole IaaS offering space of each cloud provider and attempted to create mappings from each value of the *number of cores* feature to the respective minimum and maximum value that has been anticipated for the rest of the features, including *cost*. This led to the definition of the following form of constraints:

$$\textbf{if } (f_2 == v_{f_2} \wedge p == 1) \textbf{ then}$$
$$(\min v_{f_1} \leq f_1 \leq \max v_{f_1}) \wedge (\min v_{f_3} \leq f_3 \leq \max v_{f_3})$$
$$\ldots \wedge (\min v_{f_m} \leq f_m \leq \max v_{f_m})$$

where f_2 is the *number of cores* feature and p is a variable that denotes a certain IaaS provider.

By combining the above two constraint forms, the solution space is reduced as cost feature is automatically calculated by a function while the different values of the core number feature guide the solution process and enable us to pick more correct values for the remaining IaaS features. This leads to a smarter solution space exploration that can rapidly diverge to the optimal solution.

3.2   Solution Post-processing

The produced solution may not be a valid one. The combination of IaaS feature values in the context of a certain IaaS provider does not guarantee that exactly a real IaaS offering can be designated. The introduction of smart constraints remedies slightly this but there is still a need for correcting this derived solution.

Such a correction or alignment is performed by examining the IaaS offering space of all providers to find a real offering which is as much as possible close to the derived virtual one. This involves first finding only the most relevant offerings from all providers via a normal matchmaking step, which can be performed ultra rapidly by employing unary matchmakers like the one in [16], and then performing the local search over them to find the most appropriate real IaaS offering.

The distance between the virtual and a real IaaS offering is calculated according to the following definition: $D\,(\text{real}, \text{virtual}) = \Delta_{\text{utility}}\,(\text{real}, \text{virtual}) + \Delta_{\text{position}}\,(\text{real}, \text{virtual})$, where Δ is a difference function. The first factor attempts to penalise the real IaaS offering based on the actual parameters that participate in the optimisation objectives of the IaaS selection problem. While the second factor attempts to penalise the real IaaS offering based on the distance of the position of the respective IaaS offering feature value within the (ordered) value domain of that feature.

By considering that the respective optimisation objective is only cost, the first term of the distance function could take the following form:

$$\Delta_{\text{utility}}\,(\text{real}, \text{virtual}) = \frac{cost_{\text{real}}}{cost_{\text{virtual}}} \cdot 100000$$

where $cost_{\text{real}}$ and $cost_{\text{virtual}}$ represent the cost of the two offerings. On the other hand, the second term of the distance function can be expressed as:

$$\Delta_{\text{position}}\,(\text{real}, \text{virtual}) = \sum_{b} \left| I_b\,(f_{b,\text{virtual}}) - I_b\,(f_{b,\text{real}}) \right| \cdot 1000$$

where $I_b(\cdot)$ represents the index function of the feature numbered as b which returns the position in the feature's (ordered) value domain for a specific value of that feature. The feature value is represented by $f_{b,\text{virtual}}$ and $f_{b,\text{real}}$ in the case of the virtual and real offering, respectively.

As it can be seen, the distance formula attempts to penalise more when we move far away from the expected utility of the solution and less when we pick more distant values for each feature with respect to its ordered value domain. This leads to imposing two levels of penalisation. As it will be shown in the evaluation section, this distance measure was enough for finding the right real solution out of a virtual one.

3.3   Optimisation Problem Formulation

The general process for solving the IaaS selection problem according to our approach follows three main steps: (a) problem formulation; (b) problem solving; (c) solution alignment, where the last step applies the respective distance-based search (see Sect. 3.2) for each application component with respect to the virtual IaaS offering derived for it.

In this subsection, we focus on the first process step by attempting to modify the formulation of the classical IaaS selection problem (see Sect. 2.2). Please note, though, that the same principles are followed which regard the use of the AHP and SAW techniques as well as linear utility functions.

The classical IaaS selection problem is, first of all, relaxed by replacing the binary decision variables with variables based on the smart constraints. The main decision variables of the relaxed optimisation problem comprise:

(a) component-to-feature variables of the form $x_{i,b}$ indicating that a certain value from the domain of feature b has been selected with respect to application component i. Thus, in contrast to the original problem, the domain of such variables now is a certain value set and not the boolean domain with just two possible values; and

(b) instance number variables for components as in the case of the original/class problem formulation; and

(c) variable p which denotes the IaaS provider.

This means that we have the introduction of one new decision variable, the modification of the first variable kind and the maintenance of the second with respect to the original problem.

The original constraints of the problem, (3)–(4) remain the same, and we are still maximising the overall utility (5). However, we do have a differentiation on the concrete level with respect to (4). In particular, the value of the different parameters at the global level can be actually easily computed from the sum of these parameters at the local level for each application component multiplied by the number of instances of that component (as we are considering mainly resource characteristics). For instance, the overall cost could be computed by the following formula: $v_1 = \sum_i x_{i,1} \cdot n_i$ if we consider that v_1 is the value of *cost* parameter which is indexed as 1 while $x_{i,1}$ maps to the local cost of the virtual IaaS offering for component i.

However, we do have now the introduction of new constraints, the smart ones, as indicated in Sect. 3.1.

$$\textbf{if } (p == P) \textbf{ then } x_{i,1} = R_p \left(x_{i,2}, x_{i,3}, \dots x_{i,|\mathbb{J}_P|} \right) \quad \text{for all } i, P \quad (6)$$

$$\textbf{if } (x_{i,2} == v_{2,l} \wedge p == P) \textbf{ then} \quad (7)$$

$$\min v_{x_{i,1}} \le x_{i,1} \le \max v_{x_{i,1}} \wedge \min v_{x_{i,3}} \le x_{i,3} \le \max v_{x_{i,3}}$$

$$\dots \wedge \min v_{x_{i,|\mathbb{J}_P|}} \le x_{i,|\mathbb{J}_P|} \le \max v_{x_{i,|\mathbb{J}_P|}} \quad \text{for all } l, P$$

Constraint (6) indicates that if a certain IaaS provider P is selected, the cost for each application component should be computed by applying the regression function for that provider over the remaining VM features. While Constraint (7) introduces the smart constraints reflecting the dependencies between the *number of cores* and the rest of IaaS offerings for IaaS provider P.

Discussion and Implementation Details. As it can be seen from the above formulation, the optimisation problem does include a greater number of constraints which, however, enable to better explore as well as filter the solution space.

Such a problem is not linear so it cannot be solved by employing different exhaustive technique kinds. On the contrary, CP seems to be the most suitable candidate as it can handle both non-linear and logic-based constraints, while it is also able to cater for the introduction of both integer- and float-based variables.

Based on this analysis, our implementation has relied on using the MiniZinc language for specifying the constraint optimisation problem as well as different kinds of CP solvers which can be deemed as best for the new IaaS selection problem formulation depending on the number of optimisation objectives involved. The use of MiniZinc enabled us to easily evaluate a great set of CP solvers and find those that have the best possible performance.

4 Evaluation

The goal of the experimental evaluation was to assess whether the performance and optimality of our proposed approach does advance the state-of-the-art. To conduct such evaluation we have relied on a certain experimental framework able to control the way the optimisation problem is formulated according to certain configuration parameters. The experiments were performed in a laptop with the following characteristics: (CPU: Inter Core i5-2430M with 2 cores and 2.4 GHz frequency, RAM: 6 GB, Disk: 500 GB SSD).

4.1 Experiment Configuration

Three main evaluation parameters were considered:

- cost as a parameter for evaluating the optimality of the examined approaches for only single objective optimisation problems;
- the solution utility as the parameter for evaluating the optimality of the examined approaches for multi-objective optimisation problems
- the solving time, i.e., the time required for solving a certain model of an optimisation problem, including any kind of solution post-processing time.

Each experiment was conducted in a series of steps by step-wisely varying one configuration parameter while leaving the rest stable. Each experiment step was computed (30) times and average values from the raw data were calculated for each approach considered and each from the above evaluation parameters.

The examined approaches were the following: (a) a classical problem formulation approach denoted as *OLD*; (b) a new problem formulation approach based on our work without the solution post-processing denoted as *NEW*; (c) the same approach as the previous one along with the solution post-processing denoted as *NEW_FIXED*. Each approach was implemented in Java and relied on the use of the best possible solver according to the actual problem at hand (variation point is the number of objectives as indicated in the previous section). To not make each solver run forever, a certain time limit was introduced (100 s) for the solving process in order to also reduce the execution time of the experiments.

The experimental framework involves using different configuration parameters to control the way the optimisation problem is generated: (a) the number of application components; (b) the number of cloud providers; (c) the number and kind of IaaS features; (d) the number of optimisation objectives. To keep the problem complexity low so as to also evaluate in an error-free manner the *OLD* approach, the cloud provider number was kept to the minimum (1, the Amazon provider) while the kind of IaaS features considered were the most common (core number, memory & disk size). Thus, to conduct the experiments, we varied mainly the component and optimisation objective number. We should also note that we have taken as a base all the actual real IaaS offerings available at the time of the experiments for Amazon AWS.

As there is no actual benchmark for evaluating IaaS selection approaches, we have relied on randomly creating IaaS service requests for each application component in each experiment step execution. Each such request attempts to randomly select a specific value from the value domain of each IaaS feature considered (out of the 3 ones in the current experiment configuration). This looks like a more correct way to produce the respective requests as we can consider that there is already widespread knowledge about which are the most suitable values for each IaaS feature across the whole developer community.

4.2   Experiment Analysis

Two main experiments have been conducted, which are now analysed below, having as their main variation point the number of optimisation objectives.

First Experiment. In this experiment, we consider only *cost* as the main optimisation objective and attempt to vary the number of application components from 1 to 6. The respective experiment results are depicted in Fig. 1.

The solving time results are quite expected. The two variants of the proposed approach seem to scale much better than the classical approach. Further, the classical approach already reaches the time limit when the component number equals to 5. The performance of the two proposed approach variants is similar. This means that the post-processing step does not occupy a great proportion of the overall approach execution time. In fact, the respective search time is mainly proportional to the number of matched IaaS offerings and application components. So, as the application component number linearly increases and the match number remains more or less stable, the post-processing time also increases linearly. So, the exponential behaviour in the two variants' performance is mainly due to the exponential increase of the solution space.

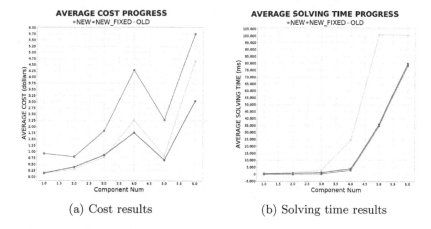

(a) Cost results   (b) Solving time results

Fig. 1. 1st experiment results

Concerning cost, i.e., the current optimality parameter, we can see that the non-aligned approach variant does not perform so well with respect to the rest of the approaches. This is mainly related to the precision of the linear regression function. As this precision is imperfect, we expect that the difference between the utility derived by this approach variant and the utility of the other approaches will be increased when the application component number increases. This is the actual case in the experiment results. With the sole exception that the utility difference between *NEW* and *OLD* gets reduced at some time point, mainly due to the deterioration of the utility on the side of the *OLD* approach.

Such a deterioration is mainly due to the fact that the *OLD* approach is starting to have a hard time in better exploring the solution space. Such that when the time limit is eventually reached, the quality of the solution deteriorates significantly. This gives the opportunity for the overall proposed approach, the *NEW_FIXED* to surpass the *OLD* one when the component number becomes 4.

Second Experiment. In the second experiment, the same control parameter is varied (from 1 to 3) but the number of optimisation objectives is now 2. These objectives include *cost* and *total number of cores*. The combination of these objectives make sense as there is usually a trade-off between computation power and cost. The respective results from this experiment are shown in Fig. 2.

As it can be seen, the *OLD* approach already reaches its time limit when the component number is two. This signifies that the increase in the number of objectives makes the exploration of the solution space more time consuming such that the exponential increase in that space's size makes the respective solver to more rapidly exceed the time limit posed. On the other hand, the two variants of the proposed approach are much more scalable while their solving time is always below 2 seconds. The time difference is again quite small between these variants, mainly due to the post-processing time penalty. This time penalty seems to be increased quite slightly with the increase in the component number.

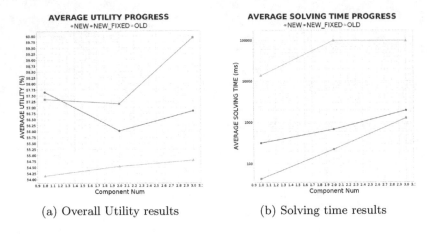

(a) Overall Utility results   (b) Solving time results

Fig. 2. 2nd experiment results

The overall utility results seem a little bit surprising. As we can see, the best approach is now *NEW* followed by *NEW_FIXED* and *OLD*. This looks more correct as *NEW* has more freedom to find the virtual solution exhibiting the best possible trade-off while *NEW_FIXED* is restrained over the capabilities of the current offerings locally matching each application component. Such capabilities might thus be less performant than those of the virtual solution found. The bad utility result of *OLD* is mainly due to its hard time to explore the solution space. Which is rather immediate than in the case of single-objective problems. While not shown here, due to page restriction reasons, the only case where *OLD* is better than the rest of the approaches is with respect to the overall cost (i.e., a part of the objective set) and only when the component number equals to 1.

4.3   Discussion

As it can be observed from the experiment results, our novel approach is much scalable and performant than the classical IaaS selection approach. Further, it is able to find a better solution in most of the cases, due to the solution space restrictions that the classical approach is facing. Only when the solution space is quite small, the classical approach could be considered as slightly better in optimality but such a case is not so frequent in reality. This validates the superiority of our approach which opens up new opportunities for solving IaaS and service selection problems in general in a much more optimal and rapid way.

5   Conclusions

This paper has presented a novel approach which exhibits a better trade-off between optimality and solving time for the IaaS selection problem. In particular, this approach models differently this optimisation problem and enables as such the scalable use of state-of-the-art exhaustive solvers for optimally solving it. The approach involves changing the decision variables as well as introducing smart constraints in the model of the optimisation problem. This enables to reduce the solution space significantly as well as have a better way to explore it. Due to a side-effect of the modified problem modelling, the proposed approach involves a solution post-processing step which attempts to guarantee that the components of the application at hand are mapped to real IaaS offerings.

The following future work directions will be pursued. First, we plan to support more cloud providers apart from Amazon and Google in our implementation as well as more thoroughly evaluate our approach in the increased solution space that will be formulated. Second, we plan to expand the modelling of the optimisation problem to cover multiple levels of abstraction. Third, we will explore whether a learning-based method could be additionally employed to further reduce the solving time of our approach. Finally, we will investigate whether additional smart constraints can be incorporated into the optimisation problem model such that the solution post-processing can be avoided.

Acknowledgements. The research leading to these results has received funding from European Union's Horizon 2020 programme under grant agreement No 731664 (concerning the Melodic EU project).

References

1. Sun, L., Dong, H., Hussain, F.K., Hussain, O.K., Chang, E.: Cloud service selection: state-of-the-art and future research directions. J. Netw. Comput. Appl. **45**, 134–150 (2014)
2. Dong, J., Jin, X., Wang, H., Li, Y., Zhang, P., Cheng, S.: Energy-saving virtual machine placement in cloud data centers. In: CCGrid, pp. 618–624. IEEE/ACM (2013)
3. Casalicchio, E., Menascé, D.A., Aldhalaan, A.: Autonomic resource provisioning in cloud systems with availability goals. In: CAC, Miami, Florida, USA, vol. 1(1–1), p. 10. ACM (2013)
4. Jayasinghe, D., Pu, C., Eilam, T., Steinder, M., Whally, I., Snible, E.: Improving performance and availability of services hosted on IaaS clouds with structural constraint-aware virtual machine placement. In: SCC, Washington, DC, USA, pp. 72–79. IEEE Computer Society (2011)
5. Rossi, F., van Beek, P., Walsh, T.: Handbook of Constraint Programming. Elsevier Science Inc., New York (2006)
6. Van Hentenryck, P., Saraswat, V.: Strategic directions in constraint programming. ACM Comput. Surv. **28**(4), 701–726 (1996)
7. Dastjerdi, A.V., Buyya, R.: Compatibility-aware cloud service composition under fuzzy preferences of users. IEEE Trans. Cloud Comput. **2**(1), 1–13 (2014)
8. Chaisiri, S., Lee, B.S., Niyato, D.: Optimization of resource provisioning cost in cloud computing. IEEE Trans. Serv. Comput. **5**(2), 164–177 (2012)
9. Soltani, S., Elgazzar, K., Martin, P.: QuARAM service recommender: a platform for IaaS service selection. In: UCC, Shanghai, China, pp. 422–425. ACM (2016)
10. Klein, A., Ishikawa, F., Honiden, S.: Towards network-aware service composition in the cloud. In: WWW (2012)

11. Kritikos, K., Plexousakis, D.: Multi-cloud application design through cloud service composition. In: Cloud, pp. 686–693. IEEE Computer Society, June 2015
12. Horn, G.: A vision for a stochastic reasoner for autonomic cloud deployment. In: Second Nordic Symposium on Cloud Computing & Internet Technologies (Nordi-Cloud 2013), pp. 46–53. ACM, September 2013
13. Kritikos, K., Magoutis, K., Plexousakis, D.: Towards knowledge-based assisted IaaS selection. In: CloudCom, pp. 431–439. IEEE Computer Society, December 2016
14. Hwang, C., Yoon, K.: Multiple Criteria Decision Making. Lecture Notes in Economics and Mathematical Systems. Springer, Heidelberg (1981). https://doi.org/10.1007/978-3-642-48318-9
15. Saati, T.: The Analytic Hierarchy Process. McGraw-Hill, New York (1980)
16. Kritikos, K., Plexousakis, D.: Novel optimal and scalable nonfunctional service matchmaking techniques. IEEE Trans. Serv. Comput. **7**(4), 614–627 (2014)

An Innovative MapReduce-Based Approach of Dijkstra's Algorithm for SDN Routing in Hybrid Cloud, Edge and IoT Scenarios

Alina Buzachis, Antonino Galletta, Antonio Celesti$^{(\boxtimes)}$, and Massimo Villari

MIFT Department, University of Messina, Messina, Italy
{abuzachis,angalletta,acelesti,mvillari}@unime.it

Abstract. Nowadays, with the advent of Cloud/Edge Computing and Internet of Things (IoT) technologies, we are facing with a tremendous increase of network connections required by different new cutting-edge distributed applications spread over a wide geographical area. Specifically, the proliferation of IoT devices used by such applications and associated data streams require a highly dynamic network ecosystem; the traditional network technologies are not adequate to efficiently support them in terms of routing strategies. In order to deploy such applications, providers need an advanced awareness of the Cloud/Edge and IoT networks in terms of flexible packets routing that can compute the paths according to different parameters including, e.g., hops, latency, and energy efficiency policies. In this context, Software Defined Networking (SDN) has emerged as the answer to these needs decoupling control and data planes, using a logically centralized controller able to manage the underlying networking resources. In this paper, we focus on the adoption of Dijkstra's algorithm in SDN environments to support applications deployed in Cloud/Edge and IoT scenarios. Specifically, considering a highly scalable network topology that includes thousands of network devices, in order to reduce the path computation, we propose a revised MapReduce approach of Dijkstra's algorithm. Experiments show that, compared to the sequential implementation, the MapReduce approach drastically reduces the shortest path computation performance when considering a complex Cloud/Edge and IoT network topology including thousands of virtual network devices.

Keywords: SDN · MapReduce · Dijkstra · Cloud computing
Edge computing · Internet of Things

A. Celesti—On behalf of Gruppo Nazionale Per il Calcolo Scientifico (GNCS) - INdAM.

K. Kritikos et al. (Eds.): ESOCC 2018, LNCS 11116, pp. 185–198, 2018.
https://doi.org/10.1007/978-3-319-99819-0_14

1   Introduction

Nowadays, in the era of Internet of Things (IoT), we are observing a proliferation of new cutting-edge pervasive applications. In this panorama, Gartner
[1] predicts that there will be 26 billion of IoT devices by 2020 representing an
almost 30-fold increase from 900 million in 2009. Despite the rapid advances
of IoT technologies, due to hardware limitations, applications deployed on IoT
devices (e.g. Single Board Computers (SBCs), mobile phones, tablets, etc.) have
to interact with the microservice architecture hosted by the central Cloud Computing [2,3] data centers and, in order to reduce network latency, also by devices
distributed in an intermediate layer called Edge Computing [4].

The microservice architecture is a variant of the traditional Service-Oriented
Architecture (SOA) that structures an application as a collection of loosely coupled fine-grained services (i.e., microservices) based on lightweight protocols. The
decomposition of applications into different smaller services allows to improve
modularity, making them simpler and more resilient. Specifically, applications
require the interaction of different smaller services or microservices generally
spread in the Cloud, Edge and IoT layers over a wide geographical network.
This introduces an important issue: ICT operators must flexibly manage the
network in order to meet the requirements of today's emerging applications. In
fact, network awareness [5] is fundamental during the deployment of microservices on Cloud, Edge and IoT devices. Unfortunately, ICT operators are not able
to have a view of the whole network topology and to think about quickly changing the setup of the physical network assets, if needed, in order to meet the
requirements of their hybrid Cloud/Edge/IoT applications [6–8], because network connections are generally shared among different providers. Furthermore,
this would cause management problems for Internet Service Providers (ISPs).
Therefore, ICT operators need an alternative solution that allows them to gain
an advanced awareness of Cloud/Edge and IoT networks in terms of flexible
packets routing in order to compute paths according to different parameters
including, e.g., hops, latency, and energy efficiency policies.

Driving the need for a new networking solution, Network Function Virtualization (NFV) was introduced with the purpose of building networks without
being dependent on ISPs. In particular, Software Defined Networking (SDN) has
emerged as the answer to these needs by decoupling control and data planes,
using a logically centralized controller able to manage the underlying physical
resources of the network, abstracting them to allow ICT operators to perform
rapid and automatic configuration of network routing. The ability to dynamically
define the behavior of a network via SDN gives ICT operators the flexibility to
adapt the network to applications' requirements, without complex and expensive
reconfiguration tasks on physical network devices.

One of the main algorithms adopted for network routing is Dijkstra that
allows to find the shortest path between two nodes. This algorithm has been
recently adopted in SDN environments.

In this paper, unlike the scientific works available in the literature, in order to
address a Cloud/Edge and IoT scenario that includes a large number of network

nodes, we propose a revised MapReduce version of Dijkstra's algorithm to optimize the connections required by applications whose microservices are deployed over Cloud/Edge and IoT environments.

The experiments carried out haves shown that, with a minimal configuration of the Hadoop cluster - 3 computational nodes and an input dataset describing a complex Cloud/Edge and an IoT network topology with 10.000 virtual network devices, since the number of devices present within the network increases the path computation time performed with the MapReduce approach drastically improves up to approximately 92% compared to the the sequential one.

The remainder of the paper is organized as follows. In Sect. 2, we present an overview of related works and contributions. Motivation is discussed in Sect. 3. In Sect. 4, we introduce some preliminary knowledge regarding the SDN concept. Starting with a sequential implementation of Dijkstra's algorithm for SDN environments, a revised MapReduce version is presented in Sect. 5. Section 6 shows the simulation results and observations. Finally, this paper is concluded with Sect. 7.

2 Related Work

Recently, several initiatives have been proposed regarding the application of the Dijkstra's algorithm in SDN. The limits of traditional hierarchical architecture design principles based on Dijkstra's algorithm in the perspective of emerging Cloud/Edge computing systems are highlighted in [9]. One of the major challenges is the mapping of virtual networks onto physical network infrastructures, which is defined as a Virtual Network Embedding (VNE) problem. In this context, a surviving virtual network mapping problem was formulated and solved using an SVE Survivable Heuristic (GRC-SVNE) algorithm based on the Dijkstra's algorithm proposed in [10]. Furthermore, an alternative GRC-M algorithm in combination in combination with the Multicommodity Flow (MCF) algorithm is discussed in [11].

The application of the Dijkstra's algorithm in SDN raises numerous challenges in terms of reliability, capacity control and scalability. The application of network virtualization in Fiber-wireless (FiWi) networks with the purpose to alleviate bandwidth tension when a physical link serving different virtual networks fail is discussed in [12]. In particular, a shared protection mechanism is embedded within the Dijkstra's routing algorithm in order to improve its reliability when a physical link fails. A reliable security-oriented SDN routing mechanism, named RouteGuardian, which considers the capabilities of SDN switch nodes combined with a piece of Network Security Virtualization framework is proposed in [13]. In particular, it overcomes the limits of the traditional routing mechanisms in SDN, based on the Dijkstra's shortest path, in terms of capacity control in order to prevent network congestion. A self-adjusting architecture based on Pairing heap to scale SDN network overcoming scalability issues due to a centralized control plane is proposed in [14]. By using Network Virtualization Function (NVF), the whole network is viewed as a huge heap and divide it into several sub heaps repeatedly until get the basic units of physical switches in the network. In this context, the Dijkstra's algorithm is applied and optimized based on Pairing heap outperforming the original one when the network is dense.

Dijkstra's Algorithm has been recently used in many emerging applications based on SDN. In [15], an autonomous agent based shortest path load balancing using the Dijkstra's algorithm was proposed to find the shortest path to virtual machines when a Cloud services saturates its processing capabilities. A piece of framework to lightweight process the 3D shape based on Web Browser considering Web3D technology areas in the era of "Internet plus" is discussed in [11]. This framework is based on Mesh Segmentation. Therefore, a new Dijkstra-based mesh segmentation approach is presented. The application of SDN/Open-Flow in an Internet Protocol Television (IPTV) multicasting implementation is proposed in [16]. In this context, an important function of IPTV multicasting is the Joint/Leave request of client in a multicast group. In order to obtain an efficient IPTV service routing, Dijkstra's and Prim's algorithms were used to comparatively calculate minimum total edge weight. Moreover, the Mininet environment is used to emulate the system, that consists of Open vSwitch and a POX controller. Experiments compare the transmission time of the first joint/receive packet to a client when using Dijkstra's and Prim's algorithms. In [17], the Service Function Chaining (SFC) was used as a model of the Shortest Path Tour Problem in order to find the minimum transmission cost path by exploiting a constructed multistage graph. In particular, the minimum transmission cost paths for multiple SFC classes is derived using the Dijkstra's Shortest Path Algorithm with resource constraints in a flexible way. Finally, some experiments are carried out and the results show the effectiveness and efficiency of our proposed method.

Differently from the scientific work available in literature, in this paper, we focus on a Cloud scenario based on SDN in which the Dijkstra algorithm can benefit from parallel processing in order process a huge amount of virtual network nodes in order to assess best paths.

3   Motivation

With reference to those applications whose structure obeys the microservice architecture in which microservices are deployed on devices across the Cloud, Edge and IoT layers, there is the need to optimize certain network parameters to align applications requirements in terms of latency and energy consumption with network connections.

Figure 1 illustrates a scenario that includes two hosts, H_1 and H_2, that need to communicate through a network topology including switches S_1, S_2, S_3 and S_4. Moreover, we consider two applications App_1 and App_2 that run on both host H_1 and host H_2. App_1 consists of microservice MS_1, while App_2 consists of microservice MS_2.

Suppose App_1 wants to take care of energy consumption, while App_2 wants to take care of latency minimization; applying the shortest path routing approach

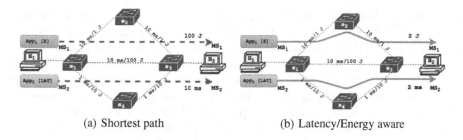

(a) Shortest path   (b) Latency/Energy aware

Fig. 1. Routing approaches

shown in Fig. 1(a), the connections between H_1 and H_2 pass through the switches S_1 and S_3. This approach is not the best in terms of energy consumption and latency minimization because we obtain $100J$ of energy for App_1 and $10ms$ of latency for App_2.

Figure 1(b) shows an alternative latency/energy aware routing approach that allows to better optimize network resources and paths according to different application requirements. In fact, although they share the same source and destination hosts, App_1 and App_2 are routed separately according to their requirements. In particular, with regard to App_1, the connections between H_1 and H_2 pass through S_1, S_4 and S_3 with $2J$ of energy consumption, while as regards App_2, connections between H_1 and H_2 pass through S_1, S_2 and S_3 with $2ms$ of latency. Furthermore, it is possible to organize customized network connections between H_1 and H_2 for each application such as:

- **Simplex.** Transmission is allowed in only one direction: H_1 always acts as a transmitter, while H_2 acts as receiver.
- **Half Duplex.** Transmission is allowed in both directions, but not simultaneously: when H_1 acts as a transmitter, H_2 acts as a receiver.
- **Full Duplex.** Transmission is allowed in both directions at the same time: both H_1 and H_2 act, at the same time, as transmitter and receiver.

The objective of this paper is to combine shortest path and latency/energy aware routing approaches for SDN environments supporting Cloud, Edge and IoT scenarios. In order to achieve this, we adopt the Dijkstra's algorithm. Although several scientific works have been recently proposed focusing on the adoption of Dijkstra's algorithm in SDN, in this paper, we focus on a revised MapReduce approach of this algorithm that can improve processing times when thousands of Cloud, Edge and IoT devices are considered.

4   SDN Overview

SDN technology is an emerging network architecture in which network control is decoupled from forwarding and directly programmable. The migration of control logic, closely linked to individual network devices, to accessible Cloud, Edge and

IoT devices, allows to abstract the underlying networking infrastructure giving, to applications, a virtual vision of the network. Management is centralized in a purely software SDN controller that has a global view of the network. As a result, the network appears to applications as a single logical switch. With SDN, it is possible to achieve the control of the network, from a single point, regardless of ISPs and network assets, simplifying network design and usage. Moreover, SDN abstraction also simplifies the operation of the network devices, as they no longer need to understand and process thousands of standard protocols, but they simply have to accept instructions from the SDN controller.

Basic SDN operations are performed by a standard protocol that allows the SDN controller to send instructions to the various switches. OpenFlow is one of main open protocols that allows an intermediate communication plane between the SDN controller, i.e., the control plane device, and routers/switches, i.e., data plane devices, that enforces network policies. In particular, OpenFlow routers and/or switches include one or more flow tables and/or group tables updated by an OpenFlow controller that can add or delete flow entries responsively or proactively. Several OpenFlow controller solutions are OpenDaylight, Floodlight, POX, Pyretic, and so on.

Figure 2 shows the general architecture of latency/energy aware applications over OpenFlow. Looking up at the top of Fig. 2, different applications with specific network requirements interact with the OpenFlow controller that monitors their network latency and energy consumption by receiving information from OpenFlow network devices. If a particular network latency and energy consumption parameter does not meet the requirements of an application, the OpenFlow controller enforces network changes to OpenFlow devices.

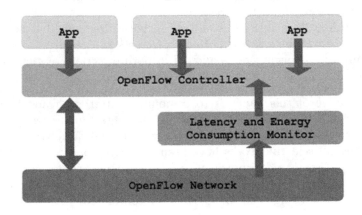

Fig. 2. Architecture of latency/energy aware applications.

5   Dijkstra's Algorithm

Dijkstra's algorithm is very useful in deriving the best routing path for sending packets from a specific source node to a destination node in an SDN environment where different parameters (such as hops, latency and energy consumption) associated to each link in the network must be considered in order to meet the application requirements deployed in Cloud/Edge and IoT scenarios. Suppose we can derive from the SDN topology a graph $G = (V, E)$, which is weighted, directed and connected. Figure 3 shows an example of a real/virtual network through a weighted, directed and connected graph. Therefore, V represent the set of network devices and E the set of network links, while to each link is associated a weight $w[e]$ quantifying different network parameters.

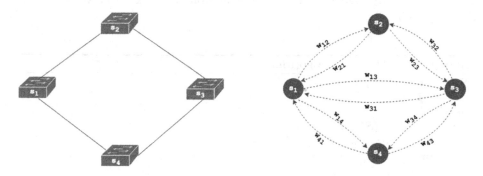

Fig. 3. Representation of an SDN topology through a weighted, directed and connected graph.

A full duplex connection between two network devices can be arranged as a pair of simplex connections each represented as a directed edge. Given that, we suppose there is at least a path between a network device to each other. Considering the latency minimization as an application preference, we assume that $w[e]$ quantify the latency associated to the edge that connects two nodes. A latency-oriented application will be provided with a path with lowest latency between the source and intended destination microservice deployed in the Cloud, Edge or IoT layers. Allocated virtual paths will be periodically updated as underlying physical network changes to ensure a given latency requirement.

Considering that there are many factors that affect the properties of the connections, network changes are more and more varied and unpredictable because the Cloud/Edge and IoT networking scenarios are very complex. This complexity is due to the fact that virtual paths that directly connect two nodes, actually pass through tunnels and/or overlay networks, built on different physical network devices distributed in the Cloud, Edge and IoT layers, that can frequently change.

5.1   Sequential Approach

One of the most common problems in graph theory is represented by the single-source shortest path problem. Moreover, the task deals to find the shortest paths from a source node to all other nodes in the graph. In particular, edges are associated with costs or weights, in which case the task is to compute lowest-cost or lowest-weight paths.

Given a weighted, directed and connected graph $G = (V, E)$, with V the set of vertexes and E the set of edges, the Dijkstra's algorithm uses a Greedy strategy to solve the problem of minimum paths with single source s of the graph $G = (V, E)$ if all the weights are non-negative.

Algorithm 1 shows the sequential Dijkstra's algorithm pseudo-code, whose input is a given connected graph $G = (V, E)$ represented with adjacency lists and $w(u, v) \geq 0$ representing the edge weight from a vertex u to a vertex v, and the single source node s.

Algorithm 1. Dijkstra's Algorithm

INPUT $G = (V, E)$, s
OUTPUT $d|V|$
$\quad d[s] \leftarrow \emptyset$
$\quad$ **for all** $v \in V - \{S\}$ **do**
$\quad\quad d[v] \leftarrow \infty$, for each $v \neq s$, $v \in V$
$\quad$ **end for**
$\quad S \leftarrow \emptyset$
$\quad$ **while** $q \neq \emptyset$ **do**
$\quad\quad u \leftarrow Extract - Min(Q, d)$
$\quad\quad S \leftarrow S \cup \{u\}$
$\quad\quad$ **for all** $v \in neighbours[u]$ **do**
$\quad\quad\quad$ **if** $d[v] > d[u] + w(u, v)$ **then**
$\quad\quad\quad\quad d[v] \leftarrow d[u] + w(u, v)$
$\quad\quad\quad$ **end if**
$\quad\quad$ **end for**
$\quad$ **end while**
$\quad$ **return** d

The algorithm maintains a set S that contains the vertexes whose minimum path weight from the source s has already been determined, i.e., for each vertex $v \in S$ it is worth $d[v] = d(s, v)$. The algorithm repeatedly selects the vertexes $u \in V - S$ with the minimum shortest path estimation, inserts u into S, and releases all the edges outgoing from u. Moreover, a queue with priority Q that contains all the nodes $V - S$ is kept, using the respective values d as key.

5.2   MapReduce Approach

The MapReduce approach of the Dijkstra's algorithm is implemented in Hadoop. From an architectural point of view, there are two types of nodes that control the job execution: one JobTracker and several TaskTrackers. The first acts as master node and coordinates all job executions by scheduling all tasks to different TaskTrakers that act as workers. TaskTrackers perform the assigned tasks and send back to the JobTracker reports on the processing status. If a task fails, the JobTracker reschedules it on another TaskTracker. When a MapReduce job is invoked by an user, the JobTracker divides the job into a set of tasks that are assigned to TaskTrackers to process the job in parallel.

As previously discussed, in the sequential approach the key element is represented by the priority queue Q that keeps a globally-sorted list of vertexes by current distance. This is not possible in MapReduce, as the programming model does not provide a mechanism for exchanging global data. Therefore, we adopted a brute force approach known as parallel breadth-first search. First of all, as a simplification, we assumed that all edges have associated unit weights. This assumption allows us to make the algorithm easier to be understood. The basic idea of the MapReduce Dijkstra's algorithm is that iteratively the distance of all vertexes directly connected to the source vertexes is one; the distance of all vertexes directly connected to those is two; and so on.

Suppose we want to compute the shortest path to vertex n. The shortest path must go through one of the vertexes in M that contains an outgoing edge to n. Therefore, we need to examine all $m \in M$ to find m_s, the vertex with the shortest distance. The shortest distance to n is the distance to $m_s + 1$.

The pseudo-code of the parallel breadth-first search algorithm is provided in the Algorithms 2 and 3. As already assumed for the sequential approach of the Dijkstra's algorithm, we consider a connected, directed graph represented with adjacency lists. Distance to each vertex is directly stored alongside the adjacency list of that vertex, and initialized with distance $d[v]$, $v \in V$ to ∞, except for the source vertex, whose distance to itself is zero. Therefore, in the pseudo-code, n denotes the *nodeid* (i.e., an integer) and N denoted the node's corresponding to the adjacency list. Substantially, the algorithm works by mapping over all vertexes and emitting a key-value pair for each neighbor on the vertex's adjacency list. Therefore, the key will contain the *nodeid* of the neighbor, and the value will be the current distance plus one.

To achieve the implementation of the Dijkstra's algorithm using the MapReduce programming model it has been necessary to implement the $Map()$ and $Reduce()$ functions as follows.

- **Map()** is invoked in the Mapper task for each available vertex within the graph. The output of the Mapper produces different key-value pairs - a key value pair having as key the source vertex, and as value the adjacent vertexes and another key-value pair where the key is given by the source vertex and the value represents the minimum distance value.

– **Reduce()** for each key vertex all distances are gathered together and the minimum between them is chosen. Gathering of distances is performed by the Hadoop framework while the choice of the minimum distance is implemented by the user. The output of the Reducer produces another key-value pair where the key is represented by the respective selected vertex and the value is the minimum distance.

Parallel breadth-first search is an iterative algorithm, in which each iteration corresponds to a MapReduce job. At the first iteration, the algorithm discovers all vertexes that are connected to the source. At the second iteration, all vertexes connected to those are discovered, and so on. With each iteration, the algorithm expands the search frontier by one hop.

A crucial aspect of the algorithm, is the determination of the number of iterations that it needs in order to finish the computation. Typically, there are *six degrees of separation* suggesting that everyone on the planet is connected to everyone else by at most six steps (the people a person knows are one step away, people that they know are two steps away, etc.). In practical terms, we will iterate our algorithm until there are no more vertex distances that are ∞.

The execution of an iterative MapReduce algorithm requires a non-MapReduce "driver" program, which submits a MapReduce job in order to iterate the algorithm, checks to see if a termination condition has been met, and if not, repeats. The iterative approach is realized using the Hadoop API to construct "counters", which, can be used for counting events that occur during the execution, e.g., number of corrupt records, number of times a certain condition is met, or anything that the programmer desires. Counters can be defined to count the number of vertexes that have distances of ∞: at the end of the job, the final counter value is checked in order to see if another iteration is necessary. The counter values of each worker are periodically propagated to the master. It brings together the values from the completion of the mapping operations and reducing and subsequently returned to the user. The Mapper and Reducer through the use of Reporter can communicate the progress.

Algorithm 2. Mapper Class Pseudo-code

Class $MAPPER$
method $MAP(nid\ n,\ node\ N)$
  $d \leftarrow N.Distance$
  $EMIT(nid\ n, N)$
  for all $nodeid\ m \in N.ADJACENCYLIST$ **do**
    $EMIT(nid\ m,\ d+1)$
  end for

Algorithm 3. Reducer Class Pseudo-code

Class *REDUCER*
method *REDUCE*($nid\ m$, $[d_1, d_2, ...]$)
  $d \leftarrow \infty$
  $M \leftarrow \emptyset$
  for all $d \in counts\ [d_1, d_2, ...]$ **do**
    if *ISNODE*(d) **then**
      $M \leftarrow d$
    else
      if $d < d_{min}$ **then**
        $d_{min} \leftarrow d$
      end if
    end if
  end for
  $M.DISTANCE \leftarrow d_{min}$
  EMIT($nid\ m$,$node\ M$)

6   Experiments

We carried out a scalability analysis in order to investigate the performance of our sequential and MapReduce implementations of Dijkstra's algorithm. In particular, the scalability analysis is based on the input dataset size to evaluate the average execution time of both implemented approaches. Specifically, we generated several input datasets representing network topologies describing different hybrid Cloud, Edge and IoT scenarios, and of different size (i) 10, (ii) 100, (iii) 1000, and (iv) 10000 vertexes respectively. We remark that in each proposed scenario the vertexes are randomly connected to each other in order to create a weighted, directed and connected graph. In order to have truthful results we performed 30 subsequent iterations of the algorithm for both distributed and sequential approaches and calculated mean values and 95% confidence intervals respectively

6.1   Experimental Setup

We use three server nodes to deploy the Hadoop MapReduce cluster. Each node has 4 vCPUs at 2.9 GHz, 8 GB of RAM and Ubuntu Server 16.04 LTS, all servers install Apache Hadoop 2.6.1 and JDK version 1.8. The sequential approach of Dijkstra's algorithm, implemented in Java, runs on another server node having the same software and hardware features.

Figure 4(a) illustrates the trend of both distributed and sequential approaches using an input dataset that describes a topology composed of 10 network devices. The execution times of the distributed approach are very large respect to those obtained with the sequential one. This behavior is due to the overhead introduced by the intra-cluster nodes communications. In fact, the MapReduce approach requires roughly 77 s respect to the sequential one which requires only few milliseconds.

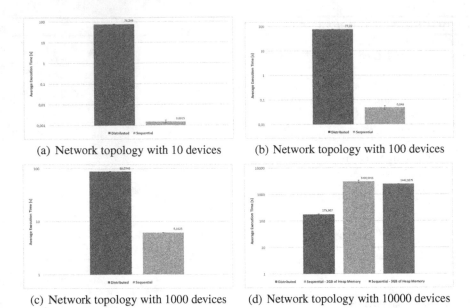

(a) Network topology with 10 devices   (b) Network topology with 100 devices

(c) Network topology with 1000 devices   (d) Network topology with 10000 devices

Fig. 4. Execution Times [s] of the Sequential/MapReduce Approach of Dijkstra's Algorithm (Color figure online)

Figure 4(b) illustrates the mean execution time of both distributed and sequential approaches using an input dataset that describes a topology composed of 100 network devices. The trend is very similar to that obtained in the Fig. 4(a), with the difference that there is a slight variation of execution times. In particular, the execution time of the distributed approach ranges around 79 s, while for the sequential one increases by a couple of milliseconds

Figure 4(c) illustrates the mean execution time of both distributed and sequential approach using an input dataset that describes a topology composed of 1000 network devices. The trend is similar to that illustrated previous two figures. In fact, the execution time registered with the distributed approach increases sligthly by 10 s, the sequential one still be more efficient.

Figure 4(d) illustrates the mean execution time of both distributed and sequential approaches using an input dataset describing a network topology with 10000 network devices. In this configuration, the trend is different. In particular, the execution times collected using the distributed approach are slower - circa 170 s, compared to those obtained through the sequential one.

This behavior is evident also performing a vertical scalability by increasing the heap memory of the JVM from $2\,GB$ to $3\,GB$. Indeed, with reference to orange and green bars of Fig. 4(d) representing the mean response times of the sequential approach of Dijkstra's algorithm with respectively 2 GB and 3 GB of heap memory reserved for the JVM, the mean processing times are roughly constant and greater than 1000 s. In conclusion, the distributed approach of Dijkstra's algorithm is suitable for huge network topologies (10000 network devices) being 95% and 92% faster than the sequential one configured with $2\,GB$ and $3\,GB$ of heap memory reserved for the JVM.

7   Conclusion and Future Work

In this paper, we considered a scalable SDN scenario, where Cloud, Edge and IoT devices must communicate efficiently to met the application requirements to minimize different network parameters such as hops number, latency, energy consumption, produced CO_2 and so on.

In this complex scenario, a single centralized routing policy can not meet all application requirements at the same time. To achieve this, we considered an SDN environment running a Dijkstra's algorithm to produce routing tables that minimize application network latency.

To address a scalable scenario that includes a huge amount of Cloud, Edge and IoT network devices, in addition to considering a sequential implementation of Dijkstra's algorithm, we also considered a MapReduce implementation to minimize processing times. Specifically, considering small network topologies (up to 1000 network devices), such as that of an intra-building scenario, the sequential Dijkstra's algorithm presents a better mean processing time than the MapReduce one, whereas in a more complex network topology, such as that of an intra-campus or smart cities scenario, in which roughly 10000 network devices are considered, the MapReduce approach represents the optimal solution.

Our future work involves the improvement of our distributed Dijkstra's algorithm implementation to address reliability issues when physical links fail, network capability control, and scalability due to a single control plane.

Acknowledgment. This work has been supported by FP7 Project the Cloud for Europe, grant agreement number FP7-610650.

References

1. Gartner Says the Internet of Things Installed Base Will Grow to 26 Billion Units By 2020. https://www.gartner.com/newsroom/id/2636073
2. Celesti, A., Galletta, A., Carnevale, L., Fazio, M., Lay-Ekuakille, A., Villari, M.: An IoT cloud system for traffic monitoring and vehicular accidents prevention based on mobile sensor data processing. IEEE Sens. J. **18**, 4795–4802 (2018)
3. Galletta, A., Carnevale, L., Celesti, A., Fazio, M., Villari, M.: A cloud-based system for improving retention marketing loyalty programs in industry 4.0: a study on big data storage implications. IEEE Access **6**, 5485–5492 (2017)
4. Ahmed, E., Ahmed, A., Yaqoob, I., Shuja, J., Gani, A., Imran, M., Shoaib, M.: Bringing computation closer toward the user network: is edge computing the solution? IEEE Commun. Mag. **55**, 138–144 (2017)
5. Liotta, A.: The cognitive net is coming. IEEE Spectr. **50**, 26–31 (2013)
6. Celesti, A., Tusa, F., Villari, M., Puliafito, A.: How the dataweb can support cloud federation: service representation and secure data exchange. In: Proceedings - IEEE 2nd Symposium on Network Cloud Computing and Applications, NCCA 2012, pp. 73–79 (2012)

7. Fazio, M., Celesti, A., Marquez, F., Glikson, A., Villari, M.: Exploiting the fiware cloud platform to develop a remote patient monitoring system. In: Proceedings - IEEE Symposium on Computers and Communications, vol. 2016, pp. 264–270 (2016)
8. Mulfari, D., Celesti, A., Villari, M., Puliafito, A.: How cloud computing can support on-demand assistive services. In: W4A 2013 - International Cross-Disciplinary Conference on Web Accessibility (2013)
9. Lin, C., Xue, C., Hu, J., Li, W.Z.: Hierarchical architecture design of computer system. Jisuanji Xuebao/Chin. J. Comput. **40**, 1996–2017 (2017)
10. Zheng, X., Tian, J., Xiao, X., Cui, X., Yu, X.: A heuristic survivable virtual network mapping algorithm. Soft Comput. 1–11 (2018)
11. Zhou, W., Jia, J.: Lightweight Web3D visualization framework using Dijkstra-based mesh segmentation. In: Tian, F., Gatzidis, C., El Rhalibi, A., Tang, W., Charles, F. (eds.) Edutainment 2017. LNCS, vol. 10345, pp. 138–151. Springer, Cham (2017). https://doi.org/10.1007/978-3-319-65849-0_15
12. Liu, Z., Yang, H., Kou, S.: Shared Protection Algorithm Based on Virtual Network Embedding Framework In Fiber-wireless Access Network (2017)
13. Wang, M., Liu, J., Mao, J., Cheng, H., Chen, J., Qi, C.: Routeguardian: Constructing. Tsinghua Sci. Technol. **22**, 400–412 (2017)
14. Wang, C., Yan, S.: Scaling SDN Network With Self-adjusting Architecture, pp. 116–120 (2017)
15. Vig, A., Kushwah, R., Tomar, R., Kushwah, S.: Autonomous Agent Based Shortest Path Load Balancing in Cloud, pp. 33–37 (2017)
16. Rattanawadee, P., Ruengsakulrach, N., Saivichit, C.: The Transmission Time Analysis of IPTV Multicast Service in SDN/OpenFlow Environments (2015)
17. Liu, F., Chen, X., An, W., Peng, Y., Cao, J., Zhang, Y.: Minimizing Transmission Cost for Multiple Service Function Chains in SDN/NFV Networks, vol. 2017, pp. 1–6 (2018)

Little Boxes: A Dynamic Optimization Approach for Enhanced Cloud Infrastructures

Ronny Hans[1], Björn Richerzhagen[1], Amr Rizk[1(✉)], Ulrich Lampe[1],
Ralf Steinmetz[1], Sabrina Klos (née Müller)[2], and Anja Klein[2]

[1] Multimedia Communications Lab (KOM), Technische Universität Darmstadt,
Darmstadt, Germany
{Ronny.Hans,amr.riz}@KOM.tu-darmstadt.de
[2] Communications Engineering Lab, Technische Universität Darmstadt, Darmstadt,
Germany

Abstract. The increasing demand for diverse, mobile applications with various degrees of Quality of Service requirements meets the increasing elasticity of on-demand resource provisioning in virtualized cloud computing infrastructures. This paper provides a dynamic optimization approach for enhanced cloud infrastructures, based on the concept of cloudlets, which are located at hotspot areas throughout a metropolitan area. In conjunction, we consider classical remote data centers that are rigid with respect to QoS but provide nearly abundant computation resources.

Keywords: Cloud computing · Data center · Cloudlet
Quality of service · Multimedia · Service · Dynamic · Optimization

1 Introduction

Over the last decade, the development of Information Technology (IT) has been shaped by different trends. One of these trends is cloud computing, which started as a paradigm for monetizing surplus IT resources to become a cornerstone paradigm in resource provisioning for business as well as private customers. In addition to these trend, we observed another major trend of increasing dissemination of mobile devices over the past few years. Omnipresent smartphones are heavily used today to consume multimedia services, communicate, and play massive real-time online games.

Combining these two trends together, i.e., *(i)* the demand for more diverse services – especially given device mobility – together with *(ii)* the elastic on-demand service (resource) provisioning of the cloud computing paradigm, we arrive at the mobile cloud computing paradigm. This paradigm imposes many new challenges, specifically regarding the Quality of Service (QoS) requirements of mobile services. Strict QoS requirements while providing multimedia services

© IFIP International Federation for Information Processing 2018
Published by Springer Nature Switzerland AG 2018. All Rights Reserved
K. Kritikos et al. (Eds.): ESOCC 2018, LNCS 11116, pp. 199–206, 2018.
https://doi.org/10.1007/978-3-319-99819-0_15

stand in contrast to the usual concentration of computational resources in a small number of large, centralized cloud data centers. To reduce the latency between data centers and users, research showed that a higher service quality can be achieved with an increased number of data centers. This obviously causes immense additional costs and oppose the *economies of scale* advantage of cloud computing [1,2].

Mobile devices using LTE networks suffer from higher latency [6] and high energy consumption [4]. Such problems can be addressed by utilizing (miniature) data centers or computation resources in proximity to the user. In the best case, such resources are accessible via Wi-Fi and offer interfaces to offload the computation of intensive tasks. These resources at the edge of the network are referred to as *cloudlets* [5]. In the work at hand, we investigate a *cost-efficient* and *QoS-aware* placement of cloudlet resources using a time dynamic, multi-period optimization model. The remainder of the paper is structured as follows: In Sect. 2, we provide the problem statement from a provider's perspective. Subsequently, in Sect. 3 we present an optimization approach for the given problem. In Sect. 4 a conclusion of the work at hand is given.

The subsequently presented optimization problem constitutes a Mixed Integer Program (MIP), which is NP-hard. To solve any corresponding problem instances in polynomial time, we publish a heuristic approach as part of an extended technical report [3]. This technical report includes the exact and heuristic solution approaches, as well as, an elaborate evaluation.

2   Problem Statement

In this work, we assume the role of a cloud infrastructure provider that aims to provide resources for higher layer application service providers. We assume that the provider owns the cloud infrastructure at hand and, thus, has free disposure over all of its resources. For premium services with rigid QoS constraints, the provider aims to augment his infrastructure using cloudlets within a metropolitan area. Therefore, we consider stationary cloudlets with permanently installed hardware, which are connected to the same Local Area Network (LAN), i. e., Wi-Fi, as the users [5,7]. Hence, the users benefit from a low propagation delay and a high bandwidth. As deployment method, we assume a top-down approach, where the provider owns and offers cloudlets and, hence, bears the entrepreneurial risk [5]. We consider cloudlet locations at existing restaurants or cafes (e. g., Starbucks stores) in Manhattan. Obviously, such deployments require contractual agreements. Since we are focusing on the optimization approaches, the underlying business models are out of scope for this paper.

In the following, we aggregate all users covered by a local Wi-Fi into a user cluster with a defined demand for services. Naturally, this user demand is fluctuating over time. As depicted in Fig. 1, a user cluster comprises different types of network connections.

First, a hard-wired LAN connects the Wi-Fi hotspot, a possibly installed cloudlet, and the router to communicate to external remote resources. Second, Wi-Fi connections that connect the mobile devices to the Wi-Fi hotspot.

Since we are assuming a higher bandwidth on the wired LAN compared to the wireless Wi-Fi hotspot, we do not consider the LAN as a limiting factor.

The third network component connects a user cluster to a central router within the Metropolitan Area Network (MAN) and hence, to other user clusters, cloudlets, and remote data centers. Figure 1 shows the basic structure of a cloudlet, the networks, and the connection to a remote cloud data center. The provider may place cloudlets and the corresponding resources at different locations. When putting a new location into service, fixed infrastructure cost will arise. Each cloudlet can be equipped with a number of servers up to an upper capacity bound. The capacity is restricted by limited physical space, limited feasibility for cooling, or restrictions regarding the overall energy consumption. For each deployed server, fixed hardware costs occur. Furthermore, for each resource unit variable costs arise, e.g., for electricity and cooling. Since such costs may fluctuate over time, e.g., due to varying energy prices, a provider needs to consider a planning time horizon that is captured here through multiple time periods. If a resource migration, e.g., in form of VM migration, is required, migration costs arise. We assume that these costs are independent of the type of cloudlet or the distance between the cloudlets. In real world scenarios, service migrations can be time aligned with data transfer. Therefore, we consider different migration costs depending on the service class.

In our model, penalty costs arise if a specific user demand cannot be fulfilled.

Data centers provide different QoS guarantees with respect to each user cluster, i.e., with respect to the end-to-end latency that depends on the distance between the data center and the user cluster. Therefore, a provider needs to differentiate between the different types of data centers for service placement, i.e., local cloudlets and remote data centers. The latter one generally possesses a higher latency.

By the means of the provided infrastructure, users access various services. We distinguish between three different service classes, whereby each class possesses specific QoS requirements: *(i)* Cloud services that can be easily used via a

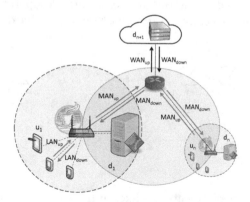

Fig. 1. Integration of cloudlets within a network topology

cellular network, i.e., services with low QoS requirements regarding latency and bandwidth, for example messaging tools. *(ii)* Cloud services that can be easily used via broadband internet, i.e., services with high bandwidth requirement, but not necessarily realtime constraints, such as on-demand video streaming. *(iii)* Cloud services with high computational effort, realtime constraints, and high bandwidth requirements, e.g., cloud gaming.

The first class of services plays a minor role in our scenario, since cloudlets only offer marginal additional benefits to such services. Nevertheless, these services can by provided by cloudlets if free capacities are available. For the second class of services, cloudlets increase the users' quality of experience through a high bandwidth to demanded content. For the third class of services, we note that cloudlets are required to ensure appropriate quality of service guarantees.

The purpose of this optimization, which is based on a provider's perspective, is to place resources in data centers and take decisions regarding the required capacity while providing QoS guarantees. Thereby, the goal is a minimization of the overall provisioning costs. In the following, we refer to this problem as *Dynamic Cloudlet Placement and Selection Problem (DCPSP)*.

3   Exact Optimization Approach

Next, we present a Mixed Integer Linear Program (MILP) formulation for the dynamic cloudlet placement and selection problem. In order to efficiently solve the problem, we provide a heuristic solution approach in the extended version of this paper [3]. To provide a mathematical model, we introduce the formal notation in Table 1. The objective here is the minimization of the total monetary cost associated with the cloudlet placement and selection.

3.1   Optimization Goal

The objective function aiming to minimize the total costs is given in Eq. 1. These costs are split into fixed infrastructure cost, variable operating cost, variable reservation cost, penalty cost, migration cost, and fixed hardware cost.

$$\min \ C =$$

$$\sum_{\lambda=1..\Lambda} x_{d_\lambda} \times C_{d_\lambda}^{fix} + \sum_{o=1..O} \left(\sum_{\substack{\lambda=1..\Lambda \\ \mu=1..M \\ \nu=1..N}} y_{d_\lambda,u_\mu,s_\nu,t_o} \times C_{d_\lambda,t_o}^{op} + \sum_{\substack{\mu=1..M \\ \nu=1..N}} y_{u_\mu,s_\nu,t_o}^{pen} \times C_{u_\mu,s_\nu}^{pen} \right)$$

$$+ \sum_{o=2}^{O} \sum_{\substack{\lambda=1..\Lambda \\ \mu=1..M \\ \nu=1..N}} y_{d_\lambda,u_\mu,s_\nu,t_o}^{mig} \times C_{s_\nu}^{mig} + \sum_{\lambda=1..\Lambda} z_{d_\lambda} \times C_{d_\lambda}^{hw} \tag{1}$$

The first summand represents the fixed infrastructure cost that depends on the selected data centers represented by the decision variable x_{d_λ} and the corresponding value for the individual fixed cost $C_{d_\lambda}^{fix}$. Such resource-agnostic cost occurs once for each planning period when a data center is placed. The second part of the term summarizes to the variable operational costs $C^{op}_{d_\lambda,t_o}$ that are caused by the provided resource units $y_{d_\lambda,u_\mu,s_\nu,t_o}$. The operational costs depend on the selected data center and may well vary over time. The third summand refers to capacities requested by a user cluster u_μ that are unfulfilled by the selected data centers. These capacities, $y^{pen}_{u_\mu,s_\nu,t_o}$, cause penalty cost $C^{pen}_{u_\mu,s_\nu}$. Penalty cost may be financial penalties defined in a *Service Level Agreement* but also may reflect opportunity cost for lost revenues. The migration cost is expressed in the fourth summand. Such migration cost $C^{mig}_{u_\mu,s_\nu}$ includes the data transfer cost from one data center to another. Assuming that launching a new service does not cause migration cost, such cost only occurs from the second time period on.

Equation 2 expresses the number of resource units to be migrated. To calculate the total amount, we distinguish two different cases: *(i)* The amount of resources that is provided to a specific user cluster u_μ w.r.t. a specific service is either constant or increases between two subsequent time periods, while the resource share provided by specific data center decreases. *(ii)* the aggregated amount of resources provided to a specific user cluster u_μ w.r.t. a specific service decreases between to time slots, while the resource share provided by a specific data center increases. To model and implement the optimization problem, this case differentiation requires a transformation into a linear equation system. However, due to space restrictions, this transformation is not part of the work at hand.

$$
y^{mig}_{d_\lambda,u_\mu,s_\nu,t_o} = \begin{cases} y_{d_\lambda,u_\mu,s_\nu,t_o-1} - y_{d_\lambda,u_\mu,s_\nu,t_o} & \text{if} \\ \quad \sum_{\alpha=1..\Lambda} y_{d_\alpha,u_\mu,s_\nu,t_o} \geq \sum_{\alpha=1..\Lambda} y_{d_\alpha,u_\mu,s_\nu,t_o-1} \\ \quad \wedge\ y_{d_\lambda,u_\mu,s_\nu,t_o} \leq y_{d_\lambda,u_\mu,s_\nu,t_o-1} \\ y_{d_\lambda,u_\mu,s_\nu,t_o} - y_{d_\lambda,u_\mu,s_\nu,t_o-1} & \text{if} \\ \quad \sum_{\alpha=1..\Lambda} y_{d_\alpha,u_\mu,s_\nu,t_o} < \sum_{\alpha=1..\Lambda} y_{d_\alpha,u_\mu,s_\nu,t_o-1} \\ \quad \wedge\ y_{d_\lambda,u_\mu,s_\nu,t_o} > y_{d_\lambda,u_\mu,s_\nu,t_o-1} \\ 0 & \text{else} \end{cases}
$$

$$\forall d_\lambda \in D, \forall u_\mu \in U, \forall s_\nu \in S, \forall t_o \in T \tag{2}$$

Note that the last summand in Eq. 1 refers to the provided hardware units z_{d_λ} in each data center. Providing servers leads to hardware cost $C^{hw}_{d_\lambda}$.

3.2 Constraints

In the following, we present the required constraints to ensure a valid solution of this optimization problem. The first constraint in Eq. 3 concerns the user cluster demand V_{u_μ,s_ν,t_o}. Since a provider has the choice either to fulfill the demand or cause a penalty, the summation of provided and unfulfilled capacities must be equal or greater to the resource demand of all user clusters for all services at each point in time.

Table 1. Formal notations

Symbol	Description
d_λ	Represents a specific data center and encompasses cloud data centers and cloudlets
u_μ	Represents a specific user cluser
s_ν	Represents a specific service
q_ξ	Represents a specific QoS attribute
t_o	Represents a specific time slot within the planning period
V_{u_μ,s_ν,t_o}	Service demand of user u_μ for service s_ν at time t_o
$K_{d_\lambda}^{min}$	Minimal capacity of data center d_λ
$K_{d_\lambda}^{max}$	Maximal capacity of data center d_λ
$K_{u_\mu}^{LAN_{down}}$	LAN downlink capacity of user cluster u_μ
$K_{u_\mu}^{LAN_{up}}$	LAN uplink capacity of user cluster u_μ
$K_{u_\mu}^{MAN_{down}}$	WAN downlink capacity of user cluster u_μ
$K_{u_\mu}^{MAN_{up}}$	WAN uplink capacity of user cluster u_μ
$C_{d_\lambda}^{fix}$	Fixed cost of selecting data center d_λ
$C_{d_\lambda}^{hw}$	Fixed costs for buying or leasing hardware for data center d_λ
C_{d_λ,t_o}^{op}	Variable cost for operating one resource unit for one time unit in data center d_λ at time t_o
$C_{s_\nu}^{mig}$	Migration cost for moving service s_ν from one data center to another between two subsequent time periods t and $t+1$
C_{u_μ,s_ν}^{pen}	Penalty cost per service unit not provided to user u_μ w.r.t. service s_ν
$Q_{d_\lambda,u_\mu,q_\xi}^{gua}$	QoS guarantee of data center d_i w.r.t. user u_j for QoS attribute q_ξ
$Q_{u_\mu,s_\nu,q_\xi}^{req}$	QoS requirement of user u_i w.r.t. service s_ν for QoS attribute q_ξ
$L_{s_\nu}^{down}$	Required downstream capacity for service s_ν
$L_{s_\nu}^{up}$	Required upstream capacity for service s_ν
x_{d_λ}	Variable $\in \{0,1\}$ indicates whether a data center d_λ will be used or not
$y_{d_\lambda,u_\mu,s_\nu,t_o}$	Number of resources a data center d_λ provides to a user cluster u_μ regarding a service s_ν in time period t_o
$y_{d_\lambda,u_\mu,s_\nu,t_o}^{mig}$	Number of resources that are migrated from one to another data center in between the time periods t_{o-1} and t_o
$y_{u_\mu,s_\nu,t_o}^{pen}$	Demand that is not satisfied by the provider and that will cause penalty costs
z_{d_λ}	Number of hardware resource units provided within a data center d_λ

$$y_{u_\mu,s_\nu,t_o}^{pen} + \sum_{\lambda=1..\Lambda} y_{d_\lambda,u_\mu,s_\nu,t_o} \geq V_{u_\mu,s_\nu,t_o} \quad \forall u_\mu \in U, \forall s_\nu \in S, \forall t_o \in T \quad (3)$$

The available data center resources are limited by a maximal capacity constraint $K_{d_\lambda}^{max}$, e.g., by the available space or cooling. Further, we consider a lower capacity bound $K_{d_\lambda}^{min}$ reflecting the economic necessity of a cost-efficient operation of data centers. As cloudlets can be established with few hardware resources, e. g., a single server, this bound could also be set to zero. These conditions determine the number of hardware resources z_{d_λ} that can be installed within a data center d_λ (cf. Eqs. 4 and 5).

$$\sum_{\substack{m=1..n \\ \nu=1..N}} y_{d_\lambda,u_\mu,s_\nu,t_o} \le z_{d_\lambda} \quad \forall d_\lambda \in D, \forall t_o \in T \tag{4}$$

$$z_{d_\lambda} \le x_{d_\lambda} \times K_{d_\lambda}^{max} \quad \forall d_\lambda \in D, z_{d_\lambda} \ge x_{d_\lambda} \times K_{d_\lambda}^{min} \quad \forall d_\lambda \in D \tag{5}$$

The adherence to QoS requirements is expressed by the binary variable $p_{d_\lambda,u_\mu,s_\nu}$. If all QoS guarantees $Q_{d_\lambda,u_\mu,q_\xi}^{gua}$ are fulfilled, the variable is set to *one* (cf. Eq. 6). Otherwise, a data center cannot provide any resources (cf. Eq. 7).

$$p_{d_\lambda,u_\mu,s_\nu} = \begin{cases} 1 & \text{if } Q_{d_\lambda,u_\mu,q_\xi}^{gua} \ge Q_{u_\mu,s_\nu,q_\xi}^{req} \forall q_\xi \in Q \\ 0 & \text{else} \end{cases} \tag{6}$$

$$y_{d_\lambda,u_\mu,s_\nu,t_o} \le p_{d_\lambda,u_\mu,s_\nu} \times K_{d_\lambda}^{max} \quad \forall d_\lambda \in D, \forall u_\mu \in U, \forall s_\nu \in S, \forall t_o \in T \tag{7}$$

As described earlier, each user cluster is connected to two types of networks, a LAN, i. e., Wi-Fi, and a MAN that connects the different user clusters with each other and to remote cloud data centers. All services that are consumed require a specific average amount of bandwidth. Note that the required bandwidth most be lower or equal than the available bandwidth. Since services may have different requirements regarding download and upload capacities, we differentiate between these two (cf. Eqs. 8 and 9).

$$\sum_{\lambda=1..\Lambda} \sum_{\nu=1..N} y_{d_\lambda,u_\mu,s_\nu,t_o} \times L_{s_\nu}^{down} \le K_{u_\mu}^{LAN_{down}}$$
$$\forall u_\mu \in U, \forall s_\nu \in S, \forall t_o \in T \tag{8}$$

$$\sum_{\lambda=1..\Lambda} \sum_{\nu=1..N} y_{d_\lambda,u_\mu,s_\nu,t_o} \times L_{s_\nu}^{up} \le K_{u_\mu}^{LAN_{up}}$$
$$\forall u_\mu \in U, \forall s_\nu \in S, \forall t_o \in T \tag{9}$$

The MAN connection is required to provide services from remote resources to a local user cluster, and may be necessary to provide services from a local cloudlet to remote users. For services that are provided by the *local* cloudlet and consumed by the *local* users, no MAN capacities are required at all. Equations 10 and 11 represent the corresponding constraints. Further, we differentiate between download and upload capacities to take specific service requirements and network characteristics into account.

$$\sum_{\substack{\lambda=1..\Lambda \\ \lambda \ne \alpha}} \sum_{\nu=1..N} y_{d_\lambda,u_\alpha,s_\nu,t_o} \times L_{s_\nu}^{down} + \sum_{\substack{\mu=1..M \\ \mu \ne \alpha}} \sum_{\nu=1..N} y_{d_\alpha,u_\mu,s_\nu,t_o} \times L_{s_\nu}^{up} \le K_{u_\alpha}^{MAN_{down}}$$
$$\forall d_\alpha \in D, \forall u_\alpha \in U, \forall s_\nu \in S, \forall t_o \in T \tag{10}$$

$$\sum_{\substack{\lambda=1..\Lambda \\ \lambda \neq \alpha}} \sum_{\nu=1..N} y_{d_\lambda, u_\alpha, s_\nu, t_o} \times L_{s_\nu}^{up} + \sum_{\substack{\mu=1..M \\ \mu \neq \alpha}} \sum_{\nu=1..N} y_{d_\alpha, u_\mu, s_\nu, t_o} \times L_{s_\nu}^{down} \leq K_{u_\alpha}^{MAN_{up}}$$

$$\forall d_\alpha \in D, \forall u_\alpha \in U, \forall s_\nu \in S, \forall t_o \in T \tag{11}$$

The presented optimization problem constitutes a Mixed Integer Program (MIP) and is NP-hard. In the extended version of this work [3], we describe a heuristic solution approach to obtain solutions to this problem with reasonable effort.

4   Conclusion

To provide services with stringent QoS requirements, an augmentation of the centralized cloud infrastructure by locally installed cloudlets is a promising approach. Since the utilization of decentralized micro data center is costly, we examined the *Dynamic Cloudlet Placement and Selection Problem* to provide the means of a cost-efficient infrastructure augmentation. We formulate a mixed integer optimization problem to compute the exact solution to the dynamic cloudlet placement and selection problem. In the extended version of this work [3], we provide different heuristic approaches to overcome the problem of high computational effort where we significantly reduce the computation time while maintaining a high solution quality under slightly increased costs.

Acknowledgment. This work has been sponsored in part by the German Federal Ministry of Education and Research (BMBF) under grant no. 01IS12054, by E-Finance Lab e.V., Frankfurt a.M., Germany (www.efinancelab.de), and by the German Research Foundation (DFG) in the Collaborative Research Center (SFB) 1053 – MAKI.

References

1. Choy, S., Wong, B., Simon, G., Rosenberg, C.: The brewing storm in cloud gaming: a measurement study on cloud to end-user latency. In: 11th Annual Workshop on Network and Systems Support for Games (2012)
2. Goiri, I.n., Le, K., Guitart, J., Torres, J., Bianchini, R.: Intelligent placement of datacenters for internet services. In: 31st International Conference on Distributed Computing Systems (2011)
3. Hans, R., et al.: Little boxes: A dynamic optimization approach for enhanced cloud infrastructures. arXiv preprint - http://arxiv.org/abs/1807.02615 (2018)
4. Huang, J., Qian, F., Gerber, A., Mao, Z.M., Sen, S., Spatscheck, O.: A close examination of performance and power characteristics of 4G LTE networks. In: 10th International Conference on Mobile Systems, Applications, and Services (2012)
5. Satyanarayanan, M., Bahl, P., Caceres, R., Davies, N.: The case for VM-based cloudlets in mobile computing. Pervasive Comput. **8**(4), 14–23 (2009)
6. Sommers, J., Barford, P.: Cell vs. WiFi: on the performance of metro area mobile connections. In: 2012 Conference on Internet Measurement (2012)
7. Verbelen, T., Simoens, P., De Turck, F., Dhoedt, B.: Cloudlets: bringing the cloud to the mobile user. In: 3rd ACM Workshop on Mobile Cloud Computing and Services (2012)

Cloud Topology and Orchestration Using TOSCA: A Systematic Literature Review

Julian Bellendorf[✉] and Zoltán Ádám Mann

paluno – The Ruhr Institute for Software Technology,
University of Duisburg-Essen, Essen, Germany
{julian.bellendorf,zoltan.mann}@paluno.uni-due.de

Abstract. Topology and Orchestration Specification for Cloud Applications (TOSCA) is a standard for specifying the topology of cloud applications, their deployment on cloud resources, and their orchestration. In recent years, the cloud research community has shown increasing interest in TOSCA, leading to an increasing number of publications. These publications address different topics around TOSCA, e.g., devise cloud orchestration methods using TOSCA, extend the language of TOSCA, or present tools for manipulating TOSCA models. To help researchers and practitioners overview this multifaceted area of research, this paper presents the results of a systematic survey of the relevant literature.

Keywords: TOSCA · Cloud · Topology · Orchestration

1 Introduction

Cloud applications may comprise many components with different technical dependencies and constraints, making their deployment and ongoing management complicated and error-prone [27]. Also, the interoperability between management tools has become challenging [4]. Thus, the need arose to describe cloud applications and related management tasks on a higher level of abstraction, in a standardized format. To address these issues, the Organization for the Advancement of Structured Information Standards (OASIS) published the Topology and Orchestration Specification for Cloud Applications (TOSCA) standard in 2013 [30]. TOSCA is a modeling language addressing the deployment and portability of applications, and the reusability of application components [2,13]. The original TOSCA specification was based on XML; the simplified TOSCA profile, released in 2016, used YAML [32].

TOSCA describes (i) the structure of composite cloud applications as *topology graphs* and (ii) *management plans* for deploying and maintaining cloud applications. In topology graphs, nodes represent components, which include management operations e.g. for creating, configuring or starting the component [19]. The topology graph also contains relationships between components; e.g., a "hosted-on" relation indicates the allocation of virtual to physical components.

© IFIP International Federation for Information Processing 2018
Published by Springer Nature Switzerland AG 2018. All Rights Reserved
K. Kritikos et al. (Eds.): ESOCC 2018, LNCS 11116, pp. 207–215, 2018.
https://doi.org/10.1007/978-3-319-99819-0_16

In *imperative processing*, a Management Plan defines the management operations and their execution order, using a workflow language such as Business Process Model and Notation [31] or Business Process Execution Language [29]. In *declarative processing*, no Management Plans are defined; instead, a runtime system infers the necessary steps for typical operations (e.g., deployment) from the application topology based on some conventions [5].

TOSCA has played various roles in different research approaches: some used TOSCA as part of a more general methodology, others extended the modeling capabilities of TOSCA or designed tools to manipulate TOSCA models. The multifaceted use of TOSCA and the growing number of relevant papers make it hard to track all related research. The aim of this paper is to give an overview of the use of TOSCA in the research community. We performed a systematic literature survey to devise a taxonomy of the main research topics that have been addressed in connection with TOSCA.

To identify relevant papers, we first used Scopus[1] with the search string `"Topology and Orchestration Specification for Cloud Applications" AND (ABS(tosca) OR TITLE (tosca))`. Here, `ABS(tosca) OR TITLE (tosca)` means that the word TOSCA must be contained in the abstract or title, ensuring that TOSCA is a main aspect of the paper. In addition, we are looking for the full term (Topology and Orchestration Specification for Cloud Applications) to exclude papers that use the word TOSCA in another meaning. We focused on the period 2012–2017, since the first TOSCA papers were published in 2012, and 2017 was the last full year until the time of writing. We found 89 papers. We excluded 6 very short papers (less than 4 pages). Using Google Scholar[2], we found 8 more papers that were not in Scopus but fit our search string. This led to a total of 91 papers. Afterwards, we read each paper and categorized it using open coding. By continuously refining our coding scheme, we built up a taxonomy in a bottom-up fashion. Finally, we analyzed the results to identify focal points of existing research and directions for further research.

2   Survey Results

Figure 1 presents the taxonomy that we developed based on the analyzed papers. On the highest level, we categorized the papers based on their *main contribution regarding TOSCA*. We identified the following categories:

1. **Tools**: papers describing a tool for TOSCA. Further categorization is possible based on the type of tool; in particular, this includes modeling tools, tools for deployment automation, and run-time environments.
2. **Extension of language**: approaches that extend the TOSCA language. The extension may relate to topologies, Management Plans, or both. Furthermore, extensions aiming at a visual notation also belong to this category.

---

[1] https://www.scopus.com.
[2] https://scholar.google.com.

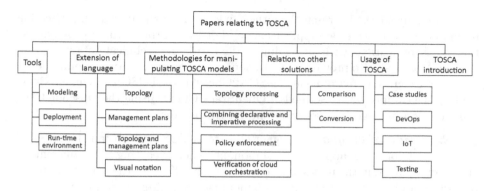

Fig. 1. Taxonomy for categorizing the processed papers

3. **Methodologies for manipulating TOSCA models**: papers describing a methodology for processing TOSCA models. The identified sub-categories are: papers about processing TOSCA topology models, approaches that combine declarative and imperative processing, solutions to enforce some given policies, and verification of cloud orchestration.

4. **Relation to other solutions**: papers about a relation – comparison or conversion – between TOSCA and some other technique.

5. **Usage of TOSCA**: papers demonstrating the use of TOSCA. This includes case studies that showcase the practical applicability of TOSCA, papers about the contribution of TOSCA to DevOps, papers about the use of TOSCA in an IoT (Internet of Things) setting, as well as papers about the use of TOSCA models for testing purposes.

6. **TOSCA introduction**: papers that introduce TOSCA or some of the concepts within TOSCA.

The following paragraphs describe some representative papers in each category of the taxonomy of Fig. 1, except for the category "TOSCA introduction." (Due to space limitation we cannot describe all found papers in detail.)

(1) Tools. The Tools category consists of papers mainly presenting tools for describing, deploying, and instantiating cloud applications using TOSCA. Prototypes that only serve to evaluate an approach are not assigned to this category.

Kopp et al. present the web-based modeling tool Winery [23]. First, Winery includes the Topology Modeler, with which components can be combined to form an application topology. Second, Winery contains the Element Manager, which can be used to create, modify, and delete components. Kopp et al. propose an extension to Winery that can be used to model Management Plans [24].

Binz et al. describe OpenTOSCA, a runtime for imperative processing of TOSCA applications [1]. This tool executes the defined Management Plans respectively the operations described within the nodes. Wettinger et al. present an extension to OpenTOSCA in the form of a unified invocation interface [40].

Breitenbücher et al. present Vinothek, which offers the user an interface for providing an instance of an application [7]. For this purpose, the user is offered the set of applications without having to deal with the technical details.

Katsaros et al. also provide a tool to deploy and manage software components [21]. The execution environment TOSCA2Chef parses TOSCA documents and deploys the components described in OpenStack Clouds using the Opscode Chef configuration management software and BPEL processes.

(2) Extension of language. Brogi et al. extend TOSCA by means for specifying the behavior of the application components when executing the management operations defined in the nodes [9]. Considering the effects of the operations to be performed and the states that the components assume after execution, makes the validation of Management Plans possible. Breitenbücher et al. propose a visual notation to unify the presentation of nodes within the topology [8]. Kopp et al. extend the BPMN to provide direct access to the topology elements [22]. The extension, called BPMN4TOSCA, can be transformed into standards-compliant BPMN.

(3) Methodologies for manipulating TOSCA models. Various approaches have been proposed to work with TOSCA models. Some focus on the processing of topologies, whereas others also take Management Plans into account to enforce policies, to verify the orchestration of the components, or to combine declarative and imperative processing.

Processing of Topologies. Brogi and Soldani describe an approach that involves matching between individual Node Types and Service Templates [11,12]. This matching allows sets of Node Types to be grouped together in a topology to reduce its complexity. In addition, proven combinations of Node Types can be reused in new application topologies. Service Templates which do not fit exactly can be adapted to create a template that matches exactly to a given node type.

Binz et al. observed that container components (e.g. virtual machines) are often underutilized by a single application component, so that additional components can be hosted by these containers [3]. For this purpose, the topologies from two applications that use the same container components are merged into one topology in which both applications retain their respective functionality. Saatkamp et al. present an approach for adapting the application topology when a provider specifies a new offer and certain components of the application need to be migrated to new container components [33].

Multiple approaches for topology completion were proposed, with the aim that an application developer only has to model the business-relevant components and the underlying infrastructure is automatically added. The approach of Hirmer et al. is based on a repository of nodes and relationships to fill in incomplete topologies [20]. Brogi et al. present an approach to collect information about suitable cloud offerings by crawling the network and storing their TOSCA representation in a repository [10]. This representation can be used by application developers to complete the topology. Soldani et al. propose TOSCAMart, an approach to reuse proven topologies in new environments [35]. The developer of a composite application defines a node in the topology that describes the requirements for the fragment being inserted. TOSCAMart then selects a solution suitable for these requirements from a repository of various existing topologies.

Combining Declarative and Imperative Processing. Breitenbücher et al. propose an approach that combines declarative and imperative processing to achieve hybrid processing [5,6]. The defined application topologies are interpreted and finally, the associated Management Plans are generated. Calcaterra et al. present a similar approach, also based on interpreting a topology and providing the appropriate Management Plan [14].

Policy Enforcement. Waizenegger et al. present a TOSCA runtime extension to enforce policies describing non-functional requirements, specifically security properties, such as the encryption of a database or the geographic positioning of privacy-related data [37,38]. Policies can be defined using both single-node management operations and Management Plans.

Verification of Cloud Orchestration. Yoshida et al. describe an approach to the formal verification of TOSCA topologies that can be used to test the achievement of a target state in the declarative processing of the TOSCA model [42]. The execution of the management operation is described by a state transition system in which a state with a certain property is to be reached. Chareonsuk and Vatanawood use Model Checking to verify security properties for imperative processing [15]. The approach of Tsigkanos and Kehrer is about defining patterns and anti-patterns and finally checking their presence or absence in the topology of a service template so that quality aspects can be proven [36].

(4) Relation to other solutions. A comparison between TOSCA and the Heat Orchestration Template (HOT) is provided by Di Martino et al. [17]. HOT is the template format used to define the structure of an application for declarative processing by the OpenStack orchestrator Heat. The main difference between the two approaches is that HOT is declarative while TOSCA supports both declarative and imperative processing. Also, similarities are shown, for example, both provide a catalog of nodes and resources that can be composed to applications.

Yongsiriwit et al. address the interoperability of standards for describing cloud resources: TOSCA, Open Cloud Computing Interface (OCCI) and Cloud Infrastructure Management Interface (CIMI) [41]. For interoperability, ontologies are defined that describe the resources noted in each standard. In addition, an upper-level ontology is presented to describe cloud resources regardless of the used standards. Using inference rules, the special descriptions can be translated into this higher-level format and vice versa, which also allows the translation from one standard to another. Using the upper ontology, a knowledge base could be created, providing insights into relationships and possible inconsistencies.

(5) Usage of TOSCA. This category consists of approaches that use the existing TOSCA notation. Kostoska et al. present a case study of the use of

TOSCA for specifying the University Management System iKnow [25]. This system offers professors and students a platform to exchange electronic information and provide electronic services. Besides a detailed description of node and relationship types, this paper also mentions the challenges of using TOSCA for the specification of this application.

A different domain for using TOSCA is the specification of Internet of Things (IoT) applications. Li et al. show how TOSCA can be used for an IoT application: an Air Handling Unit (AHU) that controls air circulation in modern buildings [26]. Da Silva et al. demonstrate the feasibility of defining IoT applications using TOSCA, in the context of different technologies [16]. In another paper, Da Silva et al. address the multitude of sensor data produced in IoT [34]. The authors describe how Complex Event Processing Systems can be deployed using TOSCA to process the incoming data and efficiently use network resources.

3 Discussion

Our survey shows the *versatility* of TOSCA: its use in different domains (also beyond cloud computing), for different purposes, in different phases of the service lifecycle, by different groups of users. This versatility is mainly due to (i) the possibility to define custom types for nodes, relationships, and capabilities and (ii) the possibility to define and manipulate partial topologies. However, this versatility also poses the risk of the proliferation of incompatible TOSCA dialects. Hence we expect that *interoperability* will play an increasingly important role.

Some further topics received limited attention so far and represent important targets for future research. First, given the enormous importance of *security* in cloud computing, it is striking that very few papers address it so far (although several authors mentioned it as future work [33,41]). Also, TOSCA support for other related topics like *data protection* needs to be investigated [28]. Second, the topic of *verification and validation* (V&V) is also addressed by few papers. Given the importance of V&V, we expect to see more work on how TOSCA can be used to improve V&V. Third, partial topologies open many possibilities for *optimization*, from which only a little has been investigated, mainly in connection with cost minimization. Many other aspects of optimization, e.g., related to performance and reliability, are yet to be explored. Finally, TOSCA has been shown to be useful in areas such as IoT and DevOps [39]. We expect to see TOSCA being applied to new domains like *network function virtualization* [18] or *fog and edge computing*.

Acknowledgment. This work received funding from the European Union's Horizon 2020 research and innovation programme (grant agreement 731678 (RestAssured)).

References

1. Binz, T., et al.: OpenTOSCA – a runtime for TOSCA-based cloud applications. In: Basu, S., Pautasso, C., Zhang, L., Fu, X. (eds.) ICSOC 2013. LNCS, vol. 8274, pp. 692–695. Springer, Heidelberg (2013). https://doi.org/10.1007/978-3-642-45005-1_62
2. Binz, T., Breitenbücher, U., Kopp, O., Leymann, F.: TOSCA: portable automated deployment and management of cloud applications. In: Bouguettaya, A., Sheng, Q., Daniel, F. (eds.) Advanced Web Services, pp. 527–549. Springer, New York (2014). https://doi.org/10.1007/978-1-4614-7535-4_22
3. Binz, T., Breitenbücher, U., Kopp, O., Leymann, F., Weiß, A.: Improve resource-sharing through functionality-preserving merge of cloud application topologies. In: Proceedings of the CLOSER 2013, pp. 96–103 (2013)
4. Binz, T., Breiter, G., Leyman, F., Spatzier, T.: Portable cloud services using TOSCA. IEEE Internet Comput. **16**(3), 80–85 (2012)
5. Breitenbücher, U., Binz, T., Képes, K., Kopp, O., Leymann, F., Wettinger, J.: Combining declarative and imperative cloud application provisioning based on TOSCA. In: Proceedings of the IC2E 2014, pp. 87–96 (2014)
6. Breitenbücher, U., Binz, T., Kopp, O., Képes, K., Leymann, F., Wettinger, J.: Hybrid TOSCA provisioning plans: integrating declarative and imperative cloud application provisioning technologies. In: Helfert, M., Méndez Muñoz, V., Ferguson, D. (eds.) CLOSER 2015. CCIS, vol. 581, pp. 239–262. Springer, Cham (2016). https://doi.org/10.1007/978-3-319-29582-4_13
7. Breitenbücher, U., Binz, T., Kopp, O., Leymann, F.: Vinothek - a self-service portal for TOSCA. In: Proceedings of the ZEUS 2014, pp. 72–75 (2014)
8. Breitenbücher, U., Binz, T., Kopp, O., Leymann, F., Schumm, D.: Vino4TOSCA: a visual notation for application topologies based on TOSCA. In: Meersman, R., et al. (eds.) OTM 2012. LNCS, vol. 7565, pp. 416–424. Springer, Heidelberg (2012). https://doi.org/10.1007/978-3-642-33606-5_25
9. Brogi, A., Canciani, A., Soldani, J.: Modelling and analysing cloud application management. In: Dustdar, S., Leymann, F., Villari, M. (eds.) ESOCC 2015. LNCS, vol. 9306, pp. 19–33. Springer, Cham (2015). https://doi.org/10.1007/978-3-319-24072-5_2
10. Brogi, A., Cifariello, P., Soldani, J.: DrACO: discovering available cloud offerings. Comput. Sci. Res. Dev. **32**(3–4), 269–279 (2017)
11. Brogi, A., Soldani, J.: Matching cloud services with TOSCA. In: Canal, C., Villari, M. (eds.) ESOCC 2013. CCIS, vol. 393, pp. 218–232. Springer, Heidelberg (2013). https://doi.org/10.1007/978-3-642-45364-9_18
12. Brogi, A., Soldani, J.: Finding available services in TOSCA-compliant clouds. Sci. Comput. Program. **115–116**, 177–198 (2016)
13. Brogi, A., Soldani, J., Wang, P.W.: TOSCA in a nutshell: promises and perspectives. In: Villari, M., Zimmermann, W., Lau, K.-K. (eds.) ESOCC 2014. LNCS, vol. 8745, pp. 171–186. Springer, Heidelberg (2014). https://doi.org/10.1007/978-3-662-44879-3_13
14. Calcaterra, D., Cartelli, V., Di Modica, G., Tomarchio, O.: Combining TOSCA and BPMN to enable automated cloud service provisioning. In: Proceedings of the CLOSER 2017, pp. 159–168 (2017)
15. Chareonsuk, W., Vatanawood, W.: Formal verification of cloud orchestration design with TOSCA and BPEL. In: Proceedings of the ECTI-CON 2016, pp. 1–5 (2016)

16. Da Silva, A., et al.: Internet of Things out of the box: using TOSCA for automating the deployment of IoT environments. In: Proceedings of the CLOSER 2017, pp. 330–339 (2017)

17. Di Martino, B., Cretella, G., Esposito, A.: Defining cloud services workflow: a comparison between TOSCA and OpenStack Hot. In: Proceedings of the CISIS 2015, pp. 541–546 (2015)

18. Dräxler, S., Karl, H., Mann, Z.A.: Joint optimization of scaling and placement of virtual network services. In: Proceedings of the CCGrid 2017, pp. 365–370 (2017)

19. Haupt, F., Leymann, F., Nowak, A., Wagner, S.: Lego4TOSCA: composable building blocks for cloud applications. In: Proceedings of the CLOUD 2014, pp. 160–167 (2014)

20. Hirmer, P., Breitenbücher, U., Binz, T., Leymann, F.: Automatic topology completion of TOSCA-based cloud applications. In: Proceedings of the Informatik 2014, pp. 247–258 (2014)

21. Katsaros, G., Menzel, M., Lenk, A., Rake-Revelant, J., Skipp, R., Eberhardt, J.: Cloud application portability with TOSCA, Chef and Openstack: experiences from a proof-of-concept implementation. In: Proceedings of the IC2E 2014, pp. 295–302 (2014)

22. Kopp, O., Binz, T., Breitenbücher, U., Leymann, F.: BPMN4TOSCA: a domain-specific language to model management plans for composite applications. In: Mendling, J., Weidlich, M. (eds.) BPMN 2012. LNBIP, vol. 125, pp. 38–52. Springer, Heidelberg (2012). https://doi.org/10.1007/978-3-642-33155-8_4

23. Kopp, O., Binz, T., Breitenbücher, U., Leymann, F.: Winery – a modeling tool for TOSCA-based cloud applications. In: Basu, S., Pautasso, C., Zhang, L., Fu, X. (eds.) ICSOC 2013. LNCS, vol. 8274, pp. 700–704. Springer, Heidelberg (2013). https://doi.org/10.1007/978-3-642-45005-1_64

24. Kopp, O., Binz, T., Breitenbücher, U., Leymann, F., Michelbach, T.: A domain-specific modeling tool to model management plans for composite applications. In: Proceedings of the ZEUS 2015, pp. 51–54 (2015)

25. Kostoska, M., Chorbev, I., Gusev, M.: Creating portable TOSCA archive for iKnow university management system. In: Proceedings of the FedCSIS 2014, pp. 761–768 (2014)

26. Li, F., Vögler, M., Claeßens, M., Dustdar, S.: Towards automated IoT application deployment by a cloud-based approach. In: Proceedings of the SOCA 2013, pp. 61–68 (2013)

27. Mann, Z.Á.: Resource optimization across the cloud stack. IEEE Trans. Parallel Distrib. Syst. **29**(1), 169–182 (2018)

28. Mann, Z.Á., Metzger, A.: Optimized cloud deployment of multi-tenant software considering data protection concerns. In: Proceedings of the CCGrid 2017, pp. 609–618 (2017)

29. OASIS: Web Services Business Process Execution Language Version 2.0, April 2007. OASIS Standard

30. OASIS: Topology and Orchestration Specification for Cloud Applications Version 1.0, November 2013. OASIS Standard. http://docs.oasis-open.org/tosca/TOSCA/v1.0/os/TOSCA-v1.0-os.html

31. OMG: Business Process Model and Notation (BPMN) Version 2.0, January 2011. OMG Document Number: formal/2011-01-03

32. Palma, D., Rutkowski, M., Spatzier, T.: TOSCA Simple Profile in YAML Version 1.0, December 2016. OASIS Standard. http://docs.oasis-open.org/tosca/TOSCA-Simple-Profile-YAML/v1.0/TOSCA-Simple-Profile-YAML-v1.0.html

33. Saatkamp, K., Breitenbücher, U., Kopp, O., Leymann, F.: Topology splitting and matching for multi-cloud deployments. In: Proceedings of the CLOSER 2017, pp. 247–258 (2017)
34. Franco da Silva, A., Hirmer, P., Breitenbücher, U., Kopp, O., Mitschang, B.: Customization and provisioning of complex event processing using TOSCA. Comput. Sci. Res. Dev. **33**, 1–11 (2017)
35. Soldani, J., Binz, T., Breitenbücher, U., Leymann, F., Brogi, A.: ToscaMart: a method for adapting and reusing cloud applications. J. Syst. Softw. **113**, 395–406 (2016)
36. Tsigkanos, C., Kehrer, T.: On formalizing and identifying patterns in cloud workload specifications. In: Proceedings of the WICSA 2016, pp. 262–267 (2016)
37. Waizenegger, T., et al.: Policy4TOSCA: a policy-aware cloud service provisioning approach to enable secure cloud computing. In: Meersman, R., et al. (eds.) OTM 2013. LNCS, vol. 8185, pp. 360–376. Springer, Heidelberg (2013). https://doi.org/10.1007/978-3-642-41030-7_26
38. Waizenegger, T., Wieland, M., Binz, T., Breitenbücher, U., Leymann, F.: Towards a policy-framework for the deployment and management of cloud services. In: Proceedings of the SECURWARE 2013, pp. 14–18 (2013)
39. Wettinger, J., et al.: Integrating configuration management with model-driven cloud management based on TOSCA. In: Proceedings of the CLOSER 2013, pp. 437–446 (2013)
40. Wettinger, J., Binz, T., Breitenbücher, U., Kopp, O., Leymann, F., Zimmermann, M.: Unified invocation of scripts and services for provisioning, deployment and management of cloud applications based on TOSCA. In: Proceedings of the CLOSER 2014, pp. 559–568 (2014)
41. Yongsiriwit, K., Sellami, M., Gaaloul, W.: A semantic framework supporting cloud resource descriptions interoperability. In: Proceedings of the CLOUD 2016, pp. 585–592 (2017)
42. Yoshida, H., Ogata, K., Futatsugi, K.: Formalization and verification of declarative cloud orchestration. In: Butler, M., Conchon, S., Zaïdi, F. (eds.) ICFEM 2015. LNCS, vol. 9407, pp. 33–49. Springer, Cham (2015). https://doi.org/10.1007/978-3-319-25423-4_3

Author Index

Printed in the United States
By Bookmasters